Young Republican

Young Republican

Douglas Putnam

Copyright © 2013
by Douglas Putnam
1969 Kentwell Road
Columbus, OH 43221-1903
Phone: 614-457-2597
E-mail: putnamdoug@gmail.com

Back cover photography by Nikki's Portraits and Design
Copyright © by Nikki McCool

All rights reserved. No part of the material protected by this copyright notice may be reproduced or utilized in any form or by any means, electronic or mechanical, including photocopying, recording or by any informational storage and retrieval system without written permission from the copyright owner.

ISBN: 978-0-615-81506-0

Printed and bound in the United States of America by
Maverick Publications ● Bend, Oregon

Author's Note

Young Republican could not have been produced without the help of many people. To each of them I extend my appreciation. They all tried, with courage and candor, to tell their versions of the truth about the remarkable life journey of Terry Stratton.

I remind readers that each of the narrators of this oral history has a unique perspective on a flawed but profoundly human man, and on his meteoric rise and brutal fall in the world of politics.

Please also note that many people pivotal in Terry's life chose not to communicate with me in any way during the course of this project. They include his adoptive parents Jean Polk and Gale Stratton, his biological children, daughter Carol and son Rhody, his second wife Pamela Lee Stratton, Governor James Rhodes, Representative Milo Forbes, friends and family of Dana Plato, and President and Mrs. Ronald Reagan.

Terry himself speaks directly only through three written documents placed in the text. There are virtually no tangible records of his personal, political or financial activities.

Notes on narrators: Cletus "Clee" Harris died in Clarksburg, WV of AIDS-related complications on November 1st, 1992, at age forty-three. I never made direct contact with Clee. The excerpt from his audio memoirs, recorded in the last months of his life, is reproduced here with permission of his mother, Cecile Harris.

Coach Tim Frame is currently incarcerated in Wallens Ridge State Prison in Big Stone Gap, VA. He and I exchanged a series of written letters in 2005.

Since sharing their memories of Terry with me, three narrators have died: Commissioner Red Yenser in 2011, political operative Mac McKenzie in 2009, and Reagan White House aide Michael Deaver in 2007. To the best of my knowledge, all other narrators remain among the living.

                                                  Douglas Putnam
                                                  August 19th, 2013
                                                  Washington, D.C.

One / Marietta 1948–1966

Ruth Toops

Jean and Gale were a year into their marriage and squabbling like demons when an angel swooped down from heaven one May morning and left a baby on their front porch. In a black cherry cradle, in the middle of the swinging love seat, between her bamboo sewing box and his stack of baseball magazines. The boy was three months old, as peaceful as a dove, and wrapped in a chocolate brown blanket that matched his eyes.

They named him Terence Charles, after Jean's grandfather and Gale's older brother, and called him Terry.

The sweet-natured child brought good feelings to the household. The squabbling ceased, the marriage righted itself, and the Stratton family bloomed in the summer of 1948 in the white clapboard house with black shutters at 333 Warren Street in Marietta, Ohio.

That was how Jean cheerfully told the story to the assembled mothers of the neighborhood in my living room on the scorching hot Fourth of July of 1955. I accent cheerfully because she wasn't that way often. Most of the time she was anxious and fretful, rubbing her nails and wringing her hands, hovering at her kitchen window, or on her front porch, or along the edge of whatever gathering she was part of.

I lived three doors down from her for twenty-three years. I can count on one hand the occasions I saw Jean Stratton looking like she was enjoying herself.

Her father was a big part of her burden. The Reverend Robert White was head minister at First United Church of Christ on Front Street, and he was the one who'd brought her the baby. When Jean called him an angel, she was being wry. The Reverend may have been an angel to his flock, but to his wife and daughters he was anything but. The man was utterly stuck on himself. He'd been a star athlete in high school and college, battled the Hun in France under Black Jack Pershing, then played pro football with Jim Thorpe and the Canton Bulldogs before going to seminary. He ardently desired male progeny to mold into a crackerjack squad of muscular Christians. As he and his wife Nell moved early in his career from one church to the next throughout the Midwest, she birthed Jean and three more girls in less than eight years.

After that, I guess they stopped trying for a boy. I'm not sure the Reverend ever forgave Nell—or his daughters—for being female.

Jean's sisters dutifully married themselves off to devout, athletic boys from proper, Protestant families. Jean took a different path. She sowed some wild oats up in Columbus at Ohio State, came home to become head of circulation at the public library, dated several men of less than sterling character, then all of a sudden out of the blue married Gale Stratton. A lapsed Baptist of all things, an amiable, dark-eyed son of a coal miner she met playing bridge one night at Murphy's Supper Club on Greene Street.

The problem was, he didn't fit in with the White family at all.

Gale was what people today call a couch potato, a smoker and drinker who followed scads of sports on radio and bird-dogged the Cincinnati Reds on WTOP-TV. But he didn't even cut his own postage stamp of a lawn. He paid one of my boys, and later on Terry, two dollars a week to do it for him. And he never played *any* game that required an ounce of exertion.

That was shameful enough in the Reverend's eyes. But when he and the rest of the family learned nine months after the wedding that Gale had damaged sperm ducts and was incapable of fathering children, the Reverend grieved. He probably thought it was God's punishment on him for allowing his daughter to marry an unworthy man. At least that was the theory passing through the neighborhood and the pews at First United.

He contacted some church connections down in Charleston and arranged for the adoption of Terry. Two years later, Jean asked him for a girl, and he brought her a baby who became Ramsay, Terry's younger sister.

Jean held on to her job, embraced motherhood, and never looked back. Gale went into a shell. I imagine he felt crushed by his situation. And he blurted out to my face in my back yard that sweltering Fourth of July that he detested his swarm of pious in-laws, who looked down on him because of his flimsy faith and deep mountain roots.

"I'm an atheist," he said to me.

"A real, honest-to-God atheist?"

He nodded his head. "Imagine a heathen hillbilly like me ending up in a righteous family like the Whites."

"You don't believe in *anything*?"

"Religion is mumbo jumbo," he said. "You have no soul. And after you die your body rots in the muck unless somebody has the good sense to burn it first."

"You've had too much to drink. Why don't you go home?"

He eyeballed me hard for a long moment and took a deep drag on his Camel. "I don't want to go home," he said.

"Why not?"

"Home is nothing but a hotel full of strangers," he said. "I've just been passing through all these years."

"Do you love Jean?"

"No."

"Have you *ever* loved Jean?"

"No. And if you tell anybody that I'll pee on your tomato plants."

"Then why did you marry her?"

"I was sick to almighty death of being alone."

He stepped out into the alley, tamped his butt into a mound of dirt and gravel, and headed into my kitchen for another bottle of Pabst Blue Ribbon.

During the war, he'd been stationed at the Kaiser Shipyards in San Francisco. He had taken in a bit of the world beyond the backwaters, and he liked it. In his mind, he was designed for fancier places. So he lived a life of quiet desperation—keeping books at the People's Bank, attending services at First United to keep the family peace, and nipping bourbon by the bucket full in his basement cubbyhole while Jean and Terry and Ramsay went on with their lives upstairs without him.

Gale was a trapped rat, dying to burst out of his cage. Soon enough he did.

Ramsay Stratton

On Warren Street, Terry slept in the sunny, square bedroom at the top of the stairs, with a window looking out over the back yard and alley that ran behind the house. His space was always neat as a pin and, wondrously, he didn't mind his messed-up kid sister hanging out there.

Gale had given him a bunch of colorful historical maps from the Smithsonian in Washington, and Terry had mounted them on his walls with thumb tacks. When I was six and seven and eight, I'd slip in there while he was out of the house, plop down on his gigantic soft blue comforter, and gaze up at the Northwest Territory, the original thirteen colonies, and the Louisiana Purchase, imagining the two of us on a wooden raft, floating down the Mississippi River to New Orleans like Huck Finn and Jim. I'd be so wrapped up in my reveries that I wouldn't even hear him come in the back door and up the stairs.

He didn't get mad and order me out of his domain. He just laid this bemused, wan, grown-up kind of smile on me, like a dad indulging a toddler in search of some attention. Then he'd scoot his hardback chair up to his little roll top desk and start reading the copy of *Time* or *Life* or *Business Week* he'd brought up from the kitchen.

I confessed to Jean when I was nine that I wanted to marry him.

"You *can't* marry your brother."

"Why not?"

"It's a sin."

"*Why* is it a sin?"

"You're violating God's will."

"*Why* am I violating God's will?"

She spun around from the sink and shot me a look. "It isn't natural."

"He's the most handsome boy in school."

"I imagine so."

"He has the most beautiful brown eyes I've ever seen. And he's going to an important person someday."

"Yes, he is."

"So why *shouldn't* I marry him?"

She dropped her dishrag, came across the room, and swatted me on the butt. "Shush now. You are *not* going to marry your brother and that's the end of that."

Two years after my confession, we went through the grand unveiling of the truth with Jean and Gale and Reverend Robert. Given what I'd told her about my feelings for Terry, I can't believe it was Jean's choice to come clean about the situation that early on—if ever. But Reverend Robert was a huge believer in coming clean, and I imagine he bullied her into it.

After that, Terry and I knew we were adopted, and that we came from different birth parents. But neither we nor the adults had any idea who they were. As I stumbled into adolescence, the situation got fiendishly difficult. The physical attraction grew. And at least in the beginning, I think it ran both ways.

He was strong enough to resist me. That's the crux of the matter. Any lust he may have felt for me was an unwanted complication that he locked away in an airtight chamber, a mile deep in his brain. I was weak, and if he had been as weak as me, we would have ended up having some sex.

Commissioner Red Yenser

In the spring of 1956, I was a thirty-three-year-old hardware store owner seeking election as Washington County Commissioner. I'd never run for public office. I was raw, energetic, immature—and hugely aroused by the intoxication of politics.

The party needed a candidate to oppose a popular incumbent named Bill Flowers. We don't elect many Democrats in Washington County, but Bill was one of them. All the Republicans in the county with stature said no to the race. In the spirit of sacrifice, I offered my services. The central committee endorsed me. I ran in the primary in May against two fringe candidates and won seventy-five percent of the vote.

Bill ignored me all summer, figuring I'd fade into the woodwork. But I hustled my tail off and turned it into a contest. After Labor Day, he realized he was going to have to work to get re-elected. And so one chilly Friday morning in late October, he and I found ourselves together up on the cramped, dusty stage in the auditorium of Marion Elementary School.

The steam heater was whistling hard, the room was stuffy as the devil, and half the seats or so were filled with teachers, the older students, and a few parents. We gave our talks, then opened the floor to questions. This scrawny boy with a thick shock of red-brown hair springs out of the back row, bounds up the aisle and stops at the foot of the stage. His eyes are big and bright and alive, and he's wearing a crisp, white button down shirt, dress slacks, and wingtips. Picture a kid that young in *wingtips*. He was so fresh and square and earnest it damn near hurt to look at him.

"I support Dwight David Eisenhower for president," he says. "I support Marietta's native son William O'Neill for governor. And I support *this man right here*, Mr. Red Yenser, for commissioner." His voice is calm and modulated, like a radio announcer's. But it seems to be packed with ten thousand volts of electricity. "Republicans are going to win a great victory on November 6th!"

There's scattered clapping, and a ripple of laughter. The crowd is astir. Here's this seven, eight-year old coming on like Edward R. Murrow. Up on the stage, Bill and I look at each other and crack up.

"Thank you, young man," Bill says. "We need more people with your kind of enthusiasm in public life. Can I convince you to change parties?"

The kid looks Bill straight in the eye and doesn't miss a beat. "No, sir. Eisenhower stands strong against Communism."

Bill wags a playful finger at him. "No stronger than Roosevelt and Truman."

"Republicans cut government fat."

"They cut muscle, too."

"And Republicans are leading the revival of the Ohio River Valley!"

He scoots back up the aisle to his seat and stays quiet for the rest of the program. After it was over, he hung around for a few minutes, and we got acquainted. That was the beginning of our friendship.

"You're going to *win*, Mr. Yenser."

"You think so?"

"Yes, sir. I feel it in my bones."

"I'm the underdog, you know."

"Sometimes underdogs win," he said. "If we *knew* who was going to get elected we wouldn't have to vote, would we?"

"I guess we wouldn't."

It was mighty strange, getting the most vigorous pep talk of my campaign from a fifth grader. I couldn't help but wonder what the source of it all was. In any case, young Terry turned out to be right. Eleven days later, Ike rode the crest of a tidal wave to his second term, O'Neill won the governorship, and Republicans swept all the other statewide offices. The surge rolled all the way down to Washington County and I beat Bill by a hundred and three votes.

I didn't lose another election for sixteen years.

Ruth Toops

On February 12th, 1957, Marietta celebrated the grandest event in its history, and Terry got a beautiful souvenir on his ninth birthday.

That was the day Rock Hudson came to town for the world premiere of his movie *Battle Hymn.* At that point, he was one of the biggest stars in Hollywood. The year before, he'd done *Giant* with Elizabeth Taylor and James Dean. A year later, he'd do *Pillow Talk* with Doris Day.

The town went utterly ape. School was dismissed for the day. We had ten thousand people lining the streets between the Hotel Lafayette, where Rock was staying, and the Grand Theater. The teenagers—girls *and* boys—were screeching like primates in heat. A group from the neighborhood was gathered in the parking lot of Flick's Market, right across from the theater.

Suddenly, Terry slipped away from us and headed down Front Street toward the Lafayette.

"Where are you going?" I said.

He beamed at me. "To track down Rock Hudson!" he said.

"You've got your nerve, boy."

"I'm dying to *touch* him," he said. "I need to see what Rock Hudson *feels* like."

"About the same as any other human being, I expect."

"I'm going to find him right now!"

Amazingly, he did. At the rear end of the Lafayette, on a wooden bench outside the service entrance, chatting up a bunch of reporters until a silver Cadillac convertible rolled in to pick him up for the motorcade to the Grand.

Terry strolled up and said good morning, Mr. Hudson. Today is my ninth birthday and I would love to shake your hand.

Rock said, let's get us a picture of that birthday handshake.

A photographer snapped the two of them together on the bench, and the next morning they showed up on the front page of the *Marietta Times*. A week later, the photo ran again, nationwide in the *National Enquirer*.

He adored that picture. We all did. He carried a reprint in his wallet, framed a big one to mount on his bedroom wall, and took it with him when he left home for college.

Now here's the craziest thing you've ever heard—thirty-six years later, it ended up in my hands.

Ramsay Stratton

On the afternoon JFK was killed, the schools closed at two o'clock and there was a steady line of kids streaming down Warren Street. I was already home, sitting in the front living room window with Jean. We could see Terry coming down the sidewalk toward us, alone, carrying the bulky, black briefcase he'd started using that year. He was fifteen, a sophomore in high school.

As he came up onto the porch, I saw a swatch of oozy blood under his nose, and his busted-up, bloated lip. He walked in the front door and laid his briefcase on the hall table.

"What happened to you?" Jean asked.

"A couple of the Catholic goons smacked me in the mouth."

"What in the world for?" Jean said.

"For daring to suggest we'll all be better off in America without Kennedy as our president."

"What are you talking about?" Jean said.

"He was an appeaser," Terry said. He pulled a handkerchief out of his pants pocket, balled it up, and pressed it against his nostrils.

Jean snorted. "He faced down Khrushchev and got the missiles out of Cuba."

"He made secret deals with the Communist Party," Terry said. "And he wanted to turn this country over to the United Nations."

Jean stomped into the kitchen. She rattled around in the fridge, and called back at him through the doorway. "Are you *glad* he's dead? Is that what you're saying?"

"I'm glad he isn't president anymore," Terry said.

"What an *awful* thing to say," Jean said. "Get upstairs and clean yourself up."

I was just as freaked as Jean was. The Terry I knew was a lover, not a fighter. Reserved, tactful, easygoing—and way too bright to get his face messed up by *anybody*, for *any* reason. I had no clue where the right-wing, John Birch Society bullshit was coming from. He wasn't mimicking the viewpoints of his parents, like most kids. Jean voted Republican because everybody else did, but I don't remember her ever uttering a passionate word about politics. And Gale had the same view of it as he did of religion. Politics was a pile of horse manure. Politicians were thieving for themselves and the cronies who put them in office. There was no reason for Joe Six Pack to take sides because Joe Six Pack was screwed up the yahoo no matter who was in or out.

Terry's lip took forever to heal up. The only time I ever saw it look that bad again was the morning he and Jack Cutler and the soldier boy mixed it up out at the cemetery.

Jack Cutler

Terry's sister nicknamed us the Magnificent Three, but we were never a gang, never a clique. You could make a plausible argument that we weren't even *friends*. The strange, twisted desire to brutalize ourselves by running two to three hours at a stretch was all we really had in common.

Running then wasn't like running now. It was not a faithful ritual practiced by tens of millions of white bread suburbanites. Distance runners were rare creatures. The high school didn't even have a cross country team—and track was nothing but a way to keep all the choice jocks in shape for football and basketball.

It was Reverend White who turned us on to the Ohio Valley Striders. That's a highfalutin name for a bunch of loonies who got together at various locales along the river to do twelve, fifteen, twenty mile runs. A couple of dozen guys and one eighty-eight-pound girl from Belpre we nicknamed the Biafra Kid. That's where Terry and I and Freddy Toops headed most Saturday mornings during junior year, pooling together to the start point in Freddy's loud, smoky beater of a Camaro or Terry's Fairlane.

There wasn't a whole lot to Freddy. He was an awesome physical specimen and that's about all he was. He possessed this ornery, defiant attitude that infuriated coaches and got him booted off every team he'd ever been on. So he found his own outlet. He could have been a fabulous 10K man, even a marathoner, but he didn't take care of himself. Freddy could only stick to one regimen—shoot the bull, watch the tube, pass the bottle around. He got by in running on raw animal strength—and exuberance.

Terry was more of a mystery. He was far less gifted physically than Freddy, but he worked his ass off. And he was grim about it, like he was punishing himself for some horrible act he'd committed. I ran with the two of them thirty times over the course of a couple of years, and I never once saw Freddy beat him. After the five hundred yard kick to the finish, it was always me third, Freddy second, Terry first.

I think Terry was spurred on by all those demons that came to possess him further down the pike.

Ramsay Stratton

In August, before the start of my sophomore year in high school, Jean and Gale split up.

Gale had gone to a bankers' conference in Cleveland and met a guy in the hotel bar who was a big wheel at a big bank in Atlanta. They bonded over bourbon and baseball, and he ended up offering Gale a job in his credit card department.

The big wheel was high on credit cards. He thought the concept of buying things with a piece of plastic was going to get *huge,* and he was giving a small town guy a shot at moving to the big city and getting in on the ground floor of the greatest invention since the light bulb. The small town guy didn't have to think about it long.

I was crushed. Completely blown away. Gale consumed an ocean of Jim Beam and Blue Ribbon down in his cubbyhole. He bickered with

Jean constantly. Any resemblance to Ward Cleaver or Ozzie Nelson or Jim Anderson was strictly coincidental. But he wasn't violent or dysfunctional, and he was decent to me. *Better* than decent compared to the fathers of some of my friends.

I had it out with him late one night in the kitchen as he packed up boxes of dishes and utensils for his move south. "What's wrong with you," I sobbed. "Why can't you stay married like everyone else?"

"I held on as long as I could."

"What the hell does that mean?"

"Your mother and I aren't right for each other," he said. "We never should have gotten married in the first place."

"Do you love her?"

"Yes, I do."

"Then why can't you work it out?"

"It's too late to work it out," he said.

"Then what the hell, Gale –"

"You won't call me *dad* anymore?"

"I'm goddam sorry I *ever* called you dad."

All I could do was curl up with a ratty blanket on the couch in the basement and wail. There were no cries of anguish from anyone else. For Jean, this was a chance to end the thing civilly, with a minimum of rancor. The prospect of being free from the man had her flitting around the house as light and fluffy as a potato. And Terry was so matter-of-fact about the whole thing it was spooky.

"What's going to happen to us?" I asked him.

"*Nothing* is going to happen to us."

"What are we going to do for money?"

"Mom works," he said. "I'll get a job. And Dad will send child support."

"Don't you hate the asshole's guts for doing this?"

"Dad deserves to be happy," Terry said. "Maybe he will be now."

"He has to make us all miserable to be happy?"

"I'm not miserable," Terry said. "I don't think Mom is either."

"This is the sorriest excuse for a family I've ever seen," I said. "I'm going to find my birth parents as soon as I can."

"You might be better off without them."

"Aren't you curious?"

"Of course," he said. "But what if they're monsters?"

"You're not a monster. Why would they be?"

Terry looked down at the floor. "Sister," he said. "I'm not really sure *what* I am."

Commissioner Red Yenser

One summer afternoon, Terry came to see me at the courthouse.

Nine years had passed since our encounter in the school auditorium. During that time we'd seen each other around town and exchanged helloes, not much more. But I followed community news and I knew about his achievements—Debate Club champion; President, Young Americans for Freedom (YAF), Southeastern Ohio Chapter; Runner of the Year, Ohio Valley Striders.

On top of all that, he was a good-looking kid. He had nice thick hair, a pair of big brown eyes, and a calm, steady gaze that immediately put you at ease. If you owned a face like Terry's, you could get a lot of folks to do a lot of things for you that maybe they otherwise wouldn't do. I think he was learning to use that to his advantage.

The purpose of his visit was to ask me to serve as his sponsor in a program called Youth in Government. If I could find something useful for him to do, he could get out of class at one o'clock every day of fall semester, work for me for three or four hours in the afternoon, and get academic credit at the same time.

"Tell me something about YAF," I said.

"Yes, sir?"

"Are you guys going to stop boycotting Firestone for building their rubber factory in Rumania?"

His smile bloomed, and his eyes lit up. I was hitting him where he lived. "I had to break ranks with the group on that issue," he said.

"That's never easy," I said. "Especially when you're president of the group."

"I respectfully submit to the will of the majority. But personally, I don't support our Firestone boycott."

"No?"

"I believe in the free market, Mr. Yenser. Free means *free*. As far as I'm concerned, Firestone can build their rubber factory on the moon. Or in the middle of Red Square in Moscow."

"What about fighting Communism?"

"The way to fight Communism is to promote capitalism," he said. "If we do that, it will collapse under the weight of its own inferiority."

"And the Berlin Wall will come tumbling down?"

His face flushed and he looked down at his wingtips. "Can I be honest with you, Mr. Yenser?"

"Aren't you always?"

"I'm tired of boycotts and debates," he said. "I want to get into *real* politics. See how it *really* works."

I was happy to oblige him. I knew his parents had just split up, and thought a new pursuit might help his frame of mind. I wanted to give Youth in Government a boost. And I did have something useful for him to do—helping re-elect Gil Brown, my Republican colleague on the board of commissioners. We controlled the board two to one; Gil's seat was the only one on the ballot in November. We had to win to keep control. The Democrats had a viable challenger, a township trustee named Dick Finn. Our campaign needed to be stronger than theirs.

Terry wrote up a proposal and got it approved. The week after Labor Day, Gil and I took him out to dinner at the Gun Room in the Lafayette and brought him into the fold. We put him to work posting yard signs, dropping literature, stuffing envelopes, manning our primitive phone bank. He did a spectacular job.

Three weeks before the election, an envelope arrived at my house in the mail. Inside was a single-page mimeographed copy of a typewritten flier:

To the Voters of Washington County:

Dick Finn, Franklin Township Trustee and current Democrat candidate for county commissioner, was recently arrested by police and charged with public urination and loitering at Berliner Park in Columbus. Why would Mr. Finn be at Berliner Park in Columbus? Could he be participating in the repulsive acts of homosexual perversion that are known to occur there on a regular basis? We believe Mr. Finn owes us all of us a complete and immediate explanation.

Your Concerned Neighbors

I was stunned. I had no idea who had written the thing, or whether the allegation was true. I did discover that nearly three hundred people got the same flier. But that's all I *ever* found out for sure.

I saw Finn three days later at the Kiwanis Club forum. He looked like he'd been jabbed in the gut with a jackhammer. His campaign withered on the vine, and Gil won going away with more than sixty percent of the vote.

The day after the election, I loaned Terry my pickup truck, and he headed out onto the highways to pick up Gil's yard signs. We didn't want people complaining about the mess we'd left all over the county. That night, he drove the truck back to my house. Along with Gil's signs, there were dozens of Finn's piled in the bed, too.

"What are you doing with those?" I asked.

He smirked. "I don't want the poor little fairy to get a reputation as a litterbug," he said. "He's got enough problems, don't you think?"

Fifteen months after the election, Finn resigned as township trustee, divorced his wife, and moved down to a cabin near Lake Cumberland in Kentucky. A couple of years later, he went out into the woods, put a shotgun in his mouth, and pulled the trigger.

No doubt that sordid piece of crap I got in the mail had something to do with it.

Ruth Toops

We threw a graduation party for Freddy. I was overjoyed he'd made it through high school and gotten his diploma. We invited people to come by on Sunday afternoon, after the ceremony.

Fifty or sixty people showed up through the course of the evening. It got pretty lively in the house and out in the yard. Jean Stratton came in alone. I told you I could count on one hand the times I saw her enjoying herself. That night was one of them.

She was immensely proud of Terry. He'd weathered her split from Gale with flying colors, he was working for Red Yenser at the courthouse, and he was going to Ohio State in the fall with scholarship money from the Chamber of Commerce, Firestone, and First United Church.

Later on, Terry came in with Jack Cutler. Freddy hauled them onto the back porch and threw his arms around them in front of me.

Mom, he said, these are my running buddies. Runners are the greatest people in the world. You are the greatest mother in the world. And this is the greatest night of my life.

Gentlemen, he said. Let us make a pledge in front of my mother that we will get together and *run*. We have lost our way. We must run together one more time and rekindle the glory of our yesterday!

The three of them pumped their fists in the air. Freddy took my hand and gave me an awkward peck on the cheek.

It was a corny moment that moved me to tears. For a day or two, I actually believed what he was trying to tell me—look, Mom, I'm not turning out so bad after all. I'm going to make it in life. If I wasn't going to make it in life, I wouldn't have these two smart, polite, great-looking guys from good families coming to my graduation party.

Of course, we were deluding ourselves. His dad was sick of him and wanted him out of the house as soon as possible. Freddy had a job lined up at Remington Rand, working the graveyard shift, but he had trouble holding onto jobs because he couldn't get along with his bosses. Higher education was not an option. We didn't have the money. He didn't have the smarts.

Freddy was going to move into some dumpy apartment, drink beer, and race hot rods through the hills for a year or so. Then, after he turned nineteen, he was going to get drafted into the Army and shipped off to Vietnam.

We knew that. We didn't talk about it.

Steve Kerth

I was twenty-five years old that summer, working as an emergency room nurse at St. Joseph Hospital in Parkersburg. Single, unattached, deep in the closet.

So deep in the closet that I expected to wake up one morning on the doorstep of the earth's core surrounded by molten lava and hell fire, with a million fingers of the devil pointed straight at my worthless, pitiful faggot ass.

To cope with the tension of having a secret life, I ran with the Ohio Valley Striders. One dawn in July twenty of us met in the town of Neptune, along the river, and did a twelve-mile loop run on a wood chip and asphalt trail through the Milhoan Ridge. It was sunny and sweltering. We were watering the wilderness with rivers of sweat. At the ten-mile mark he was a hundred yards ahead of me, alone. I broke away from my pack, reeled him in with an easy, tender move, and caught him right at eleven.

We motored stride for stride for a minute or so, a long hot silence hanging between us. I tried to pass. He stuck to me. I tried again. He refused to let me break away.

I was six-foot two, one seventy-five, and maybe ten percent of it was fat. I could pass damn near anybody I wanted, especially a guy who looked to be five-nine, five-ten, one forty tops. But this son of a gun would not yield. In the last quarter mile, I had to find a new gear and hit the turbo all the way to the finish line to beat him by five steps.

He was alone that day. His buddies weren't with him. We toweled off in the parking lot and shucked through some macho jive before we both admitted how exhausted we were.

"I'm spent," is what he said. I love that word, *spent.*

My place in Belleville was just a few miles away. I asked him if he wanted to stop there and scrub up before he made the trek back to Marietta.

After a moment of hesitation, he said sure.

It turned into a memorable afternoon. We each took a shower, cracked beers, and ate cold fried chicken and potato salad out on my back porch. I always smoke a few brimming bowls of ganja after a long run, and I asked him if he wanted to join me.

"I've tried the stuff. It doesn't do much for me."

"You're smoking dirt weed," I said. "Have a couple hits of this and it'll sure enough do something for you."

He got high all right. We both did. I put on the Byrds *Fifth Dimension* and showed him my books and albums in the bedroom. He stood in front of the big window, looking at the woods behind my house, and my loins surged at the sight of his ass. I came up behind him, slipped two fingers down the back of his shorts, and grazed the crevice between his cheeks. His knees wobbled, and he let out a little cry.

I spoke softly into his ear. "Have you ever made it with a girl?"

"Three times with the same girl. Always with a rubber."

"What about sucking cock?"

"No, never."

"Is that something you want to try? It can be as good as making it with a girl. Or better."

He turned around and nodded.

I pulled the window shade down, stripped naked, and sat down on the edge of the bed. He got down on the hardwood floor in front of me, put two pillows under his knees, and tilted his head up.

It wasn't a timid exchange. He didn't mind taking orders, and he didn't mind going a long time. He worked me every which way but loose for ten minutes before I offered up a gushing load. He swallowed every drop of it down and barely flinched. I could hardly believe he was a virgin.

We switched out, and I did to him exactly what he'd done to me. I rarely reciprocate, and when I do, it isn't out of the goodness of my heart. It's because I want a taste of the guy. He was as sweet and succulent as fresh pineapple.

He stopped by my place one more time that summer, after a half-marathon in Charleston. He had a thick wad of twenties and wanted to take as much ganja off my hands as I was willing to part with. I sold him a dry quarter-pound with huge buds and very little lumber for a better than decent price. Basically, I was fucking myself over, but I didn't mind. He stuffed it all into the bottom of his gear bag, wrapped up tight in a black plastic raincoat.

"Why don't we smoke some right now?" I said.

"Later would be better," he said. "Right now I want you to spread me out on the bed, lube me up, and fuck me in the ass. And when you do that, I'd like *both* of us to be sober."

I fulfilled his request. Afterwards, we sat out on the back porch and ate roast beef sandwiches and cole slaw. Then he left. That was the last time I ever saw Terry Stratton.

Ramsay Stratton

One rainy afternoon, a few weeks before he left for Ohio State, I went into his room to talk and ended up bawling my eyes out on his bed like a five-year-old.

I couldn't help it. The tears had been damming up all summer long, and they gushed out of me. The thought of him gone and me alone in the house with Jean was almost making me physically ill.

He let me cry. He didn't try to stop me. After I calmed down, he pulled me up off the bed and hugged me long and hard. I'd never had a hug like that in my life. I felt fifty thousand percent better.

Jean was at work. He pulled a lockbox out from under his bed and laid it on his desk. He opened it and took out a pack of matches, a small wooden pipe, and a plastic baggie of grass.

"Would you like some?" he asked. He filled the pipe, handed it to me, and lit it. "Inhale a tiny bit," he said. "Hold it in your lungs as long as you can. It'll relax you."

That was the first time I ever got stoned. We spent cocktail hour cooking spaghetti and meatballs and listening to Dylan's *Blonde on Blonde* with the volume cranked up and the windows shut so we wouldn't bug the neighbors.

Before he left for college, he gifted me an ounce of his stash. It was a powerfully humane act on his part. Because grass led me to music, music gave me the courage to draw, and drawing gave me a meaningful life. I've seen my cartoons everywhere now—books, magazines, coffee mugs, billboards, tea towels, cocktail napkins, magnets. And whenever and wherever I see one, I always thank big bro for giving me my first nudge in that direction.

Jack Cutler

It took all summer, but the Magnificent Three fulfilled the pledge we'd made to each other at Freddy's house on graduation night. We set up a Saturday morning run in Wayne National Forest, a few days before Terry and I were going to leave town. We agreed to go up together, but on Friday night Terry called me and said he wanted to drive separately. He said he'd meet us in the parking lot at the trailhead.

It was a freakishly cool September morning, with temperatures in the low fifties. Overcast, dry, windless. Perfect for a long run. Freddy and I got to the trailhead a few minutes late and Terry wasn't there. That was odd because he was virtually always on time. We warmed up and stretched. Finally, we took off without him.

We were heavy and slow and horribly out of shape. Freddy looked so strung out I thought he was going to collapse. We struggled through twelve miles in a little less than two hours. I kept thinking we'd hook up with Terry somewhere along the trail, and that the three of us would finish up together.

But Terry was nowhere to be found. He never showed up.

Two / Columbus 1968–1981

Kris Lamborn

Terry didn't have me at hello. He had me *before* hello—light years before. He was the most attractive guy I'd ever seen in my life. I felt a craving to cleave to him the first time our eyes locked.

He was at every football game during the fall of my freshman year at Ohio State, ten or so rows behind me in the student section, at the closed end of the Horseshoe. I twisted around in my seat and snuck glances at him constantly. We looked so much alike we could have been brother and sister: thick auburn hair, wide-set brown eyes, high cheekbones, big foreheads, slender body frames. I spent a grotesque amount of time daydreaming about how beautiful our children were going to be. And at that point I had not said word *one* to him.

At the Michigan game at the end of the season, I decided to approach him. I hadn't run into him anywhere else on campus, and I thought I might never see him again.

We'd been passing a flask of gin up and down our row all afternoon. I'd been a good girl and just said no, but in the last minutes of the fourth quarter, as the crowd went banzai over the Buckeye romp, I took two sips for courage. When the flask came back my way, I took two more.

The game ended, thousands of fans surged through the police lines onto the field, and I broke away from my friends and pushed up the concrete steps through the crush of bodies, toward Terry's seat. But I couldn't spot him. I'd lost sight of him in the chaos.

Two bellowing rowdies came charging hard down the aisle from above. My head spun, my knees knocked, and just as they were about to trample me, a strong pair of arms wrapped me up from behind and pulled me out of their path.

It was him. I *knew* that before I turned around.

"Are you all right?" he said.

"Yes," I stammered. "Thank you."

"I don't mean to scare you," he said. "But you were about to get hurt."

An exotic way to break the ice with my future husband. Him bear hugging me in the middle of a slow motion riot in a football stadium. I was a shivering wreck at first because I was so nervous, but he seemed like he *wanted* to talk to me. That—and the gin—took a lot of the nervousness away.

We left the Horseshoe and moved with the throng across Woodruff, then through the walkway between St. John Arena and the ice rink. Behind the 7-Eleven on Lane, he had a bike chain-locked to the foot of a dumpster. That surprised me because there weren't many bikers on campus, and nearly all of them were hippie freaks or science geeks. From the looks of him, Terry was neither.

"Where are you heading?" I said.

"The Jai-Lai." That was a huge, popular restaurant a half-mile south of the stadium.

"To eat?"

"To work."

"You work and go to school at the same time?"

He gave me an indulgent smile, the kind a worldly junior gives a naive freshman. I blushed hard.

"I wash dishes Friday and Saturday nights," he said.

"Are you going to the Rose Bowl?"

"I hope so," he said. "But I've got to find the money and get time off work. What about you?"

"I hope so, too. But I'm not sure."

Actually, at that moment, I *knew* I was going. My parents were fervent Buckeye fans, and dad had already put down deposits on a package tour for him, mom, my older sister and me. We were flying to Los Angeles on a charter DC-6 three days after Christmas.

But as Terry hopped onto his bulky, black Schwinn with wire baskets straddling the back wheel, I didn't tell him that. WASP princess jets to West Coast with mummy and daddy and sissy while working stiff stays home to wash dishes. That seemed like fifteen yards for unnecessary roughness.

So there I was, telling my first lie, fifteen minutes after we'd met. Not a deception, not a withholding of information. A bald-faced lie in response to a direct question. Terry deceived and withheld and lied to me uncountable times. For him I think it was second nature, a way of life. What other people called lying he called making his way through life. He could say anything to anyone with an absolutely straight face—and he did.

But I always dwell on the lies he told. I told my share, too.

As he pedaled off toward the Jai-Lai, he turned around on his seat and gave me this crisp, little hand salute, like a cop or a soldier—and a huge, beautiful smile.

"Let's get together again!" I yelled.

We did. But it wasn't until six weeks later, after winter quarter started in January. I found him studying in the basement of the Union one Friday night, and we went out for beer and pizza. We were pretty much inseparable after that.

Turns out Terry *did* make it to the Rose Bowl that year, with two of his gym rat friends. But our paths never crossed. I was at the Huntington Sheraton in Pasadena. He was at some fleabag motel down near LAX.

At least that's where he *claimed* to be. Of course he told me about meeting O.J. But other than that, he never said much about that trip.

O.J. Simpson

This happened on December 30th, 1968, two nights before we played Ohio State in the Rose Bowl.

The team was holed up at South Harbor Inn in Rancho Palos Verdes, next to the old Ocean Trails Golf Course. That's where we went to hunker down and focus before big games. It's getting on toward bed check time and A.C. and I are chilling on this brick patio, out behind the swimming pool. Nobody else around. Quiet as can be. Nothing but stars, surf and the hummy buzz of insects.

This white dude pops out from behind a metal storage shed out by the parking lot and sprints toward us. Slim, short hair, fit as a fiddle, and dressed like some Ken Doll: button down shirt, khaki chinos, a pair of swanky running shoes.

Buckeye fan, can you believe that? I kid you not. Drove forty-four hours straight through from Ohio with two buddies for the game. He made some phone calls and dug around in the papers, found out we were staying at South Harbor, and decided to check us out.

Ballsy of the dude to just waltz into our camp. Of course, L.A. in '68 wasn't like L.A. now, with iron gates, machine guns, ID cards, rent-a-cops, metal detectors, 24/7 cameras and the rest of the happy horseshit. The atmosphere, the vibe, *the entire way of life* was mellow, friendly, small-town.

Still. The dude is displaying moxie showing his face here. Of that there is no doubt.

Congratulations on your Heisman, he says. You *may* be the greatest running back in the history of football.

You're very kind. Thank you.

I can't believe I ran into you like this. This has *got* to be the luckiest day of my life.

A.C. says: Where are your buddies tonight?

Back at the motel. Getting down with some ladies.

Where's your lady? A.C. says.

Had to leave her in Ohio.

So I say, you're taking a solo cruise around the City of Angels tonight, just for shits and giggles. Is that what's going on?

He blushes and shoots me a big goofy grin. That's what's going on, he says. And then—O.J., could you sign an autograph for me?

No way, I say. Acting pissed off. I don't sign autographs for *Buckeye* fans. I mean, what would my teammates think? What would our *fans* think? Jesus, I shouldn't even be talking to you.

Just pulling his leg. Having some fun. You can pin some nasty shit on me, but I'll sign an autograph for *any* fan, *any*time, *any*where. But Ken Doll can't see I'm kidding. He's got this frightened, hurt look, like he drove all the way to the edge of the ocean to search me out and got *incredibly* lucky, and now he has to leave without getting what he came for.

He says, if I got you high right now on some really righteous herb, would you give me an autograph?

I'm thinking, what is going on? I am looking at maybe the straightest arrow I have ever seen.

Are you military? I ask.

Fuck military, he says. Fuck LBJ. And fuck Vietnam.

Up the ass, A.C. says. With an electric cattle prod.

Are you some kind of narc? I say.

Hell no.

Trying to set us up?

I may be a redneck hilljack from Ohio, but I am no goddam narc.

A.C. touches my elbow and gives me his secret look, saying: He's cool. Let's partake of his offering quick, right here, right now, before bed check.

We slip out onto the first fairway of the golf course, into a grove of trees. The breeze is getting stiff coming off the ocean, but Ken Doll gets his joint fired up like a seasoned stoner.

I'm San Francisco born and raised, no stranger to the finer strains of ganja. But this was the strongest shit I have ever inhaled in my *life.* An absolute bulldozer high.

We stop back at the patio behind the pool. He sprints out to his car and comes back with a notebook and a fancy gold fountain pen.

What did you say your name was? I ask.

Terry.

I sign three personal autographs "To Terry," on three separate pieces of paper.

He heads back to the parking lot and climbs into this clunker of a Fairlane with a bumper sticker on the back—*America: Love It or Leave It.* He starts the engine, yells "Go Bucks!" out the window, and rolls off into the night.

Of course I thought I'd never see the dude again. So picture this: twenty years later Nicole and I are treadmilling at Sports Club L.A. and there he is up on the balcony, sipping some concoction out of a red plastic cup at the juice bar.

I have to focus hard and do three takes to make sure. But yeah. He had a face that was hard to forget. Groovy head of hair, soft brown eyes, Grand Canyon smile.

It's him. And hanging on his arm was Gary Coleman's big sister, from that TV show. The strung-out chick who knocked off the dry cleaners in Vegas with a pellet gun. What was her name?

Dan O'Hanlon

.
He was Republican, twenty, in the middle of his junior year at Ohio State. I was Democrat, twenty-three, eighteen months out of Notre Dame. We started working as pages in the Ohio House of Representatives on the same day—January 8th, 1969.

Even in a place as full of raging careerists as the statehouse, it didn't take Stratton long to get noticed. It was his look, his attitude, the way he carried himself. Whenever he moved, he moved quickly. Remember how Pete Rose bolted to first base whenever he drew a walk? That's who Stratton looked like. And in meetings he sat ramrod straight at the table underneath the rostrum, ready to spring to his feet at the command of the chairman, scribbling notes, eyeballing documents, listening raptly to whatever brand of bullshit our distinguished lawmakers were serving up that day.

Many mornings, we'd share a cup of coffee in the cafeteria in the basement of the statehouse and hash out the events of the day. It soon became apparent that he had no ambivalence about the system. He was in it whole hog, and he was so damned *earnest* about it all. What did he think of me? He was bewildered by my skepticism, impressed by my Catholic sense of duty, and *quite* in awe of the O'Hanlons of Rocky River—my father was a corporate lawyer and major Democratic fundraiser, my mother was the Cuyahoga County treasurer, and my uncle—my father's older brother—was starting his third term in the U.S. House in Washington. At Notre Dame, I'd spent my summers interning in his office on Capitol Hill.

"Tell me, hombre," he said one morning in the cafeteria. "Do you want to make it back to Washington someday?"

"I'm not sure," I said. "The further up the line I go in this business, the worse it seems to get."

"What gets worse?"

"So many well-meaning individuals," I said. "So many bad decisions."

"If their decisions reflect the will of the people, why is that bad?"

"Because the people want quick fixes instead of real solutions. And that's what politicians give them, time and time again."

He leaned across the table and touched my wrist. "I'll share a secret if you promise not to tell."

Young Republican 27

"For my ears only."

"Washington is where I'm headed," he said. "Bad decisions, quick fixes, phony solutions and all. Washington is where *everything* happens, and that's where I want to be."

That spring, he got assigned to work on the budget bill with the Finance Committee. He was writing fiscal notes for members about the impacts of all kinds of provisions. I have no idea how he pulled that off. Pretty soon there was whispering among the aides and pages that Stratton wasn't as smart as he seemed to be, that he got the Finance assignment by going down on the chairman, on the speaker, on anybody he needed to go down on to get what he wanted.

That made zero sense to me. Yes, Stratton was an ass kisser, a sycophant. He was bewitched by power and the people who wielded it. If the right person had told him to drop to his knees and roll a cow patty up Route 4 to Lake Erie with his nose, he would have done it. But sexually servicing men in exchange for promotions? It seemed beyond ridiculous, and I didn't believe a word of it.

Back in the old days, before he got rich and famous and ruined his life, there was so much about him I didn't know.

Ruth Toops

Freddy died on May 12th, 1969, on Ap Bia Mountain, along the border between South Vietnam and Laos. The tribes living there called it the Mountain of the Crouching Beast. The American soldiers fighting there called it Hamburger Hill. That was their description of what their faces would look like after the killing was over.

Freddy's battalion was tracking down North Vietnamese troops hiding out in the jungle. They set up a command post in a clearing halfway up the mountain. Patrolling at dusk, an American Cobra helicopter mistook the post for an enemy encampment, swooped low, and sprayed it with machine gun fire. Twenty soldiers on the ground were wounded, and four were killed. Freddy was one of them.

We didn't know at the time that he had died by friendly fire. All we were told was that the post had been "attacked." We had to badger the Army for ten years before we finally learned the truth.

We did get a letter that fall from the medic who was with him at the end: "Your son took a round to the groin and a round to the chest. He went into shock quickly from massive internal bleeding. I'm sorry to say I could do nothing for him. I wish I could have done more. His last words were 'Doc, I'm going to be all right, aren't I?' I lied and told him he was going to be fine."

I wrote back to the young man and thanked him for that final act of kindness.

Jack Cutler

Fifty cars followed the hearse from First United Church to the cemetery. Freddy's plot was jammed in with hundreds of others in the low, flat section that rolled down to the river between two sloping hillsides. The bugle sounded. Old Glory fluttered in the breeze. All the Handsome Johnnies in uniform saluted, and the gravediggers lowered Freddy's tattered remains into the ground. Ramsay Stratton dropped a bouquet of red roses on top of the coffin.

After the ceremony, people hung around. Terry was thirty yards up one hillside, alone, reading markers. I hadn't talked to him since our graduation summer, the night before his no-show at the Wayne Forest run with Freddy and me. I walked up the hill and said hello. He apologized for not showing up that morning, and we made some stilted conversation and caught up with each other as the line of cars began to weave out of the cemetery.

"It's a damn shame about Freddy dying," he said.

"He didn't die," I said. "He got his balls blown off in the middle of some shit-stinking jungle for no reason."

"Jack."

"That's what happened to Freddy."

"Calm down."

"How high does the body count have to get before *you* get angry?"

"Kennedy and LBJ got us into this war," he said. "We can't just march out."

"Why not? We marched in."

"There's light at the end of the tunnel," he said. "The president is leading us there."

I was yelling now. "The only place Nixon is leading us is Cambodia!"
"Peace with honor."
"Peace with honor is a crock of shit!"
"You're acting like a creep, Jack."
"Me?"
"We're here to bury a patriot and a friend and you're flinging your juvenile rage in my face."

A bulky, zit-faced Johnny angled up the slope toward us. He pointed at me. "We'd appreciate it if you'd leave," he said.

"I'll leave when I'm damn well ready."

"Your mouth is out of line," he said. "You're offending people."

"Who?"

"*Me.*"

With three fingers, Terry nudged me hard in the neck, an inch or two below my Adam's apple. "Listen to the man," he said. "Get out of here."

I pivoted, swung hard and fast with my left fist and hit him flush on the nose. As the blood trickled out, he dropped to his knees in the grass, moaning.

I lifted my foot back to kick him, but before I could follow through, the Johnnie yanked me around and sent me ass backward onto the ground with a savage punch to the gut. I rose up to face him just as he smacked me in the mouth.

"Leave! Now!"

As everybody in the cemetery stared in silence, I staggered down the slope toward my car.

"Piece of hippie shit garbage!" the Johnnie screamed. "Cut your fucking hair!"

I bid farewell to Marietta a few years later, headed out to northern California, and never returned. The only time I ever saw Stratton's face again was on the tube five or six years ago, when he was bopping around the country, screaming about Bill Clinton and Monica Lewinsky and the stained blue dress.

My God. The depths to which the guy descended. But I have to give the phony, two-faced son of a bitch some credit. He was still running his miles.

Kris Lamborn

On the night of the first moonwalk, at the Lamborn mansion across Club Road from the second fairway at Scioto in Upper Arlington, my father introduced Terry to Governor Jim Rhodes. That was when I saw, for the first time, how serious Terry was about making it in the business of politics.

The governor and dad were kindred souls. Profit was not a dirty word for Jim Rhodes. It wasn't for Bob Lamborn, either. He owned and operated Columbus Fasteners, a wholesale distributor of nuts, bolts, clips and clamps to concerns large and small in twelve foreign countries, Guam, Puerto Rico, and all fifty states. Dad was a top-level donor to the governor's campaign fund and a staunch backer of his Jobs and Progress program.

He and mom had sent him an invitation, but they didn't really expect him to make an appearance. They were giddy when he called on Sunday morning to say he planned to drop by the house for an hour.

My parents were not social animals, and they disdained extravagant displays of wealth. But they let their hair down big time that day—three open bars, catered dinners, a five-piece Dixieland jazz band, and a sprawling red, white and blue canopy tent in the back yard. They even hired a little shuttle bus to ferry folks who had to park way down at the bottom of the hill. The first of two hundred guests arrived shortly after the *Eagle* landed on the lunar surface at four p.m. and the last of them didn't go home until the astronauts climbed back into their module at one o'clock Monday morning.

At seven o'clock, a plain vanilla Ford sedan driven by a Highway Patrol trooper braked in front of the house. The governor stepped out of the passenger seat alone. Terry watched him intently as he worked his way up the driveway through knots of well-wishers and greeted mom and dad on the back patio. That's where he and Terry shook hands.

The look on Terry's face at that moment truly disturbed me. We were only six months into our relationship, and I'd never seen it before. It was like he was gazing into the face of God. For a moment, I thought he might drop to his knees and kiss the man's feet.

Rhodes went into our kitchen. Terry excused himself and followed him inside. Through the window, I spied on them as they conversed one-on-one in the breakfast nook for five minutes before the governor moved on.

Inside, I found Terry down in the basement, messing around at the pool table in the rec room. Even in the middle of the house I grew up in, surrounded by the people who cared about me most, I wanted to be next to him all the time.

"What did you talk to the governor about?" I said.

"The new budget bill," he said. "Tax credits, investment options, rebates for small businesses."

"He seemed interested."

"I'm telling him some things he doesn't know. Useful things, I hope."

For the next forty minutes, Terry shadowed the man from a discreet distance and studied his every word and move. After the governor left, he was moody and distant in the midst of the gaiety. As nightfall came on, I dragged him out to the back edge of the property, away from all the revelers and up into the studio apartment we kept above the garage. I closed all the curtains and turned on the little black-and-white TV. We pushed off our shoes, lay down on the lumpy, single bed and watched the screen in the gathering darkness.

"What's wrong with you tonight?" I asked him.

"Jim Rhodes doesn't want anything to do with me anymore."

"Why do you say that?"

"I'm afraid I came off as a total jerk."

"How?"

"There's a time to talk, and a time to keep your mouth shut," he said. "I need to learn the difference."

"Why does it matter so much?"

"Because I can't get to where I want to go by myself," he said. "I need to hitch my wagon to a star. And Jim Rhodes is the biggest star in this town."

On the screen, Armstrong popped out of the module hatch in his big, silver suit and bounded down the ladder to the lunar surface. There was a roar from inside the house.

"This *might* be the greatest moment in the history of the human race," I said. "Could we *possibly* enjoy it together?"

I wrapped my arms around his waist from behind, unzipped him, and caressed his shaft and balls over his underpants. The man had so many exquisite features it was easy to overlook his gorgeous horn. Like always, it swelled slowly and *very* surely into my hand.

"Is this for me?" I whispered.

"For you and you alone."

We peeled off our clothes, and I climbed aboard like a space cowboy and sent him into orbit the old-fashioned way.

Howard "Mac" McKenzie

I worked for Jim Rhodes for thirty-three years. I started as an errand boy in his first run for governor in '50 and walked out of the statehouse with him in '83 at the end of his last term. I never saw him more depressed than he was after his loss to Taft in the Senate primary in '70. Jim won fifteen elections in his career; he only lost four. The loss to Taft was by far the most painful.

People say he was tired of politics at that point, that he was relieved to lose, that he wanted to invest in Florida condos and Wendy's hamburgers and get rich.

None of that is true. Rhodes lived and breathed politics every waking minute of his life. He *hated* to lose. And appearances aside, wealth didn't matter all that much to him. Florida condos and Wendy's hamburgers turned out to be nothing much more than a way to pass the time before he launched his next bid for office.

The state constitution barred him from running for governor again without sitting out four years. Jim had always had a strong dose of Potomac Fever, and he wanted to win the open seat in the Senate and move directly to Capitol Hill in Washington. Many of us were eager to move with him, including me, and Terry Stratton, who'd busted his ass like a mule during the campaign.

What stopped us in our tracks was the four kids getting killed at Kent State the day before the primary in May. Right or wrong, that ruined Jim Rhodes in the eyes of many people.

It was a violent era. An era of fear, mistrust, anger, destruction. We forget that today. Jim activated the Guard *thirty-six* times in eight years to control civil insurrections. How many insurrections do we have these days that require armed intervention by the state?

The young men who fired on the students on May 4th had spent March and April patrolling the Ohio Turnpike in jeeps and armored cars, protecting motorists during a Teamsters strike by truck drivers. From there they were reassigned to the Kent campus, after protestors torched the ROTC building. The public they were supposed to be protecting didn't give a hoot about what they were doing. Their superiors had told them they'd be going home. They'd been pushed beyond their limits. Well beyond. And it was me and my colleagues, sitting on our fat asses in our fancy suits at the statehouse, who were pushing the hardest. I felt that way. Other members of the inner circle felt that way. Deep down in his gut, I think the governor did, too.

All hell broke loose then. The militants got active on every campus in the state. We circled the wagons and put up a brave front, but we were heartsick about what happened. Don't let anybody tell you otherwise.

The blood of those four dead kids was on our hands. We had to live with that forever.

Terry Stratton

May 10th, 1970

Dear Governor Rhodes:

Thank you for the opportunity you gave me to serve on your staff during the primary campaign. The experience was immensely rewarding. The knowledge and insights I gained were invaluable.

Although the outcome of the election was not the one we wanted, we made a valiant effort. There is no shame in defeat. I hope all of us in the party can unite now and defeat the Democrats in November.

With regard to this week's tragedy at Kent State, I am confident that I speak for the vast majority of college students when I say thank you.

Your decisions to send troops to Kent State—and to Ohio University and Ohio State—were right decisions. They were just and appropriate decisions.

Order must be preserved. Laws must be obeyed. Violence and hooliganism, in the name of any cause, cannot be tolerated in a free society.

You have a duty to protect the lives and property of the state's citizens. You have chosen not to shirk that duty, whatever the consequences to you personally, or to your career. For that, millions of us are grateful.

Our friend and colleague, Bob Lamborn of Columbus Fasteners, has said it best: "The governor is making the tough calls. And he is making the right calls."

Your dedication to the people of Ohio is awe-inspiring. I stand ready to serve you in the future, wherever and however needed.

> *Sincerely,*
> *Terry Stratton*
> *Ohio State University, Class of 1970*
> *Budget Analyst / Office of the Speaker of the House*

Ramsay Stratton

A couple of weeks after Kent State, Terry called me at my dormitory at Ohio U. in Athens.

"How's the revolution going down there?" he asked.

"Campus is still closed," I said. "We've got porkies camped out on the East Green."

"They're here too," he said. "Four thousand of them. But we've reopened and we're going to class."

"My roomie and I are coming to Columbus Sunday for the Hendrix show."

"Come Saturday," he said. "We're throwing a spring bacchanal. You can crash in our attic."

Kris was gone for the weekend, visiting her sister in Chicago, and Terry was flying solo. The ramshackle ranch house he shared with three guys was west of campus, across the river, out of the curfew zone. When we arrived at six o'clock, the bash was going strong across five lawns, each with a keg flowing and a grill burning.

Things got louder and crazier as the evening unfolded. A Credence-style garage band set up in a driveway and started cranking. My roomie crossed paths with a long-lost crush from high school and disappeared. At nine o'clock, the porkies swooped in without warning and shut it *all* down: the kegs, the music, the rowdy crowd spilling into the street. It got confrontational, a bunch of guys and a chick got frisked and cuffed and hauled away in a paddy wagon, and the festivities ended with a painful thud. Maybe it was the death spirit of Kent State lingering in the air.

I fled the bad karma and climbed up through Terry's house to the attic.

I was surprised to find him there, alone, pushing a box spring and mattress into a space where I could lay out my sleeping bag.

"Bro, I'm worried about you. *How* are you going to stay out of the Army?"

"I wish I knew," he said. "Maybe divine intervention."

"You've got friends in high places. Pull strings."

"And let some other poor bastard go over there and die in my place?"

"If you have to put it that way, yes."

I dropped my bag and gear onto the mattress and peered out of the window at the chaotic scene on the street. He wouldn't say anymore. I knew he'd been calling Jean about it, and she'd told me he was in turmoil. But he blew off my overture to open up. I want to put a positive spin on it and call that being private and reserved. But Terry was *more* than that. He was secretive. Keeping secrets was an elemental part of his nature. He'd devised a plan to deal with the draft. He just wasn't going to share it with me.

I went nuts then. I don't know if it was the grass or the wine or loneliness or all of the above and then some, but I came over from the window, wrapped my arms around him, and kissed him full and open on the mouth.

I expected him to pull away. He didn't. I yanked up his T shirt, licked his nipples, and slid my hands down his stomach.

"Let's not do this," he said.

"Let's do this."

"No."

He pushed me back—*hard*—and gave me a look I'll never forget. Angry, incredulous, disdainful, disgusted. He dropped down the rickety ladder that led up to the attic, and a minute later I saw him bound out the front door. I didn't see him again for the rest of the visit.

That was the weekend that was—or wasn't. A valve closed off in me then, and I never touched him in a sexual way again. Out of the blue, the Hendrix concert was canceled on Sunday morning because of his "sudden illness" in Cincinnati. My well-laid roomie and I headed back to Athens. And Terry went back to Kris, the statehouse, and the sweet smell of success.

Commissioner Red Yenser

Terry and I crossed paths soon after he graduated and started working in the speaker's office full-time.

I went to see him with the CEOs of the county's largest employers: B.F. Goodrich, Airolite, Remington Rand, Shell Chemical. Congress had just passed the Clean Air Act. Nixon was about to create the federal EPA, Ohio was ready to launch an EPA of its own, and Jim Rhodes wasn't governor anymore. Instead we were dealing with John Gilligan, the best friend the tree huggers ever had. We were scared.

Our industries were spewing ungodly amounts of vile crud into the air. No one in their right mind could deny that. Walter Cronkite called Steubenville the dirtiest city in America, and it was just eighty miles upriver. But jobs are jobs. Lives are lives. We were facing the decimation of our economic base. That's what we believed at the time. *Nobody* could tell us what the long range implications were going to be.

The fear mongering was merciless. I heard from two dozen employees who were terrified about losing their jobs. The feeling around town was that I had some influence up in Columbus, and I wanted to be helpful in any way I could.

I called Terry on behalf of the CEOs and asked for an appointment with the speaker.

"Anything for my oldest and best hombre," he said. "Consider it done."

The next week, he ushered us all into a large, wood-paneled conference room at the statehouse. This was high altitude territory, and I was nervous. There was a portrait of U.S. Grant on the wall, and I was hoping the general might instill me with an extra shot of courage. The speaker came in with an aide, shook hands all around, and sat down at the head of the table. Our CEOs said their piece. They asked for one thing: a straight dollar-for-dollar credit on their corporation income tax for the cost of every piece of pollution control equipment the EPA was going to force them to buy over the next three years.

"We're battling environmental extremists who want to destroy the free market system."

"These people won't stop until they turn Marietta into a ghost town."

"We need this credit to protect *all* of us—employees, retirees, shareholders, and above all—*our customers.*"

"Don't forget the township trustees and school boards who are going lose tax revenue when the jobs disappear."

The speaker stood up. "I am sympathetic to your concerns," he said. "You have my word that this House will give your proposal serious consideration."

As the one who'd brokered the meeting, that was lovely music to my ears. I was in my fourth term, my zest for the job was waning and my act was wearing a bit thin. I needed to do something significant for the business community to keep my edge. Maybe this would be it.

As we were breaking up, Terry touched my sleeve. "Can I have a few minutes of your time?"

He took me into his office, a bare cubicle at the back end of the wing, next to a storage closet. I sat down in the only chair. He shut the door, leaned against a wobbly metal file cabinet and swilled a can of Tab.

"Mr. Yenser," he said. "I don't want to go into the Army."

"Of course you don't."

"I need some assistance with the draft board down home, where I'm registered."

"What's your lottery number?"

"Sixty-eight."

"Ouch."

"I've already been in for my physical," he said. "The sergeant told me to count on being inducted in three months."

"Have you got a hearing date with the board?"

"Next Friday."

I grasped his predicament. Vietnam was dragging on. The Pentagon was desperate for live bodies. There were even rumors about drafting married men. Terry's undergraduate days were over, and you couldn't get a deferment as a graduate student anymore.

"Why don't you sign up with the National Guard?" I said. "Become an officer. Get a deal for yourself."

"I don't have time to join the Guard."

"Couldn't you find time?"

"I've got other priorities," he said. "What I'm looking for is a 3A—a hardship exemption."

He put a file in my lap. Inside were copies of twenty checks he'd written to his mother over a period of six years. There were also court papers related to Gale Stratton's lapses in child support after his divorce from Jean, and a detailed record of Terry's long employment history.

A hardship exemption was a judgment call, a gray area if there ever was one. His case was weak. There were no children involved, Terry's mother had her own income, and I knew from mutual friends that she was engaged to marry a guy named Ron Polk, who taught history at the high school. If Terry had been supporting her in the past, I doubt he was doing much for her now. I figured he had no more than a slim shot at getting what he wanted.

I wasn't averse to helping. But I'd picked up plenty of talk about him being responsible for the homosexual smear on Dick Finn in the commissioner race six years before. Somebody had seen him churning the mimeograph machine in the engineer's office in the basement of the courthouse late one night. Somebody else had run into him dropping envelopes at the post office down in Belpre, where a large batch of the letters had been postmarked. The thought of him being involved made by blood boil. I'm ashamed of myself for not confronting him then and there in his office that day. But I needed his help too badly to risk alienating him, and I let it pass.

"I'll speak with each member of the board before your hearing," I said. "Put in a good word for you, make sure they've read your file."

"That would be fantastic," he said. "And rest assured, I will put in the same good word for you and your CEOs up here."

So that was the arrangement. I gave the draft board a nudge for Terry, and he gave the decision-makers at the statehouse a nudge for me and our companies. He got his hardship exemption. We didn't get our tax credit. He called me a few months later to give me the bad news.

"Things aren't rolling our way, Mr. Yenser. Gilligan is fighting us tooth and nail."

"What do we do now?"

"Try again next year."

It didn't happen then, either. By that time, the CEOs and a lot of their employees had lost faith in me. In November, Nixon buried McGovern at the top of the ticket, but I lost my try for a fifth term. To a raw, energetic kid who reminded me of myself in the old days. The Democrats won control of the House in Columbus, too, and all the jobs that went with it. Terry got booted out of the speaker's office. But he managed to land on his feet.

Politics is about survival. Terry survived. I didn't.

Dan O'Hanlon

Rhodes started his comeback the minute he left the governor's mansion. With his dream of joining the Senate in Washington shattered, he set his sights on reclaiming his old job. Stratton hired on as his man Friday, and was at his side every step of the way.

The sons of bitches got what they went after. The way we let that election slip away will haunt me for the rest of my life.

Yes, Gilligan was pompous. Stiff, uptight, prissy. The kind of guy who steps out of the shower to take a piss. But that shouldn't have mattered. Nixon had just resigned, the stench of Watergate was ripe, it was a huge Democratic year within the state, and our man was the incumbent. He had more money, media support, staff. What he didn't have was the stomach to go negative on his opponent right out of the gate.

There were a few Young Turks in the campaign who firmly believed that we needed to play hardball to defeat Rhodes. We voiced our suggestion to the older guys who were running the show.

"Governor Gilligan is an idealist," they said. "He does not engage in negative campaigning."

"If we simply *tell the truth*, it will inspire voters to take the intelligent action of supporting the governor for re-election."

"We are going to take the high road and let the chips fall where they may."

When it got down to crunch time, they took tens of thousands of votes away from us in Cuyahoga County—our own back yard. Where were we weakest? In the black wards on the East Side of Cleveland—the most reliable Democratic turf in the state. A lot of people there got convinced that our man was an arrogant, upper crust, Irish-Catholic racist who did not have their best interests at heart.

Somebody produced a flier, and dropped copies at thousands of doors. At the top was the ugliest photograph of Gilligan's pasty mug you could imagine, and below that in bold, black type:

Does Governor John Gilligan Deserve Your Vote? Judge for yourself:
1. *His new state income tax takes money out of your pocket.*
2. *He has no blacks on staff, or in his cabinet.*
3. *He's closing your schools, playgrounds, parks, and libraries.*
4. *He's turning his back on you, on Cleveland, on Cuyahoga County.*

On election night, Gilligan took a strong early lead. By eleven o'clock, Rhodes was so certain he'd lost he gave a concession speech on live television. But when the final count came in the next morning, they were up, we were down. Gilligan lost by 11,488 votes out of 3.7 million cast.

So much for taking the high road.

Stratton was involved in the flier garbage. Up to his eyeballs. He's denied it to my face and I've never been able to prove it. But I know it's true.

Clee Harris

I went up to Cleveland with you because you were scared to go alone. You had a secret assignment with your campaign, you wanted to get as deep into the East Side as you could and spread your fliers around, and you needed protection. I was bulked up to two hundred twelve pounds from three years of pumping hard iron. That caught your attention. When I told you I was still tight with a homeboy who ran a barbershop up there, you damn near *begged* me to go.

You didn't have to beg, dude. I was tantalized by you, like every other top man, 'roid monkey, speed freak, and drag queen oogling you on your treadmill at the gym. You looked straight, you acted straight, you had a steady girlfriend. All of that was a huge turn-on, especially for a proper, polite Negro boy raised in fire and brimstone by the Reverend Portis and Mrs. Cecile Harris in Clarksburg, West Virginia.

We motored up I-71 that morning in my big blue whale of a Chevy station wagon, with your fliers bundled and stacked on the back seat, heading to a place called Diamond Cuts at Superior Avenue and 71st. Inside the shop, covering one of the sidewalls, was a magnificent sports heritage mural done up with crayons and ink, with the faces of *everybody*: Jackie, Joe Louis, Jim Brown, Wilma Rudolph, Hank Aaron, Althea Gibson, Jesse Owens. The Rumble in the Jungle was about to go down in Zaire, and as we got acquainted my homeboy worked away on Ali and Foreman.

We went upstairs to his apartment. Some lady was back in the bedroom, ironing clothes, with *Wheel of Fortune* rumbling on the TV. She didn't step out to say hello. You laid your bag of ganja and your pipe out on the kitchen counter, we shared a smoke, and you explained what you wanted to do.

"Could be right up my alley," my homeboy said.

You dropped three crisp benjys onto the counter. He scooped them up and slipped them into his shirt pocket. He went into the bedroom and shut the door, turned the TV down, and made a couple of quick phone calls that we couldn't make out. When he came back, he looked as carefree as a jaybird. "Let's get moving," he said.

He closed up his shop. We piled your bundles into his El Dorado, cruised the 'hoods all day, and made our drops. A couple of brothers showed up in a Lincoln to help out. Nobody gave us an inch of hassle, the heat was nowhere in sight or sound. You were delighted and that delighted me. "This thing is going about as smooth as it's possible for a thing to go," you said.

My homeboy chuckled. "There are black folks who know how to get along with the Man and there are black folks who don't," he said. "I'm one of the ones who knows."

When we got back to my place in Columbus late that night, I got bold and invited you in to mellow out. I figured you'd say no and scoot home to your girl. My heart damn near exploded out of my chest when you followed me into my living room. It was awkward at first, but after three lines of coke and a couple of shots of Crown Royal apiece, the vibes got better. I wanted to jump you, but I minded the words of my wise-as-an-owl grandma and took things *slow*. I let you come to me and offer yourself up.

And when you did, it was exquisite.

When you left, you hesitated at the door. "I'm getting married in six weeks," you said. That hit me like a sledgehammer in the throat. "But it doesn't have to change anything. Let's get together for the fight."

We didn't. We never got together again for anything. You stopped coming to the gym. I called you what—five, six, seven times? You didn't even have the basic human courtesy to call back.

I saw you downtown a few months later, coming out of Lazarus with a shopping bag in your hand. I called out your name and ran toward you. When you saw me, you flew across the street like a cheetah.

What did I do to deserve that? Did you have to be that cruel? Did you have to be such a fucking coward?

Ramsay Stratton

On December 8th, 1974, Terry and Kris got hitched in haute WASP style at First Community Church, in the village of Marble Cliff on the edge of Columbus.

Jean and her new husband Ron Polk drove up from Fort Myers, Florida. They'd moved there from Marietta, after getting married a year earlier. Gale flew in from Atlanta with *his* brand new wife, Tanny. The Reverend Robert and Grandma Nell came from Blowing Rock in North Carolina, where they had a retirement home in the mountains.

And me and Boyfriend arrived stoned from Taos, New Mexico in our mellow yellow VW bug. Taos is where we'd migrated after college to fritter away our twenties, pretending to be adults, pretending to be artists, pretending to be a committed couple.

My not-quite All-American family had dispersed. Except for Terry, we were all Sun Belters. But for the moment we were stuck with each other in a strip motel, a mile downriver from the church and Scioto Country Club, where the reception was going to be held.

Jean didn't get along with her mother. She never had. I didn't see the Reverend say a single word to Gale all weekend. Ron Polk and Tanny scoped each other like a pair of alley cats. And they *all* detested *everything* about Boyfriend: the sneer, the ponytail, the puke green Nehru jacket, the radical B.O. and the slurping noises he made when he ate.

In a patch of woods behind the motel where he and I repaired to smoke our joints, I found a little iron horseshoe in a pile of debris. I put it prongs up, on top of the door to our room, to beckon benign spirits.

The sucker worked. We made it through the weekend without any ugly scenes. Terry was our saving grace. He played the role of groom to perfection—gallant, reserved, dignified. He and Kris were honeymooning in Acapulco, and then he was starting his new job as executive assistant to Governor Rhodes.

At the reception, Terry introduced us to his boss. Boyfriend pulled me aside and hissed in my ear: "Is this the same guy who murdered four kids at Kent State?"

"The very same," I hissed back.

"I'm going to give the bastard a piece of my mind."

"Go get another piece of cake and shut the fuck up."

I turned back to Terry and the governor but they were already across the room. The father of the bride was introducing his bright, shiny new son-in-law to a circle of gray-haired men.

Terry was twenty-six, eight years out of Marietta High School, four years out of Ohio State. He was a long way from his neat-as-a-pin bedroom on Warren Street. I couldn't see his future in any great detail. But wherever he was headed in life, he wasn't taking me or any of the rest of his family with him.

Chuck Moffo

Turd Helmet is what I called him. All that wavy hair plastered over his head. The son of a bitch cheated me. He took for himself what was rightfully mine.

I did all the grunt work. Stratton shows up in the fourth quarter of a long, brutal game, and does lunch. Where is the justice? He was a pretty face with a hot ticket wife and rich father-in-law who ran with a crowd of bigwigs eager to open their wallets for the Man. All Stratton ever did was prance around from one restaurant to the next, collecting their cash.

It was me who got the call from Mike Deaver out in L.A. Reagan was reluctant to challenge a sitting president and split the party, but he was fed up with Ford's policies and was going to fight him for the nomination. Deaver is asking around, looking for an experienced worker bee to organize Reagan in Ohio. My name has come up a few times. Am I interested?

I start hyperventilating. I'm so excited I think I'm going to puke all over the phone. "Mr. Deaver, when can I start?"

"The sooner, the better."

I'd sworn allegiance to Reagan when he made his speech on TV for Goldwater in '64.

"You and I have a rendezvous with destiny," he said.

I thought—*this man is speaking directly to me.*

"We must seek hope and faith—not defeatism and despair."

I said out loud—*'here is the leader I've been aching for.'*

"America is the last best hope for man on earth!"

I shouted at the screen—*'you're goddam right it is!'*

As a young man, Reagan saved seven lives working as a lifeguard at Lowell Park in Dixon, Illinois. He saved another one the night he delivered that speech.

I quit my job selling washers and dryers at Sears, buy two decent suits, and set up in a one-room office in the basement of the Neil House hotel, across from the statehouse. It's an uphill struggle from the get-go. Jim Rhodes lines up everyone in the state establishment behind Ford. The big shovels in Washington try to bury us. But we refuse to give up the fight, and we start winning some rounds—North Carolina, Texas, Arkansas.

Top staff decides to bring the Man through Ohio for five days in June, a week before our primary. We can't beat Ford, but the goal is to win a big percentage of the popular vote and keep momentum rolling all the way to the convention in Kansas City.

I pick him and Nancy up at the airport. Just the two of them pop out of the tunnel. No posse, handlers, aides, guards, assistants. Is that awesome or what? The rest of the team was flying in the next morning to start the road tour.

"Hello, Chuck," he says. Gripping my hand, looking me straight in the eye. "Meet my wife Nancy. Thanks so much for being here."

He looks like a million bucks. Exactly like he looked hosting *Death Valley Days*. So many people want to shake his hand it takes half an hour to get to the baggage claim. The whole scene has me quivering, dizzy, almost faint, feeling like a million bucks myself for maybe the first time in my life.

The Man had that effect. It was exhilarating to walk at his side.

I drive them downtown to the Neil House. They have the tact not to mention the piece of junk they're riding in. They need a place to freshen up and make a few calls before their business starts upstairs. I take them down to my office, and give them a few minutes alone while I run upstairs to check the meeting room on the mezzanine.

When I get back, Turd Helmet is there. His shriveled, skinny ass in *my* chair. Shooting the breeze with the Man and Nancy like they're old friends.

The Man says: "Chuck, meet Terry Stratton. Terry was just passing by, saw us, and came in to say hello."

Just passing by. What a crock of shit that was. He *knew* the Man was coming to town, *knew* where the campaign office was, *knew* that he'd probably at some point be stopping here. The creep was lying in wait, ready to pounce.

I say to him: "I've heard of you. You work for Rhodes."

"Righto."

"*Ssshhh!,*" the Man says, putting a finger to his lips.

"Then you're for Ford," I say. "What are you doing here?"

"We've already discussed that," Nancy says. "And we're not going to hold it against him."

Turd Helmet opens his wallet, pulls out a baby picture, and flashes it at us. "This is Rhodes Reagan Stratton," he says. "He'll be two months old tomorrow."

The Man takes the picture, passes it over to Nancy, and chortles like some silly ass school boy. "That young man is going to grow up to be a Republican!"

"Governor," I say. "Your room is ready. Your *friends* are eager to see you."

Stratton didn't officially come on board for four more years. But that is how he and the Man first met. On *my* watch, under *my* nose. If I hadn't gone upstairs to check on that meeting room, I could have fended him off.

Campaign grunts of the world, listen up: Never leave your candidate unattended. Not even for ten minutes. You never know what kind of vermin might creep in.

Lynn Starhawk

On the first night of that Ohio swing in June, Nancy called me from her hotel, late, after her husband was asleep.

She said they had encountered the most *marvelous* young man that morning. Slim, exquisite-looking, with strong morals, impeccable manners, and a newborn son whose middle name was Reagan.

"This young man is an Aquarius," she said. "Born on Abraham Lincoln's birthday. See what you can find out about him right now."

"Yes, ma'am."

"Ronnie may not win the nomination this year," she said. "But if we stay in politics, he looks like a top-notch person to bring on board."

I consulted my charts and cards. I couldn't believe what I saw. An hour later, I called her back.

"This is a *perfect* moment for a stranger—and an Aquarius—to enter your life," I said. "The stellium is superior. Air on air, mutable on fixed. Uranus dominating in the eleventh house as the modern ruler."

"That makes perfect sense," she said. "Because he was born on the very same day I lost my special friend so long ago."

"A word of warning."

"Tell me."

"The moon in Aquarius means this young man may have an irrational need for freedom," I said. "A fear of close relationships, even a tendency toward perversity. So he could be gone in the blink of an eye. Please, hold him close."

Apparently, she did.

Young Republican

Mac McKenzie

Terry was versatile. He could decipher the tax code, lobby the Democrats who were running the legislature, raise campaign money, handle a meeting with any group of people under the sun from giggly Girl Scouts to fired-up farmers. He also knew how to read a map, change a flat tire, and sniff out a place to get a decent bite to eat in the middle of nowhere.

The governor liked all of that. Terry talked up to him, and the governor liked that, too. Jim didn't have a son of his own, and their relationship was special. That was apparent to all of us.

We had so many old guys from Jim's first eight years who were back for the second act. Terry was a bright, enthusiastic new guy. A fucking new guy is what some people called him. That might have been the key to the thing. Maybe Jim was craving fresh, young blood to keep himself energized.

In February of '78, he dispatched Terry to the Union County Lincoln Day banquet in Marysville. Ronald Reagan, off and running for the '80 nomination, was the keynote speaker. Jim was mad at Reagan. He didn't think he had done enough to help Ford get elected in '76, and he blamed Reagan for Carter beating Ford in Ohio and going on to win the White House. He was sore enough to avoid greeting him in person, but he didn't want to totally snub him. So he sent Terry as his emissary.

Forty-five minutes after Terry left, Jim called me at home.

"You and me better get up to Marysville and say hello to Governor Reagan."

I wasn't used to Jim changing his mind. "Should I get hold of Terry and tell him we're coming?"

"It's his birthday. Just for fun, let's surprise the boy."

We headed up Route 33 in my Oldsmobile Cutlass. It was only two weeks after the Blizzard of '78 had shut the state down. Glistening sheets of hard-packed ice spread out in the dusk. We could see the remnants of dozens of hay mounds that had been dropped by helicopter to feed starving livestock trapped in the fields.

Despite the chill, a large, boisterous crowd was gathering at the armory at the county fairgrounds. There was no sign of Terry. We met an advance man from the campaign setting up extra tables. Tubby guy with a big bald spot on the crown of his head. Chuck something. He took us behind the armory to a giant black Winnebago and knocked on the door. He went in alone for a minute, then waved us inside and left.

Ronald and Nancy sat at opposite ends of a black velvet couch wrapped around a coffee table, sipping steaming drinks out of Styrofoam cups.

In between them, looking like he was about to upchuck his lunch, was Terry.

He was *damned* surprised to see us. Jim had sent him up there to shake Reagan's hand, politely decline a seat at the head table if offered, and eat dinner with the locals out on the floor. Not to schmooze the man and his wife before the show in their dressing room.

Terry was overstepping his bounds. Everybody sensed it. But Jim and I sat down for some hot tea with lemon and a birthday cupcake in honor of Terry turning thirty, and we all kept our composure.

Nancy beamed at me. "Terry is telling us how wonderful the people of Ohio are," she said.

Ronald leaned across the table and touched the governor's wrist. "Jim, can you finagle us anymore of that Cincinnati style chili?" he said. "That's the best grub I've eaten in *years*."

It was all so light and fluffy I thought we'd wondered onto the set of *Dinah!* After a few more minutes of patter, Jim stood up. We said our goodbyes, shook some hands out in the lobby, and headed home.

In the car I said: "Boss, why did we drive up here tonight?"

"To say hello to the governor."

"Six hours ago you didn't want to say hello."

"It's time for me to make my peace with Ronald Reagan," he said. "He's going to be our next president."

"Ford was the incumbent and he couldn't beat Carter. How can Reagan?"

"He's a better candidate than Ford," Jim said. "Did you see the crowd tonight? They were wild for him."

"Boss, what are we going to do about Terry?"

"What's to do?"

"What the hell was he doing in that Winnebago?"

"Having a bit of a lark, I suppose. His wife is expecting again, and he's living it up while he can."

"Did you know he was going to be in there?"

"No."

"So he's pulling this crap behind your back."

"He is, yes."

"We *cannot* have it," I said. "He works for you, and you're not endorsing anyone for the nomination."

"I expect he'll keep his distance from now on. And even if he doesn't, we'll be all right."

"Why do you tolerate it?"

Jim let out an exasperated sigh. "Goddamit Mac, I know you're right," he said. "But Terry is on his own path, and he's moving fast."

"*Too* fast," I said. "And too loose."

"Don't fret," he said. "I don't think he'll be with us much longer."

"Is he moving on?"

He turned his head away and stared out through the darkness at the ice sheets. "I'm not raising him to stay with me," he said.

I got the message. I didn't bring up the subject of Terry again.

Amy Jang

I was twenty-six, two years out of the Columbia School of Journalism, a fresh cub interning at the *Newsweek* bureau in Peking. He was thirty-one, the youngest member of the trade delegation that arrived in the summer of '79.

No civic leaders from the heartland of America were making goodwill trips to Communist China. The Ohio group led by Governor Rhodes was the first. My chief assigned me the story, and for two days I went everywhere with them: the Great Wall, the acupuncture clinic, Bob Hope's penthouse suite at the Royal Palm Hotel, the Capitol Theatre where he was filming his TV special "Road to China."

On the night of the Fourth of July, there was a party on the lawn of the American Embassy. The grounds were lit up with dozens of red, white and blue lanterns. He and I ended up alone together in the rose garden, behind the compound, talking about movies. I told him about my father being a vice-president at Universal Studios in L.A. and getting a bit role in *Battle Hymn* when I was four, playing one of the Korean war orphans Rock Hudson airlifts out of the combat zone in his cargo plane.

He opened his wallet and showed me a picture of him and Rock in his hometown during the world premiere of the movie there.

I felt an instant, overpowering connection.

My apartment was two blocks away. He walked me home and gave me a deep, long, wet kiss. My heart roared. My thighs went moist.

He asked me if he could come back later that evening, after the celebration calmed down. I said yes. Around ten, he tapped softly on my door. My place was tiny. There were units above and below and on each side. We dragged my futon into the living room, lay on the floor, and made quiet, forceful love by candlelight.

The men I had been with before cared only about their own pleasure. He was different. With his lips and tongue and shaft and shoulders and thighs, he took me places I'd never been before—or since. I did not really know what sex could feel like until that night.

He didn't lie. He told me he was married, with two young children. Did that bother me? Yes, but not as much as you might think, because I didn't know the wife. I was in the throes of the most powerful sexual attraction of my life. I simply didn't have the strength to resist.

The delegation left for Shanghai the next day. My chief needed me on another story, and I didn't go with them. I was just as glad. My experience was far from vast, but I'd already learned the cardinal rule of forbidden love. Take one long, sweet taste and break away clean.

Kris Lamborn Stratton

In December of '79, Terry and I went to Los Angeles for the Rose Bowl game between Ohio State and USC. We flew out on Pond Power's corporate jet with Governor Rhodes, Mac McKenzie and his wife and a dozen other folks, and stayed three nights in a suite in the Huntington Sheraton in Pasadena. That trip was the moment everything started to unravel.

I was a hagged-out, irritable mess. Motherhood was bearing down on me hard. I didn't enjoy *anything* anymore. Rhody was almost four; Carol was fifteen months. Those nights in California were the first I'd spent out of the house since she'd been born.

Terry was hardly ever *in* the house. He left at six in the morning to drive the governor to work, and didn't get home until eight or nine o'clock. Five minutes of conversation at breakfast and another five in bed at night made it impossible to keep the flame burning. The thought of slapping on my happy face and flying across the country to celebrate the dawn of the 80's with him and his statehouse gang made me nauseous. I *should* have been overjoyed at the chance to escape. But I wasn't. Not even close, and that disturbed me. I wanted to be somewhere else, *anywhere* else—even on my knees on the grimy, damp linoleum floor in our cramped kitchen, wiping up milk spills and other gooey messes.

The afternoon we checked in, Terry took a private phone call in the bedroom. A couple of minutes later, he came out to the living room and proceeded to shock the bejesus out of me.

"We need to change our plans for tomorrow night," he said. "We've been invited to New Year's Eve at the Reagans."

"You just found out about this *now*?"

"I've been working my contacts for weeks," he said. "Trying to get us on the list."

"Why didn't you tell me?"

"I didn't want excite you and then have it fall through."

"I'm *quivering* with excitement. Can't you tell?"

He shot me the cold, silent stare he used to let me know I was being obnoxious. "I want to manage Reagan's campaign in Ohio this year," he said quietly. "I've got a real shot at the job. Both of us meeting both of them tonight will just about nail it down."

"I don't know you anymore," I said.

"Nancy will be in her trademark red—head to toe."

"I'm not sure I ever did."

"I've been advised that the ladies should strive to *complement* her outfit—not clash with it."

"Jesus Christ, Terry."

"Especially the younger, more attractive ladies such as yourself."

"I cannot believe you're pulling this crap on me."

"There's one other thing," he said. "Nobody can know we're going."

"So we have to sneak out?"

"I don't like the word *sneak*. We'll have to be *discreet*."

The next morning, Terry told Mac and Governor Rhodes we couldn't pass up the chance to spend the evening in Westwood with dear friends from our college days. At eight o'clock, we slipped out the service entrance at the back of the hotel and into a hired car Terry had procured for the evening. The driver took us twenty miles to the Reagan residence in Pacific Palisades, to the House of the Future overlooking the ocean that General Electric built for them when he became the company's chief of public affairs.

Amidst a swelling jam of Cadillacs, Jaguars, and Rolls-Royces, we strode up the buffed, paved-brick driveway arm-in-arm, past the triple carport and into the gleaming black slate foyer. Inside the house, I could see a retractable roof for indoor-outdoor dining, and beyond that, out back, a pair of hearts marked NDR-RR on the wet cement patio next to the swimming pool.

I did my duty like the good Girl Scout I am. When my moment to shine arrived, I exchanged Big Ten football banter with the governor and celebrated the joys of raising young kids with Nancy. As we chatted, she looked me up and down and nodded approvingly. My subdued gray pantsuit and scarlet earrings and nail polish must have done the trick.

The only awkward moment came around eleven o'clock, after we'd finished a light supper. I took a wee bit too long to finish my business in the back lavatory and opened the door to find Jimmy Stewart waiting—a wee bit impatiently—to get in.

Shortly after midnight, the car whisked us back to Pasadena. I pushed off my shoes and collapsed into Terry's lap.

He kissed my lips and eyes and nose and neck. "Thank you, beautiful," he whispered. "I think we passed the audition."

Dan O'Hanlon

I was so disgusted by our defeat in the Rhodes-Gilligan race that I said goodbye to politics, to campaigns and the statehouse and Terry Stratton and the rest of his ilk. I enrolled in law school at Case Western in Cleveland, and after I passed the bar I went to work as a staff attorney for the Legal Aid Society on Lorain Avenue on the West Side, dealing every day with what I came to call the D-bombs of human existence—divorce, disease, drug abuse, drunkenness, domestic violence, deadbeat dads, death.

Then early in 1980, Speaker Vern Riffe came up to Cleveland, met me for lunch at the West Side Market, and asked me to run for the open Ohio House seat in the 55th District.

"I've never run for public office," I said.

"That won't hurt," he said. "It might even help."

"I'm an O'Hanlon. Voters don't like family dynasties."

"They like some dynasties just fine," he said. "If your mom and dad and uncle were unpopular people, it would be a problem. But they're not."

"I'm doing a mountain of good at the clinic right now," I said.

"I'm sure you are."

"Actually *helping* people," I said. "More than I ever could in Columbus."

He chewed on that a little and eyeballed the throng on the market floor. Then he swirled his head around and fixed his hawk-like gaze dead on me. "If you come to the statehouse you can put your name on a bill to fund a hundred clinics," he said. "And then a hundred more after that. There's really no telling how much good you can accomplish."

"I wish I saw it that way."

"You can act out your faith and do your duty, and help establish some justice in this sinful world."

"The problem with that strategy is the politicians are all sinners themselves."

He narrowed his eyes. "Is that what we are?"

"And *way* too connected to the world they're trying to change."

He stood up and dropped some crumpled bills onto the table. "Reagan will be at the top of the Republican ticket in November," he said. "He's going to get a ton of Democratic votes."

"Or two."

"I need my best people on the ballot to hold onto my majority," he said. "You're my best people, Dan."

"I'm humbled by that."

"You can pretend you're back in philosophy class at Notre Dame, lamenting the sorry state of the world. Or you can join us. This is your moment, partner." He turned around and walked off into the crowd.

I was thirty-four, solvent and healthy, and married to a fantastic woman who would support me in whatever I wanted to do. And I was tired of beating my boat against the current. I decided to give the O'Hanlon family business another try.

Chuck Moffo

In 1980, we foot soldiers of the revolution answer the call from the Man one more time, with feeling. Ohio is a battleground, as always. Except this time, Stratton is my boss.

The Lord High Honchos in Los Angeles and Washington hire him to manage Ohio. Turd Helmet is giving me orders, and all the while he's slicking by, hogging the phones, guzzling cans of Tab, trimming his eyebrows and nose hairs and filing his fingernails like the complete and total fag he no doubt was.

One afternoon after one of his three-hour lunches, he's so wrapped up in himself he comes back from the restroom fiddling with his hair and walks straight into the fucking wall. He hears me giggling at him, comes into my office, and shuts the door behind him.

"You're pissed off at me," he says.

"I am."

"You want my job, don't you?"

"I do."

"Stop sulking, Chuck. You're hurting morale."

"Why did they pick you instead of me?"

"Maybe because I know how to get along with people."

"Is that what they call your area of expertise?"

"What does that mean?"

"You're a suck up," I say. "A brown-nosing, boot-licking phony. You're not a true believer, and you haven't paid your dues."

"Blimp boy, you can go straight to hell."

I ignore him after that. Never utter another word to him. November is bittersweet. Ronald Wilson Reagan stomps Carter by half a million votes in Ohio and is elected fortieth president of the United States. Everybody on the campaign is trying to follow him to Washington. I'm working every angle I've got and coming up empty. I clean out my office, plop down on my living room couch, and wait for a call that never comes. Then I'm up home in Defiance one weekend and I pick up mom's *National Enquirer*. There's a profile of Nancy Reagan that says she can't *stand* to be around fat people. That she thinks fat people are ugly, disgusting, repulsive.

This thousand watt floodlight erupts in my brain.

So *that's* what's wrong with me.

The fix was in. Stratton was inside the palace, feasting on everything life had to offer. I was outside in the weeds with my dick in my hand. I quit politics after that. Never worked on another campaign. It's a young man's game and I was pushing forty. I quit the Man, too. He turned out to be the biggest fraud ever to occupy the White House. Shrink the size of government, my ass. He and his Hollywood Mafia turned D.C. into a boomtown. Reagan wasn't the solution. He was the problem. How did he fool me all those years?

As for Turd Helmet—tables turn. He got what he deserved.

Michael Deaver

Nobody wanted Stratton. Jim Baker had no use for him. Neither did Ed Meese. Duberstein and the lobbyists didn't want him because he had no experience on Capitol Hill. Atwater and the political people didn't want him because they were getting negative feedback from the field. Stratton wasn't a true conservative. He was a phony who hadn't paid his dues. He lied, he was lazy, he partied too much.

Finally, Mrs. R. asked me to find a place for him. I didn't want him any more than anyone else. But I didn't have much choice. I put him in the Office of Communications and called him the Associate Director of External Policy.

Then I tried to figure out something for him to do.

Dan O'Hanlon

With the speaker's staunch backing, I ran for the open Ohio House seat in the 55th District, and I won. A couple of weeks before Christmas, I went down to the statehouse for an orientation session for new members. During a break, I was sipping a cup of coffee by myself in the basement cafeteria when I felt a hand land lightly on my left shoulder from behind.

"Greetings, hombre."

It was Stratton, decked out in the shiniest charcoal gray power suit I'd ever seen in my life, with a maroon tie and a pair of nifty black wingtips.

"You've done your family proud," he said. "Congratulations."

"Same to you," I said. "When are you leaving for Washington?"

"As soon as we can," he said. "I start work on Inauguration Day."

He grabbed a cup of coffee for himself and sat down across from me. We gingerly tossed the old days back and forth and silently took the measure of each other. I wasn't surprised by his quick rise in the business. I don't think he was surprised by mine.

"Please don't write me off," he said. "I know you're sore at me."

"I am."

"I admit I've been overzealous at times," he said. "But always in the heat of battle. There's no reason we can't be friends again."

"Were we ever?"

"It hurts to hear that," he said. "How many hours did we spend together right here at this table, solving the problems of the world?"

"All the crap you spread around about Gilligan."

"Ancient history," he said. "But for the record, I had nothing to do with that flier."

"Just an ugly rumor, is it?"

"That's *exactly* what it is."

"Here's another one," I said. "You were the guy on Reagan's team who stole Carter's briefing book before the debate in Cleveland."

"You're kidding, right?"

"Am I?"

"A briefing book wouldn't help us anyway."

"Then why bother to steal it in the first place?"

"No need to get huffy," he said. "Is that some mordant Irish beast welling up inside you?"

"We call it a clurichaun," I said. "The surly cousin of the leprechaun, who spreads rancor and bile and ugly gossip all day long."

"Repress that nasty being," he said. "He doesn't play well on you." He stood up and laid that gentle hand on my shoulder again. "Stay in touch, hombre. There's going to come a time when we'll be quite useful to each other."

I hadn't seen the last of him. Not by a long shot.

Mac McKenzie

That January, Bob Lamborn and his wife hosted a send-off for Terry and Kris before they left for Washington. I got an invitation and stopped by their limestone manse on Club Road.

A man I thought of as a friend was starting work at the White House in two weeks. He'd left us for the Reagan campaign in a heated rush almost a year before, with a strained, awkward goodbye. I wanted to touch base and see if he still thought of me as *his* friend.

I needn't have worried. Terry was never one to burn bridges. He blushed a bit, squeezed my hand, and gave me a friendly buss on the shoulder. I was envious. Here was a guy twenty years younger than me making the big move I'd often dreamed of making myself. And he was starting at the top—1600 Pennsylvania Avenue. Terry was in his glory that afternoon, greeting the flow of well-wishers at the big oak dining room table, showing them autographs and pictures of Rock Hudson, O.J. Simpson, Bob Hope and all the other celebrities from his collection.

Kris was more subdued. I found her in the basement rec room, refereeing a game of Twister for a passel of screechy kids. She introduced me to Rhodes Reagan Stratton, her five-year-old son. They called him Rhody.

I asked him: "Are you ready to go?"

"Yes, sir!"

"Is your sister ready to go?"

"Yes, sir!"

I turned to Kris. "What about you?"

She gave the spinner to one of the older kids, grabbed my forearm and pulled me into the dark utility room, away from the noise.

"Terry can only rise so high in the world," she said. "He's going to be out of his league in Washington."

"I can hardly believe that."

"He could have a fantastic life if he just stayed put."

"I don't think he's designed that way."

"He has secrets. And temptations." Her grip on my forearm tightened. "This is an easier place to keep secrets and resist temptations than there."

"I think you're fretting over nothing," I said. "You're going to be fine."

"Tell me I'm right, Mac. Come on—*tell me I'm right*."

She didn't wait for my response. That was good because I didn't know what to say. She released my arm, went back to Twister, and left me lost in my thoughts with the washer and dryer and furnace.

 What she said startled me. I never forgot the tone of urgency—and panic—in her voice. She sounded like a trapped, frightened woman.

And in the end, I think events proved her right. Terry would have been better off staying put.

Kris Lamborn Stratton

We left for Washington on the Friday morning before the inauguration. The big orange moving van idled in the street, engine growling. In the driveway, Rhody and Carol babbled in the back seat of the packed station wagon.

We'd sold the house and wouldn't be coming back. I walked into the backyard one last time. A plastic trash bag propped up against the side of the garage had blown over and some stuff had spilled on to the patio. As I squatted down to shove it back in and retie the bag, I saw a crumpled twelve pack of Trojans lying on the pavement. I looked inside. Only four were left.

I felt sick to my stomach. Terry hadn't used a condom with me for years. I wanted to lie down on the icy, frozen grass and die.

He came up the driveway to the back of the house. I was so wrapped up in fear and despair and rage I didn't even notice him. Behind me, in a very calm voice, he said, "Everyone's ready to go."

Without standing up or turning around, I waved the box above my head. "Are these yours?"

"I found them in my bottom drawer when I was throwing things out," he said. "I didn't even remember I had them."

"So you don't need them?"

"No," he said. "That's why I threw them out."

I turned around and stood up. "You're sure?"

"Of course I'm sure."

I stared into his face. He looked scared. "You goddam well *better* be sure."

He backed up a few steps and watched me for a long moment. "Rhody and Carol and I are moving to Washington now."

"Is *that* where you're going?"

"*That's* where we're going. And we're all sort of hoping you'll come with us."

I dumped the Trojans into the garbage bag, tied it up tight, and went with them.

Three / The White House 1981-1983

The Reagan Center
17186 Ventura Boulevard
Tarzana, CA 90870

Mr. Douglas Putnam
3721 Warren Street
Washington, D.C. 20005

August 10th, 2001

Dear Mr. Putnam:

The President and Mrs. Reagan have received your letter, dated August 10th, 1997, in which you ask them to share their memories of Terry Stratton, particularly of the time he spent with them at the White House.

They will not grant your request at this time, and they foresee no time in the future when your request will be granted.

Sincerely,
Elizabeth Clark / Interim Associate Director
The Reagan Center

Vonda Vance

Mrs. R. was taken with Terence Charles. That's what she called him. Once or twice a week she would peep her head into my cubicle and whisper "Terence Charles is coming over. Shut all my doors and make sure we're not disturbed."

That wasn't easy. Her office was at the center of the White House, on the middle floor, between the East and West Wings. She spent most of her time there, perched on an arm of the massive couch or pacing the carpet, talking on her white phone with the ultra long cord.

There were three doors—one led to the central hall, one to the makeshift gym that she and the president set up after he was shot, and one to the living quarters by way of Mrs. R.'s twelve walk-in closets and cosmetics room.

I did as I was told and shut them all. Very few people were aware of what was going on. Clearly not the president, at least until the end. Mike Deaver knew because I told him. Beyond Mike, who can say?

The official denials were always so curt: "The president does not believe in astrology."

Fair enough. Perhaps he didn't. But his wife certainly did.

We'd seen it before—Mrs. R. hiring someone at the urging of one of her seers. She'd had several through the years. In this case it was her Wiccan friend Lynn Starhawk, from the old days back in Sacramento. I was acquainted with Lynn myself, because I was one of the Sacramento People. Never to be confused with that other band of Tribe Reagan, the Hollywood People.

We were staff. They were friends. The line between us was always crystal clear.

I grew up in Modesto, the youngest of four sisters. Dad was a cop, mom was a first grade teacher. You've probably seen *American Graffiti*. That was my turf, my town, my time. After I graduated from Chico State, I got married and started a job with the California Chamber of Commerce, doing public relations and lobbying out of their office on L Street, across from Capitol Park.

That's where I met Mrs. R. She came with her husband to our legislative reception in March of '67, two months after he was sworn in as governor. She was forty-five, quite beautiful, and completely unlearned in the ways of being a governor's wife. I took it upon myself to ease her burden. Later, when she started importing girlfriends from Los Angeles, I eased their burdens, too.

"We'll call Vonda at the Chamber," Mrs. R said. "Vonda can show us the ropes around here better than anybody else."

She was grateful for all I did—introducing her to rich businessmen, finding the best places to shop and dine, arranging visits to veteran hospitals, soliciting sponsors for her foster grandparents program. That might surprise you, given her reputation. But she was far less sure of herself back then, and she paid attention to the little people. She wanted to learn.

The irony is that I was so young, I barely knew what I was doing myself. We winged it together. After Governor Reagan won a second term in '70, she hired me as her personal assistant.

I always strived to look my best, and I didn't have any trouble staying slim. She loved that, and she loved having someone young to talk to. Every now and then she'd let her guard down and reminisce about the eleven movies she'd made for MGM, about Clark Gable and other men she'd dated before "Ronnie swept me off my feet like the tornado in *The Wizard of Oz.*" A few times I even got the feeling she was telling me things she'd never told anyone else in her life.

When the governor left office in '75, Mike Deaver asked me to manage Mrs. R.'s affairs out of the new Westwood branch of his public relations firm in Los Angeles. My husband refused to move. He was a pure-bred country boy from the Salmon Mountains and he wanted *no* part of L.A. I divorced him and went alone. I followed Mrs. R. through the '76 and '80 campaigns and on to Washington. Where, like everyone else, I lived in fear of her wrath.

In the White House, Mrs. R. became much more distant. She didn't drop her guard anymore. But I'd known her for fifteen years, and I honestly think she trusted me more than anyone else on the premises, except her husband and possibly Mike. That's why she had *me* close the doors whenever Terry came calling.

Don't get me wrong. She never said a word to me about what went on between them in there. I had to discover that myself.

Officially, he became her policy analyst, her research guy. That was the job she and Mike concocted for him. He worked out of Mike's shop in the West Wing. Nobody cared about what he did. The charade was beyond ridiculous. One Monday morning at a staff meeting he presented her with twenty copies of a "backgrounder" he'd prepared on the effects of television violence on children. "I'm going to send these to my best friends in the industry," she said. "To show them how serious this situation really is and get them off their duffs."

A couple of hours later, I found all the copies stuffed into the big metal trash can in the president's gym.

Terry tried. He gave it his best shot. But he was in a no-win situation. He was the queen's knave in a palace full of people who hated the queen.

Michael Deaver

I'd made peace with her astrology. But this was not astrology. She'd gone off on a seance kick, right after the election. It may well have been separation anxiety—fear of the move to Washington and all it would entail. Then Lynn Starhawk sent her a reading board. It arrived a week after the inauguration, a thinnish slab of wood about half the size of a card table, covered with black and green paint and all sorts of arrows and numbers and strange shapes and designs. A Wiccan version of a Ouija board is the best way to describe it. I wouldn't have known about it at all if I hadn't seen it with my own eyes one morning, propped up against a wall in her office, off in a corner. I don't know all of the bells and whistles that were on her *particular* board. Browse around the Internet today and you'll find a hundred different types of these damn things. But they all have the same purpose—to contact the dead and communicate with them.

I didn't want to bring it up with her, so I asked Vonda if she had the scoop.

"I wish I did," she said.

"Have you seen this Ouija board or whatever it is that Lynn sent?"

"Yes, I have."

"Try to find out what's going on," I said. "It's important I know."

At six o'clock the next morning, she called me at home. "I was tagging shoes last night in the closet next to her office," she said. "I overheard her talking to Lynn on the phone. About a man named Wyatt St. George."

"Who in the world is Wyatt St. George?"

"A beau from her earliest Hollywood days," Vonda said. "She's told me about him a couple of times. They arrived in town the same week in 1948 and fell madly in love."

"Where is he now?"

"A month after they met, he took a Corvette out to the desert near Death Valley, drifted off the road in a dusty haze, and slammed into a Joshua tree."

"I'm not hearing this," I said.

"Now Lynn has planted the notion in her head that Wyatt's spirit *has* to be reached, to protect her *and* the president here in the White House."

"This cannot be true."

"Do you think I'm making it up?"

"Find out as much as you can and get back to me."

That afternoon, she popped into my office in the West Wing and shut the door. "They've been haggling with each other all day," she said. "She wants to do her own readings but Lynn says no. So they're going to do them together, over the telephone."

"My God."

"And to facilitate things, her favorite Aquarius is going to be sitting right across from her, with the board balanced on their four knees. They're even going to burn a lavender candle to summon benevolent vibes into the room."

"Have you shared any of this with the president?"

"Of course not."

"Does anyone else know about it?"

"I don't see how they could."

The whole scenario scared the living hell out of me. Not quite the same as reading your horoscope in the newspaper every morning, I think you'll agree. We needed to keep an airtight lid on it, because there were legions of Reagan haters in the media who were hell-bent on destroying her. The last thing we needed was a leak to Brinkley or Rather or the *Times* about her channeling a dead boyfriend by way of this Wicked Witch of the West out in Sacramento, with special assistance from a handsome stud of a guy young enough to be her son.

That was Stratton's role in the administration. That's why he came to work every day.

It was sad because he could have done more. He was bright, eager, alert. To try to get involved, he jogged with Atwater. Once or twice a week, rain or shine, they'd slap on running gear in the gym and head over to the Mall together. But Lee never budged. He never let Stratton into his tree house.

I liked Stratton. I had no need for him in the grand scheme of things, but I was fond of him. Underneath the glossy exterior, he was like me—a fry cook, ditch digger, meter reader kind of guy. A small-town boy with thunder in his heart and stars in his eyes. He was in rarified air and he knew it. He wouldn't be passing this way again.

He was always bugging me to lay out our autograph collections, and one afternoon we did a little show and tell, down the hall in his cubicle. Just the two of us, a couple of kids showing off their best marbles to each other.

I'm a huge USC fan and I craved his O.J. Simpsons. I offered him five hundred bucks cash on the spot for all three of them. He told me they weren't for sale.

Vonda Vance

On the afternoon John Hinckley shot the president at the Hilton, Mrs. R. was alone in her office. She had just found out from Mike that her husband had a bullet lodged in his chest, two inches from his heart. Secret Service was about to drive her to George Washington Hospital.

Her door to the central hall was slightly ajar. I peeked in. She was standing on the coffee table in her stocking feet, clutching a butcher knife, and she looked horribly frightened. Above her, hanging by a cord from the ceiling, was a paper Red Chinese Lantern the size of a basketball that she'd brought to Washington from the house in Pacific Palisades to "ward off evil spirits."

Moaning like a possum in heat, she lifted the knife over her head and slashed the lantern six, eight, ten times. Then she slit the cord, and the tattered thing plunked onto the carpet.

Mrs. R. changed after that. In public she was valiant, but in private, as she nursed her husband's ghastly wounds, she was fearful. Her sessions with Terry became more frequent. He was with her virtually every day during the president's recovery period. In July, four months after the shooting, she insisted that Terry go with her to the royal wedding in London.

That stung. So many of us wanted to go on that trip. But the president was staying home, the entourage was bunking at the ambassador's residence instead of a hotel to save money, and space was tight.

"Terence Charles will need his own room at Winfield House."

"Mike told me to double up everyone but you and him."

"I don't care what Mike told you," she said. "Get Terence Charles a single."

"Will do."

"My office will be off-limits to *everyone.* Except you and my husband."

"Yes, ma'am."

"This is your best time to inventory my fall wardrobe. Tag *everything*."

"Everything."

"There's a vegetable tray on my desk. Help yourself."

"Thank you."

"Then take it to the kitchen and put it in the refrigerator," she said.

"Top shelf, right side."

"Wrap and save the dip."

Frankie Hodnett

There's a saying: find a bird in a bar and you'll lose her in a bar. It can be the same with mates. That's how the Squire passed in and out of my life.

I found him in July of '81, two days before Charles and Diana got married, in a club called Godiva's, on Bridle Lane near Piccadilly. I'd rented out the whole place and piled kith and kin inside to celebrate the *Eye's* first anniversary.

We were having it large that night and we deserved it. We'd defied huge odds and launched the first national newspaper in the U.K. since *The Daily Mirror* in 1903. And we'd done it our way. Blood and gore on the front page, tits and ass in the *Eye* Popper centerfold, football on the back. With mint celebrity gossip plastered throughout, compiled in expert fashion by our ace reporter Lizzy Cherry.

 I was only thirty-one, and suddenly I was a player. No longer some specky four eyes with blackheads and bad breath, running my business like a lemonade stand out of the basement of a curry shop.

The upright gentlemen of Fleet Street had christened me Filthy Frankie. Called me bad for journalism, bad for civic life, bad for moral and ethical standards of every shape and stripe. Here's the daft thing—this monster out to destroy Western civilization was still bunking at home with mum and dad and big sis in Stepney. I didn't get my own place until Lizzy and I got married a few years later. That's the God's honest truth. Yes, I had a spot at the office, with a couch and coffee table and hot plate, and I spent the odd night at Lizzy's flat. But eight evenings out of ten, I laid my head on the pillow in my bedroom on White Church Lane, surrounded by Marilyn Monroe posters, Green Bay Packers gear and Louis L'Amour novels. All of which I stockpiled in abundance because, like every other with-it English lad, I was in thrall of all things American.

So I'm holding court that night with the crew at Godiva's, at a big round table in the downstairs bar, where it's quiet. Up gallivants Lizzy with the Squire on her arm. She was always blowing my mind like that. How I convinced such a corker of a woman to marry me I'll never know. Beautiful, smart as a whip with her own money, and here she is delivering a genuine member of the First Lady's inner circle straight into my lair.

"Terry is off-duty tonight," she says. "I used my wiles to lure him out on the town to meet a few of London's finest."

They settle in for a couple of rounds. The crew is silently savoring the moment because we're working up a nasty swipe at Queen Nancy, giving her hell because of the way she's behaving over here. Refusing to curtsy for *our queen.* This sappy visit to the kids at the Spastic Society Centre. *Six* bloody vehicles to haul her people out to the Prince's polo match.

We had a lovely photo of her high heels sinking into the mud along the sidelines. Madame First Lady, one does not wear high heels to a polo match. *Especially in the fucking rain.* Dear, dear. Don't fall and break your lipstick.

We fished and pried and poked, and he was sweet as can be, but he gave us nothing whatsoever to chew on. Not that I expected him to. No man in his position worth a cup of piss would give up anything to a bunch of finks like me and the crew. And the Squire definitely appeared to be worth a cup of piss.

Lizzy and the crew headed off to the dance floor, and I snagged him alone for a few minutes in the game room. "I'm exploring the idea of expanding my business to the States."

"So I'm reading."

"Don't believe *everything* you read about me." I said. "I didn't invent the dirty magazine all by myself."

"And you're not plopped down on a velvet throne in some crumbling castle up in the moors?"

"No."

"Whipping naked girls with one hand and shooting smack between your toes with the other?"

He had me chuckling. That was a marvelous sign. "A load of people on this side of the pond are expending a load of energy trying to see me off," I said. "I want to start keeping tabs on what's happening in Washington."

"I can help you there."

"California Dream Dolls, Smarty Pants, Oriental Flames. They're all mine. And I've got a deal bubbling with Larry Flynt to publish the British edition of *Hustler.* Does any of that give you cold feet?"

"No," he said. "But something else might."

"Tell me."

"Running a nasty piece on Mrs. Reagan in the *Eye.*"

I blanched. I thought maybe Lizzy had blabbed to him. "What makes you think I'm going to do that?" I said.

"Just an educated guess," he said. "All the other tabloids are smacking her in the mouth. Can I talk you out of following along?"

"Why shouldn't I follow along?"

"She's a human being," he said. "She *does* have feelings. All this negative coverage is crushing her."

"It would be easier to crush a bag of nails."

"As tough as she is, she's having a hard time making it through the day." He looked fiercely into my eyes. "What kind of kick will you get out of making it harder?"

"It's not about me getting my kicks."

"That's a big part of it. Even if you won't admit it to yourself."

Zing. He was right. Nobody had said anything like that to my face in quite a while. I'd already figured out this man was as snazzy as they come. He had a healthy dollop of everything I lacked—grace, looks, brains, connections. If I got to know him, some of it might rub off on me. And now I could see that he wouldn't be one to pull punches, either. That was exactly the combination I was looking for.

Lizzy popped downstairs to fetch him and whisk him off. I never broached the subject with either of them, but I imagine they boffed each other that night.

He handed me his business card. "When you're ready to make your move, get in touch with me."

A couple of years later I did. And the next morning, as a gesture of respect to my new-found mate, I killed our Queen Nancy piece—and the high heels photo as well.

That pissed off the crew royally. They thought I was going pansy in my old age. But I had a hunch it would help me down the line. I was right.

Kris Lamborn Stratton

We lived in Arlington, across the Potomac from D.C., in a three-bedroom split-level house we rented on 25th Road North. There was a steep, sloping lawn that led down to the street, and a big picture window in the front of the living room. I spent hours peering through that glass at the world outside, tickling Carol on the couch, playing count the cars with Rhody, waiting for Terry to pull up the crumbling stone driveway in his Taurus.

I was lonely, angry, miserable, confused. And I was pretty sure how I'd gotten that way. It had to do with loving a man I couldn't trust.

In June of '82, he called me on a Friday afternoon from the Mayflower Hotel. Three of Nancy's girlfriends from Los Angeles were in town. He'd been escorting them around, he was tired and tipsy, and he was going to get a room there and come home in the morning.

He said he'd get back to me after he checked in. By nine o'clock, I hadn't heard from him. The hotel switchboard connected me to his room. The phone rang six times, then kicked into voice mail. I hung up without leaving a message. At midnight I did the same.

We were friendly with a retired widow who lived next door. At eight o'clock Saturday morning, I told her a friend from Columbus had arrived in D.C. unexpectedly, that I needed to make a quick trip to the

Mayflower to see her, and she agreed to watch the kids for a few hours. I called a cab because by that time I was too upset to drive.

The hotel clerk refused to give out his room number. I went into an alcove and called him from the house phone. As it was ringing, an elevator opened in the bank across the lobby, and he came out of it, walking straight toward me. I tucked in behind a wall where he couldn't see me.

He was dressed in running gear—scarlet singlet, gray shorts, a white headband. There was a very slim, very young blonde woman with him, in running gear, too, and she had her arm wrapped loosely around his waist. As they came closer, she giggled and leaned into him, and he ran his fingers across her stomach and snapped the elastic band of her shorts with his thumb.

I stepped out to the lobby, directly into their path. They were so wrapped up in each other they didn't notice me staring at them. Then he looked up and saw me, twenty yards dead ahead of him.

He stopped in his tracks. The blonde stopped with him. His face turned white, and then he grinned. The blonde turned bright red, whispered into his ear, and dashed through the revolving door to the sidewalk.

I walked up to him. "Tired and tipsy, are we?"

"You have no reason to be upset," he said. "This isn't what you think it is."

"One of the Nancy's girlfriends from Los Angeles?"

"As a matter of fact, she is."

"Bullshit. Have you fucked her yet?"

"We're going to jog up Connecticut to the zoo."

"Or do you like a hot, sweaty fuck *after* you run?"

"I'll check out right now and leave with you."

"Maybe you can shower off all your sweat together and fall spanking clean into bed."

"Give me fifteen minutes."

Through a window, I could see the blonde hovering on the north side of De Sales Street. "Don't let me spoil your plans," I said.

"Kris!"

I went outside to get a cab. On the way home, I was feeling a mixture of so many emotions I could barely breathe. Rhody opened the door for me.

"Did you have a nice visit with your friend?"

"Yes, sweetheart."

"You don't *look* like you had a nice visit with your friend."

He came in a couple of hours later, acting thoroughly ashamed of himself.

"I *didn't* sleep with her."

"You snapped the waistband of her shorts."

"That's just something runners do."

"And that's the biggest load of crap that has ever come out of your mouth."

"Are you perfect?"

"What does that have to do with it?"

I didn't talk to him or touch him for three weeks. Rhody and Carol suffered badly for it. So did he. We finally had it out one night after the kids were asleep.

"I'm sick of living like this," he said. "I want you back in my life."

"You can't have me back in your life."

"Kris, for the love of God."

"How many other woman have you had sex with since we've been married?"

"Five."

"Including the runner bitch?"

"Yes."

"So you fucked her after all."

"Yes, I did."

"Even though you told me you didn't."

"Yes."

"If you need other women, why did you marry me?"

"Because I fell in love with you," he said. "You're smart, compassionate, incredibly sexy."

"This marriage has been a farce."

"We have two beautiful children."

"I'm leaving you."

"You can't do that."

"I'm going home and I'm taking them with me."

He begged me to stay and try to work things out. But I couldn't forgive the lies, the deception, the breach of trust. I drove the kids to Columbus and left them with my sister and brother-in-law. Then dad and

I flew back to Washington and packed up a rented U-Haul while Terry was out of the house. As I rolled down the driveway for the last time, the widow next door came out to her front porch and waved goodbye.

That was the saddest day of my life. I felt nothing but utter devastation. I'd been with Terry since I was eighteen years old. I hadn't worked full-time in seven years, and the thought of what I was doing overwhelmed me. Why didn't I suck it up like millions of other women in the same position and stay with him?

It was the grin. The stupid, slobbering, shit-eating grin he gave me when I caught him in the lobby of the Mayflower with the blonde hanging all over him. Like a five-year-old with his hand in a cookie jar. Or a dog slurping water out of a toilet.

I couldn't stand the sight of his face after that.

Mac McKenzie

Terry rode Air Force One to Columbus with the president in October of '82, on a campaign swing before the mid-term elections. I met up with him in the jam-packed statehouse rotunda, minutes before Reagan and the governor stepped out onto the west portico to address the crowd.

"I trust the family is well," I said.

"Rhody has more guts than any guy I've ever known," he said. "Carol is the most beautiful girl you've ever seen in your life."

"What about Kris?"

He looked past me toward somebody on the other side of the floor "She's my world," he said. "I couldn't live without her."

"And how are all the president's men?"

"It's morning in America, Mac. The sun is shining brightly."

He averted my eyes again. As masterful a bluffer as Terry was, he couldn't quite say it with a straight face. If it was morning in America, then Ohio had a throbbing hangover. We were enduring the bleakest economic times since the Depression. The guts of the steel and rubber and auto industries were being ripped out of us, they were never coming back, and there wasn't a damn thing we could do about it.

Jim was in the last three months of his final term. Dick Celeste was going to succeed him as governor, and a horde of Democrats was ready to descend on Columbus. It was the perfect time to make a graceful exit.

We'd had an incredible run. Longer than anyone had a right to expect in politics. I was fifty-seven. I could have carried some weight as a lobbyist for ten or fifteen more years, but I wanted out. I'd seen too many guys hang on too long and turn into dotty old fools. The missus and I had lived below our means and stockpiled our cash, and we'd used a big chunk of it to buy in early on a beachfront condo on Sanibel Island in Florida, in the Gulf of Mexico off Fort Myers. That's where we were going. I was ready to pass the baton to Terry and the rest of the younger people—and I didn't envy their situation.

I found out a couple of weeks later that Kris had left him. Taken the kids, moved back to Upper Arlington, and started work as an account rep at her father's company. She was suing Terry for divorce, alimony and child support.

I didn't know the details. I didn't *want* to know. I imagine she'd discovered one too many of his secrets.

Jim left office in January. The missus and I moved down to Sanibel that summer, and I didn't hear from Terry for many years. But I followed his whole sordid saga as best I could from my outpost on the edge of the gulf.

Terry transformed himself. He turned into someone I wasn't familiar with.

Vonda Vance

I was aware of his breakup early on. He told me right after he told Mrs. R. and Mike. Divorce was not a plus in the Reagan White House, but it didn't put you at risk of losing your job as long as it didn't get ugly and public and embarrass the First Couple. Terry and his wife were discreet. A lot of people *never* found out.

He was hurting, though. He slunk up and down the central hall like a whipped dog with his tail between his legs.

"You're looking worse for wear," I said one morning. "*Far* less than your best—and then some."

"Thanks for your honesty," he said. "Are people noticing?"

"I think they are."

"The last six months have been absolute hell on Earth."

"Is there anything I can do to help you?"

"Just don't share my misery with her," he said. "That's all I ask."

She wasn't having the best time of it either. There'd been an ugly tiff with Barbara Sinatra over all the attention Mrs. R. was giving Frank during state dinners. Then in August, her stepfather Loyal Davis died in Arizona, and the very next day Alfred Bloomingdale died out in Santa Monica. Alfred's death sparked a horrific fight between his wife Betsy and his mistress Vicki Morgan. Vicki was teasing the tabloids with cryptic stories about Alfred's sex tapes, audio *and* video. The rumors about what—and *who*—was on them got raunchier by the day.

Morgan Mason flew to L.A. and tried to broker a truce. He was the son of James Mason, and the boyfriend of Belinda Carlisle of the Go-Go's, and he knew the milieu more intimately than anyone on staff. But he failed in his mission. All he did was infuriate Mrs. R, who told him and everybody else he was sticking his nose in where it didn't belong.

The situation had her on edge. And then the East Wing erupted in turmoil over Queen Elizabeth and Prince Phillip's upcoming trip to California. Mrs. R. knew she'd behaved badly with the royals in England. Oh my yes, did she ever. Their visit to her home turf was a chance for her to redeem herself. But too many people jumped into the planning process, and the whole project descended into chaos.

The only thing going well was the Just Say No campaign. There was anxiety about getting her involved in the drug issue at all. But she took a deep breath, plunged in, and brought Terry on board to calm her nerves. When the entourage left for California to greet the Queen and Prince Phillip, he was included.

He called me at the White House a week later. He was aboard the royal yacht *Britannia*, docked in Long Beach Harbor. In the background I could hear violins, tinkling glasses, festive voices.

"I have a message for you from Mrs. R.," he said. "Take the TV out of the laundry room."

"Excuse me?"

"She doesn't want the maids watching soap operas in there while they wash clothes. Get the TV and put it in the president's gym."

"Will do," I said. "Are you coming back on Tuesday?"

"No," he said. "After the Queen goes home, the First Lady and I are off to Hollywood."

Jaye Janis

I first laid eyes on Terry Stratton the day he came to Universal City with Nancy Reagan to tape the Just Say No episode of *Diff'rent Strokes*. I was three years out of Vassar, green as green can be, working the show's fifth season as a production assistant while I tried to break into the Industry as a script writer.

"Production assistant" is television jargon for a bright young person with creative aspirations wandering around the set with nothing much to do. I *did* report to work sober, at least at first. I wasn't stoned or buzzed or blitzed or tickled or mashed or frogged. On Nancy's special day I was sober as cement, and I'm glad I was because there was a throng of strangers—corporate suits, spouses, reporters, Secret Service agents, and *her* people. Terry Stratton was one of them.

At the request of the First Lady, the writers had put in a small part for him. A nerdy substitute teacher who bolts into Gary Coleman's classroom from next door, desperately seeking chalk for his blackboard. Two scenes, five lines. He was far too attractive to play a nerdy substitute teacher with *real* credibility. But we mussed up his hair and stuck a pair of glasses and a goofy tie on him, and he managed to pull it off.

All the while, off in a corner by herself, Dana Plato was hunkered down in a lawn chair, zoned out of her ever loving mind. She was nineteen by then, living on Melrose Avenue without her parents, hanging out with a heavy duty party crowd. She only had two scenes herself, and that allowed her to spend the better part of two hours *devouring* the man with her eyes. And I'd spied him more than once coming right back at her with the same.

When the taping was over, there was half an hour of social time. Forty or fifty people were milling around in clusters, sneaking glances at each other, nibbling chips and nuts, sipping soft drinks. Norman Lear arrived with great fanfare to offer an olive branch to Nancy. She was peeved over all the shots he and Ed Asner and Rob Reiner and the rest of the liberals kept taking at her husband.

With the gathering in full swing, Dana drifted off the set and headed down the hallway that led to the prop warehouse. A minute later, Terry did the same. I won't say I *followed* them. I'll just say I suddenly noticed a few boxes of stuff that had to be carried back there and put away.

There was no sign of them in the main storage area. I was up on a ladder putting the boxes away when I heard a giggly squeal somewhere on the far side of the floor. I climbed down as quietly as I could, peeked out from behind the shelves, and there they were, maybe forty yards out ahead of me, in a dimly-lighted vending nook near the loading dock. They didn't see me.

He had her pinned against the front of a big, red Coke machine. Her thick hair was tied back in a ponytail with some kind of twine. Her blouse was unbuttoned, and her bra was dangling around her waist. Up on her left shoulder, I could make out some kind of tattoo. He leaned into her, cupped her left breast in both of his hands, and planted a tender kiss on her nipple.

My fascination with Terry Stratton began that day. I wanted to know who the man was, where he came from, what he stood for, and how he ended up fondling this barely grown child celebrity in front of my astonished, astounded eyes.

I'm not sure I ever discovered *any* of that. And as close as I ended up getting to him, I never told him about what I saw that day.

Dan O'Hanlon

The engraved invitation arrived in my statehouse mailbox in Columbus in May of '83.

The President and Mrs. Ronald Reagan were requesting my attendance at the First White House Summit on Drug Abuse. I was directed to RSVP ASAP to Vonda Vance, Special Projects Associate in the Office of the First Lady, who would brief me on scheduling and security details.

My first thought was that Stratton might be playing some kind of prank on me. I reached his voice mail through the White House switchboard and left a message, trying to find out what was going on.

He got back to me late that afternoon.

"Greetings, hombre," he said. "Wonderful to hear from an old friend."

"Is this fancy piece of cardboard I just got in the mail for real?"

"As real as real can be."

"What have I done to deserve such an honor?"

"The First Lady is very impressed with the drug enforcement bill you're sponsoring out there," he said.

"It's not my bill anymore," I said. "My name is at the top of the page, but after the House passed it, the Neanderthals in the Senate turned it into *exactly* what I was trying to avoid."

"That's the reality of the legislative process," he said. "We understand that, don't we?"

"Jail terms and heavy fines for first time offenders," I said. "Crumbs for education and rehab. Maybe you should invite *those* guys instead of me."

"We're committed to recognizing some of the foot soldiers in this battle," he said.

"The situation is so dire you're even hauling in a few token Ds."

"This summit has *nothing* to do with party."

"I'm getting it now," I said. "I'm a two-fer. A foot soldier *and* a D. You kill two tokens with one invite, which frees up a slot for another hot actor. Or some sexy hunk of a doctor."

"As cynical as ever, aren't you?"

"How can I not be?"

"A thousand black kids from the D.C. schools will be joining us," he said. "They're marching up Pennsylvania Avenue from the Hill with their Just Say No banners. Is that something to be cynical about?"

"How do you like being a sitcom star?"

"I'll tell you all about it when you come over here."

Some of those cave men in the Senate *did* get upset when word got around that I was the one who'd been invited. A good number of my own caucus were ticked off, too. They saw it as aiding and abetting the enemy. But the speaker gave me his blessing, and so did Uncle Bob. I called Vonda Vance and put my name on the list.

On the morning of June 12th, after a lightning quick welcome from the president, two hundred warriors in the battle to save the nation crammed into the East Room for two hours of speeches from a host of bigwigs. From there we proceeded to the South Lawn for box lunches, networking, and photo opportunities, with musical entertainment by the Beach Boys.

The stars were out in force: Pee Wee Herman, Bette Midler, Merv Griffin, Barbara Stanwyck, Olivia Newton-John, and Clint Eastwood, whom the First Lady kept tucked on her arm all day. There were oil sheiks, too: King Fahd of Saudi Arabia, the Sultan of Brunei, and their bands of minions. I asked Stratton why they were there.

"They've come to Washington in search of a new batch of AWACS surveillance planes," he said.

"I understand. And they've suddenly developed a keen interest in the First Lady's crusade to keep America's kids clean and sober."

"Hombre, you're a quick study."

Of course Stratton had his own agenda. He'd assembled a diverse group of contacts from outside the Beltway to introduce to his best Washington friends. The fact that Uncle Bob was in Congress gave me added panache.

"Dan—meet Georgy Greco," he said. "Georgy is chief of staff for Chairman Fryer. She's our lifesaver on the Hill."

A thirtyish, dark-haired, doe-eyed woman extended her hand to me. "It's *always* an honor to meet an O'Hanlon from Rocky River," she said. "Families like yours are what make this country great."

"And this is Raj Rao," Terry said. "Raj lobbies for Golden Pharmaceutical. Golden has been an angel for us in this fight."

Raj had a short crop of thick black hair and a thoughtful, disarming smile. "I'm hearing great things about your bill and I'd love to hear more," he said.

Vonda Vance came by with a big, old-fashioned Polaroid camera and snapped a picture of the four of us, with the South Portico in the background. These days, I fantasize about grabbing the camera away from her, ripping the film out, and trampling the contraption to bits with my heel, like Sonny Corleone at his sister's wedding in the opening scene of *The Godfather*. My wife has this theory that the four of us are cursed. Maybe Nancy Reagan's astrologer put a hex on us, or Stratton picked up a dose of bad karma on the set of *Diff'rent Strokes* and brought it back to the White House. Given the misfortunes that befell him and Raj and Georgy, it's hard to shrug her theory off. It makes me wonder if the curse has anything left in the barrel for me.

Those thousand black kids Stratton had mentioned came screaming and swarming across the lawn. Their march from the Capitol was over. It soon became apparent that the planners of the summit had overlooked a critical item—there wasn't a single porta-john in sight. As the hullabaloo ramped up, I said a quick goodbye and grabbed a taxi outside the East Gate.

I was heading to the Hill to see Uncle Bob. That was *my* main agenda item for the day. He wasn't going to seek an eleventh term in the House in '84, and I wanted to succeed him. We were going to meet with the House Democratic Fundraising Caucus to gauge how much support they were willing to give my candidacy.

As the taxi pulled away I caught my last glimpse of the summit—Stratton leading Pee Wee Herman and a bunch of squawking kids past the Marine guardhouse, into the East Wing. Probably trying to find them all a place to take a leak.

I didn't know it at that moment, but his days at the White House were numbered. Something horrible must have happened, because after the summit the knives came out for him in short order. All of a sudden, he was gone.

Lynn Starhawk

Don't believe the lies about me *fixing* something to get Terry Stratton fired. About me putting a mark of the devil on him that wasn't real, tilting my board and giving a false reading, because somebody in the White House pressured me to do it to give Mrs. R. a reason to get rid of him.

You might have heard that from Deaver. He's deflecting blame from himself. Dragging me into the situation to cover his own posterior. All I ever did was *tell the truth.* Why do people have such a problem with that?

Deaver never had a clue anyway. The man was oblivious. I practice *white* magick, for the cause of good, not evil. I would never do the work of the devil for money or politics or vanity or any other reason.

Even if I *were* a black witch, why would I put a phony mark of the devil on Terry Stratton? I never met the man, or saw his picture, or even knew his name until years after the fact. To me, he was always Mrs. R's favorite Aquarius, and that's all he was.

I felt *no* need to pry into her personal affairs. You're confusing me with some of my trashier rivals. I won't name names. Thieves, parasites, charlatans, soaking up their fifteen minutes of fame for all it was worth, trying to make a buck.

I carry myself on a higher plane. The Wiccan Rede actually means something to me. I have never tilted a board in my life. The suggestion is insulting. I have been sorely *tempted* to tilt a board. Any reader who says otherwise is not being honest. We want so badly to tell our loved ones what they want to hear. But I refuse to even do so much as *shade* the truth. Not even for her.

"I have unsettling news," I said. "Your favorite Aquarius has moved outside the sacred circle of protection."

"Whatever in the world do you mean?"

"A black triangle has erupted on my board. Like some horrible chancre."

"My God, no!"

"I can no longer channel magickal energy in your direction."

"Are you telling me he needs to go?"

"I would never presume to tell you what you *need*," I said. "But this chancre destroys his link to your special friend from long ago. And if he stays now, he may actually *harm* you and your husband."

"Why, why, why, why, why?"

"I warned you about his need for freedom," I said. "And the tendency toward perversity."

"Stop!"

She dropped me after that. I never heard a single word from her again. It was the end of a thirteen-year friendship. When she stopped taking my calls, it was devastating.

I don't have many loved ones who knew me when I was a man. She was one of very few. I still wear the crystal pendant she gave me after my operation, and I still have my *I Love Nancy* button with the big red heart in the middle.

She'd had enough, I guess. Of witchcraft, of magick, spirit boards, toiling so hard every day to channel her special friend from so long ago. She wanted to move on. As for me, I played it straight as an arrow. I have nothing to hide. Nothing to explain. Nothing to be ashamed of.

Vonda Vance

On the morning before Terry resigned, Mrs. R. and the president were exercising together in their gym. She was walking on the treadmill. He was riding the stationary bike. I was halfway up the hall that led to the living quarters, tagging clothes in a walk-in closet. I firmly believe to this day that neither of them knew I was there.

The door leading from Mrs. R.'s office into the gym was open. I could hear them talking to each other over the noise of the machines. Their voices kept getting louder.

"How much time have you been spending with this kid?" the president said.

"He's helping me reach Wyatt because Wyatt can protect *us*."

"If Wyatt St. George is protecting me, how the hell did I end up with a bullet in my chest?"

"Maybe he kept it from penetrating your heart."

"Wyatt St. George has been dead for thirty-five years. Get over it!"

"That's exactly what Lynn told me to do. And I will."

"I don't give two shits about Lynn Starhawk or Wyatt St. George or Terry Stratton. Fire his ass."

"Ronnie, please."

"Lavender, frankincense. Leaving that goddam board out on the lawn under the full moon. My God."

"I'm sorry."

"Get the hell out of here and leave me the fuck alone!"

Mrs. R. began to sob. She came through her office and started up the hall toward the living quarters. I dropped flat on my stomach behind a partition and a pile of big packing boxes. She went by the closet quickly, her sobs getting louder.

On the floor, I was trembling. In sixteen years, I'd never heard them argue, never heard the president swear, never heard Mrs. R. cry. I stayed exactly where I was and didn't make a sound.

The president rode the bike a few more minutes. Then I heard grunting and heaving and pounding, and the loud snap of cracking wood. He came up the hallway past me, breathing hard.

When the coast was clear, I went into the gym. The little black-and-white TV I'd taken from the laundry room was on, tuned to *Good*

Morning America. Shoved in a corner behind the metal wastebasket was a pile of stuff: a hand broom, a small bell, black and white candles, quartz crystals—and the remains of Mrs. R.'s reading board. The president had smashed it to smithereens with a twenty-pound dumbbell.

I left all the stuff where it was. By afternoon, it was gone. I never found out what happened to it.

Terry submitted his resignation the next day, effective immediately. That was the end of his time at the White House.

Michael Deaver

People accuse me of treating my subordinates like scum. Let the record reflect that I did not treat Terry Stratton like scum. He got a raw deal. In my twenty years with the Reagans, it was the most asinine situation I was ever involved in.

I let him down as easily as I could. Mrs. R. commanded me to cut him off completely, but I defied her and left my door open. I told him he still had access to me, that he could call me any time.

Let me make one last point: I did Stratton a favor by letting him go. He wasn't cut out for life in the Great White Jail. He was a bird in a gilded cage. I set him free.

Four / Washington–Hollywood–Las Vegas/ 1983-1993

Ramsay Stratton Karnes

Bro called me many times in the fall of '83, after he left the White House and ventured out on his own. He needed a shoulder to cry on and, strangely, he picked mine.

Time and geography had eroded our bond. I hadn't seen him since his wedding nine years before, and we were camped out on opposite oceans. I'd left bohemia and bongs and Boyfriend behind in New Mexico and moved to San Jose in California, where my husband Jim Karnes was the director of Ed Levin County Park. I was thirty-three, scampering up and down our mustard stucco split level barefoot and pregnant, and loving every minute of it.

One day, Terry's voice sounded slurry and sloppy. "Where are you?" I said.

"Approaching Tyson's Corner," he said. "I'm doing circles around the Beltway in my Volvo 760. Three-position tilt steering. Aerodynamic headlights. Bosch oxygen sensor."

"You're inside a *car?*"

"On my DynaTAC 8000X."

"Your *what?*"

"My mobile phone," he said. "Hand held, cordless. Thirty five hundred for the unit, plus one fifty a month service."

"You must be working then."

"Kris's dad is still with me, bless his heart. He's brought in a few clients, but I need more."

"Can I level with you about something?"

"By all means."

"You sound *incredibly* fucked up."

"Have you ever smoked hash oil laced with coke?"

"Once or twice," I said. "A hundred years ago."

"Add a nip of Absolut every time you pass an exit, and you have the perfect combo for doing circles around the Beltway."

"Hang up now and drive to your office."

"At the moment I have no office."

"Home, then."

"Ditto."

"Jesus, Terry. Go *somewhere*."

"I promised myself I'd keep doing circles until I figure out what to do with the rest of my life."

"Get a book deal," I said. "Give the world the inside scoop on Queen Nancy."

"That would kill my so-called career," he said. "Rats are not appreciated in this town."

"Service the lonely wives of Georgetown," I said. "Be like Richard Gere in *American Gigolo*."

"Too high risk for a straight arrow like me."

"Get yourself baptized in the Potomac by some Holy Roller preacher, then rail about the decay of America in front of the White House."

"That may be worth looking into."

What a strange conversation bro and I were having.

First, the role reversal. Terry had been riding high in life from day one. All that time, I'd been adrift—place to place, job to job, man to man. Now, Terry's marriage was kaput, his White House gig was history, and he was out on the street. As for me—with a husband who acted like he wanted to stick around, a baby in my belly, and my cartoons getting published every month after two thousand rejection slips, I was on a rocket to the moon.

Second, Terry mooning over his car and phone. He'd always been a careerist, but somewhere along the line he'd acquired a taste for expensive *things*. From my angle that didn't bode well, because his financial obligations seemed heavy—child support for Rhody and Carol, alimony for Kris, living and working expenses in D.C.

Finally, the drugs. Substance abuse seemed to be rearing its ugly head. I figured him to be a regular consumer, but a functional one who could get up the next day and go to work. Now he was motoring around I-495 at ten o'clock on a Wednesday morning, sounding thoroughly smashed.

"Bro, find your mother and father. At least *try*."

"I'm better off without them."

"No you're not."

 "I need to get my act together first."

"Finding them might *help* you get your act together," I said. "It was the best move I ever made it my life."

When he got a permanent address, I sent him a mailing with information about my birth parents, and how I'd contacted them. I got a card from him after my daughter Erin was born in March, and we got together that summer for a couple of hours in Akron when Jim and I took Erin back East to meet his family.

Then we stopped communicating altogether. He'd hurled himself into the great Washington maw.

Judy Zakowski

Everybody was whispering that's him, there he is right *there*, by the TV camera, next to Pat Buchanan. And I had no idea who they were talking about. I asked a reporter and he said, that's Stratton, the guy who worked at the White House, whose autograph collection got written up in the *Post*, who was on *Diff'rent Strokes* with Nancy Reagan.

This was February of '84, in Gucci Gulch, the hallway outside the House Ways & Means Committee room. The Gulch is named after the shoes and Terry always wore an expensive pair, like the dozens of other lobbyists lined up with him to kiss Member ass.

To us they were all scum. By us I mean the *good* people on the Hill, what precious few there were left. The good people were here for the love of humanity, to make the world a better place. The scum were here to make a pile of money. We wanted to slay the monster called Status Quo. They wanted to keep it alive.

How deluded we were in our thinking. Naïve, simplistic, self-righteous, and above all, hypocritical. Because in the dark forest of our souls, all we good people really wanted to *be* lobbyists ourselves. And those of us who spewed the most venom on the scum—like me—were the same ones who ended up selling out with barely a shred of shame to the highest bidders.

That came later. When I spotted Terry in Gucci Gulch I was still an idealist, starting my fourth year in the office of Representative Milo Forbes, Democrat of Wisconsin, champion of the working class, guardian of the 12th District that spread north and west from Madison into Sauk and Iowa counties. He was a burly, bearded mountain of a man, and the only Member who played the mandolin. Mounted on his office wall on the fourth floor of Cannon was a Jethro Burns Signature Washburn, with a custom-made rosewood bridge. When he wanted to show off, or when he was homesick, he would take it down and pluck the *Hee Haw* theme or the Badger Fight Song.

Eighty-four was Milo's first year on Ways & Means. He was close to Chairman Rostenkowski and he'd beaten out several strong candidates for the vacancy. By then I'd moved up from staff assistant to policy aide to legislative director. But I wasn't prepared for the swarm of lobbyists that descended that winter. Terry was one of them. He represented a trade group called the Buckeye Generals, whose members were large-scale manufacturing companies and their suppliers and affiliates. Their agenda was to preserve and, whenever possible, expand— the depreciation allowances in the IRS code for their many types of expensive machinery and equipment.

On the afternoon of spring recess I ran into him at the Boar's Head, on Pennsylvania. We split off from the mob at the bar and ended up in a booth in the back room, by the pool tables, drinking Rolling Rock, sharing a basket of fries, and talking music, movies, football. No business whatsoever. I tried to remember the last time I'd had a bonafide conversation with a man about anything other than tax law. I couldn't.

Let me humbly confess that my hostility toward Terry Stratton disappeared in those two hours.

We must have seemed like the oddest couple in the universe. You know what Terry Stratton looked like. What did *I* look like? Splotchy skin, dishwater hair, humongous ears, a thick brown mole on the back of my neck. And sixty excess pounds worth of every form of comfort food on the planet packed onto my butt, thighs and stomach. Even my ankles and wrists were fat.

"I've got a friend coming to town next week who adores the Packers," he said. "Would you like to have dinner with us?"

I'd like to have dinner with you alone right now is what I was thinking. And I wouldn't mind if we skipped the meal and proceeded straight to the bedroom. Of course, that was nothing but a pathetic, adolescent fantasy on my part. Because every waking minute of every day there was a chant droning in the back of my head: I don't deserve to be here. I'm not chic enough or attractive enough or sexy enough to operate in this environment. People pity me. They cringe when they see me. They make fun of me behind my back because of the way I look.

I was trying so hard to back away from the refrigerator, the cupboards, the breadbox. To grab something else—*anything* else—when I felt anxious or down or lonely. Because I didn't want to eat.

I said to Terry, "I'd love to have dinner with your friend."

That was the start of my road to ruin.

Frankie Hodnett

Such an incredible rush to hook up with the Squire again. When Lizzy and I arrived in D.C. on our first visit to America as man and wife, he welcomed us with open arms.

The topper? Mr. Deaver joining us for dinner on the last night of our stay. We were in the main room at Duke Zeibert's—Lizzy, me, the Squire and Ms. Judy Zakowski from the office of Forbes of Wisconsin, a key player on the tax-writing committee. When Mr. Deaver came in and worked his way through all the movers and shakers back to our table, my palms went clammy and my heart started thumping. I actually thought I might pass out.

The Squire said to him: "Frankie owns the *Eye* in London. We remember the *Eye* from the royal wedding, don't we?"

"Indeed we do," Mr. Deaver said. "And Frankie, as a gesture of appreciation for the respect you showed our First Lady, I have something for you." He reached into his inside suit coat pocket, pulled out three football cards wrapped separately in wax paper, and handed them to me. "All original issues," he said. "Bart Starr, Paul Hornung, Jerry Kramer. All in their rookie seasons."

I damn near melted into the floor. The Squire tossed me his wryest smile, I tossed mine back, and suddenly things seemed as sweet as a nut.

Before Lizzy and I flew to Las Vegas the next morning, I had a quick bite with him at a little hole in the wall place on K Street. He agreed to be my man in Washington, the registered legislative agent for Royal Duchess Media. Fifteen thousand dollars a month, plus expenses, is the number we settled on—with a backhander now and then if he needed one.

"The price is high," I said. "But I need you. I'm moving to the States."

"Are the Fleet Street bastards finally driving you out?"

I nodded sadly. "And Lizzy's folks are aiding the effort. They can't stomach the fact that their beautiful West End princess threw herself away on a piece of East End trash like me. They want us as far away as possible."

"The South Pole would be ideal, right?"

He had me chuckling again. "Mars would be even better. But America will have to do."

It wasn't as all bloody horrible as I'm making it sound, because Lizzy and I were keen for a fresh start. We were done with print. I was selling my four glossies, turning the *Eye* over to my crew, and moving on to visuals. Something spectacular was going on there. Thanks to the glorious miracle of VHS, dirty pictures were moving out of dank, grimy theatres and into millions of living rooms and bedrooms all over the world.

Los Angeles was where it was happening. Up in the San Fernando Valley to be exact, in a place called Chatsworth. There was a new life to live and another mountain of money to be made, out on the rim of the Pacific. That's where Lizzy and I were headed.

Phil Sparrow

We both worked on the Hill, but I talked to him for the first time at Columbia Station, in Adams-Morgan. We were watching the Orioles game and he smiled at me across the bar. "I know you," he said. "You're in the Doorkeeper's Office, in the House."

He had a place on Biltmore Street, halfway down a long block toward Rock Creek Park. Top floor of a stick thin three-story brownstone, with a living room-kitchen up front and a big deck out back, behind the bedroom.

One night, after I got to know him better, we went over there to smoke weed and snort coke. After half an hour or so, he hit on me. Real casual.

"Ever done anything with a guy?"

"A few times."

"Want more?"

We didn't do much. Not that night or any other. We'd take off our clothes and wrestle on his bed, or on the thick, shaggy rug in the living room, giving each other shoulder massages, back rubs, long, lubed, luxurious handjobs.

Later on we went down on each other, with condoms. Nothing anal. He was vigilant about safe sex. He taught me how to demand it *and* enjoy it, and in spite of everything that happened between us I'm forever thankful, because he probably saved my life.

He was thirty-six. I was twenty-eight. He was ten miles above me in status, wealth, education. The White House, his law degree, his Volvo, the lobbying firm he was starting with the other mojos. All that plus being born with a silver spoon in his mouth out in Ohio, growing up in a mansion with a swimming pool and servants, getting his own Mustang when he was sixteen.

I figure half or more of what he told me was bullshit. But I could hardly complain because I gave the same back to him. Such as lettering in football at Marshall as a backup tight end and scoring a touchdown against Florida State in '74. Such as getting high with Dolly Parton in her Winnebago after a concert in Norfolk. Such as my late old man being a distinguished citizen of Carver, North Carolina, and my late mother being a saint.

None of the lies really mattered, his or mine. We had this weird bond because we both had Xs and kids, both had a boy eight and a girl six. We'd joke about getting everybody together for a picnic, giving each other's Xs a go, marrying our kids off to each other. We had the coke thing, too. But that was never the highlight. We always transacted quickly, right after I arrived at Biltmore Street, before we got down.

He took twenty grams off me like clockwork, the second Saturday of every month. Always paid in cash, always in twenties. Ultra cautious, ultra discreet, appreciative of my efforts. And fully aware of the risks I was taking.

All factors considered, he was the best customer I ever had.

Media Advisory:
For Immediate Release
July 16th, 1984

Three veteran Washington strategists are pleased to announce the formation of The L Street Team, a legal and consulting firm that will provide legislative advice to corporate clients on a wide range of tax, business, and energy issues.

In her most recent role, Georgiana "Georgy" Greco, 33, served as chief of staff to Representative Howard Fryer (D-Pennsylvania), Chairman of the House Ways & Means Commerce Subcommittee. She also is Special Adviser to the National Hellenic Council for Human Rights. A native of Pittsburgh, Greco is a graduate of Stanford University and Yale Law School.

Rajan "Raj" Rao, 35, most recently served as Director of the Washington office of Golden Pharmaceutical. He also has been Vice-President for Policy at the Foundation for Capitalism and a member of the Reagan-Bush transition team. Born and raised in Plano, Texas, Rao is a graduate of Baylor University, the London School of Economics, and Harvard Law School.

Terry Stratton, 36, was Associate Director of External Policy under Michael Deaver in the White House Office of Communications. Stratton has advised the president and senior White House staff on numerous economic and domestic policy issues. He was Ohio director of the Reagan-Bush campaign in 1980 and is a graduate of The Ohio State University.

Greco, Rao, and Stratton also have formed L Street Elections, an affiliate of The L Street Team. L Street Elections will offer campaign and fundraising services to candidates for the United States Congress.

For more information contact Media Relations Manager, The L Street Team, 1909 L Street, N.W. Suite 333, Washington, D.C. 20036. 1-202-657-6728.

Judy Zakowski

They desired me, they enticed me, they beckoned me into their world. I wasn't sure I belonged. I *never* got over the feeling of not being worthy enough to walk with Raj and Georgy as an equal.

The three of us had breakfast at the Greenbrier Resort, in White Sulphur Springs in West Virginia. This was in August of '84, after the House recessed before the Republican Convention in Dallas. Red pepper omelets and fresh-squeezed orange juice amidst the antiques in the main lobby, what the hosts call the living room. Served by a waiter in hunter green livery, who informed us that we were dining at the same table where Princess Grace always liked to have tea.

The event was called Controversies of the Tax World. Officially, it was a series of roundtable discussions among the nation's foremost fiscal experts. In reality, it was a way for forty Rs and seventy Ds to mingle with the hundred lobbyists who had ponied up six grand apiece to book the place solid for three days and hire a twelve-car train to carry us all out from Union Station in D.C. And while Members mingled, their spouses and kids played golf, tennis and croquet, roamed acres of forest, rode horses and limos up the mountain to the shooting range, and got olive oil body scrubs at the spa, all courtesy of America's most civic-minded corporations. The scene repulsed me. I was there only at the request of Milo, who despised lobbyists even more than I did and was skipping the festivities.

Raj peered at me intently across Princess Grace's table. He always gave the impression that deep thoughts were churning inside his head. "We'd love to have you come work with us at L Street."

"That is *quite* a surprise."

"I don't know why it should be," he said. "Terry thinks the world of you. We do, too."

"I can't bring you any clients."

"We have clients," he said. "What we need is your expertise. Your work ethic, your integrity."

"I'm committed to Milo's re-election campaign."

"We understand that," Georgy said. "We respect that. But where do you see yourself come January?"

"With Milo," I said. "Fighting for the people with no voice, no lobbyists, no PACs. The ones who aren't here having breakfast with us this morning."

Georgy reached across the table and gently touched my hand. It felt warm and comfortable in my own. "*Never* would we ask you to give up that fight," she said. "Raj and I certainly haven't."

"Let's call this a standing offer," Raj said. "If you get to a time and place where L Street would be a good fit for you, let us know."

Despite my hissy attitude, I left the table giddy. Beyond flattered. I dug into the tedious, technical grit of my job as deeply as I could and tried to tune out the madness swirling around me. I didn't think anyone outside of Milo's office even noticed my efforts. Now, I was seemingly being given a chance to write my own ticket off the Hill.

Did I mention that Raj and Georgy were married? To each other, that is. Excuse me, I'm being clever. Everybody in town knew, but people outside the Beltway are probably unaware. We call them mixed marriages in D.C. He being R, she being D—it was intriguing. So was the ethnic mix. They always laughed that off. She said Raj was more Greek than she was; he said Georgy was more Indian than he was.

Why did they want me? To handle client issues in Ways & Means, as simple as that. We'd passed Reagan's enormous tax cut during his first year in office, but we'd given away too much. The president *himself* realized that he'd overreached, and after he trounced Mondale in November and was into his second term, he wasn't going to put up much of a fight when Tip O'Neill played Robin Hood by clawing back a canyon full of money from corporations and the rich. The ballpark figure being bandied about the Greenbrier was two hundred billion. The Gipper wasn't going to *like* it, but he wasn't going to stand in our way.

So the battle was joined. The L Street Team had one mission, and it was strictly defensive—preserve existing tax loopholes for their clients. Make some other firm's rich bastards pay the piper. Not *their* rich bastards.

I didn't think I had the stomach for it. It was Terry who kept my interest alive. On the morning the conference was breaking up, he pulled up to the portico of the Greenbrier in a gleaming blue Volvo that looked as sturdy as a tank. I came out of the living room and made a beeline toward him.

"Long time, no see," I said. "Where have you been?"

"Out in Ohio," he said. "Visiting with my sister and her husband and their new baby. I wanted to drop by here and say hello to everyone."

"Your timing is perfect."

"Say listen," he said. "I promised Mr. Brandt and Mr. Russell a lift back to town, and I've got room for one more. Would you like to skip the train and ride with us?"

My God. Would I ever. Anybody on the premises would have lopped off an arm and a limb to be named later for five hours of private face time with two of the heaviest hitters on Ways & Means. To this day, I think Raj and Georgy arranged the whole thing to spin my head around.

I sat in the back with Mr. Brandt. Mr. Russell rode shotgun next to Terry. As we cruised home in air-conditioned comfort through the Appalachians, a thought that I'd been suppressing started gurgling around in my head.

Listen up, girl. Maybe you're misjudging this. You should reconsider selling your soul out to the scum. The life of a high-priced influence peddler might not be so bad after all.

Dan O'Hanlon

Stratton and The L Street Team worked for me in my run to succeed Uncle Bob in Congress. He was as pivotal as any single person in my winning a race that was in play right to the end.

He called me several times that summer, after I won the Democratic primary, always on his mobile phone, pitching the services of his new firm. In July, he flew out to Cleveland and took me to dinner at Fagan's Steak and Seafood on Old River Road in the Flats. We ate sirloin and shrimp outside on the deck and watched the boats cruising the water.

"You're a winner, hombre. You're going to beat Roberta Tate, do the O'Hanlons of Rocky River proud, and be a fantastic asset for *all* the people of your district."

"*Any* Republican over *any* Democrat. You told me that one time."

"I was young and naïve," he said. "My world has changed."

"You're part of a full-service operation now. Is that it?"

"That's what we are."

"You'll handle any race for any candidate, anytime, any place—as long as the price is right?"

"Let's not waste energy lamenting the flaws of the system."

"As long as you're in town, why don't you pitch Roberta Tate? Work for both candidates in the same race and not tell either of them what you're up to."

"I'll tell you why. The Buckeye Generals don't want Roberta Tate in Congress."

"Compared to *who*?"

"Sterilize welfare mothers? Make English the official language of Cuyahoga County? Not exactly our priority issues."

"She happens to be a very effective campaigner," I said. "She connects with people on a gut level."

"Which is why we need to bring Georgy Greco and Howard Fryer out to do two events for you. One here, one in Columbus."

"All that faceless money," I said. "From PACs and people I know nothing about."

"Who do you think is funding her? It's not Joe Six Pack in Parma, mailing in fifty bucks from his two-bedroom ranch with a garage."

"Do I *have* to do it the way she does?"

"National Right-to-Life, NRA, Pat Robertson. They all own a piece of the lady."

"Is this what we've spawned?"

"You and me and ten thousand co-conspirators," he said. "But we're off-purpose again, moaning about something we can't change. The Generals want you, and Kris's father tells me they'll not only endorse you—but *work* for you."

"Have those guys *ever* endorsed a Democrat?"

"Until you came along, there's never been a Democrat worth endorsing."

You hear stuff like that often enough and you start believing it. People telling you how great you are, how honest, courageous, intelligent, compassionate, forthright. I was insecure enough to need the propping up. I was far from the most compelling candidate to ever come down the pike, I was only thirty-eight years-old, and I was swimming in the deep end of the pool.

After some dithering, I hired L Street to do polling, media ads, and fundraising for the general election. Stratton didn't let me down. He arranged a meeting with the Generals in August that went spectacularly well. I got their endorsement, and their PAC raised fifty thousand dollars for me. That was a full twenty percent of what I spent, and I needed every cent of it.

Somebody was looking out for me during the last month of that campaign. It was probably the Dagda, Celtic god of magic and wisdom, giving me strength from his bottomless cauldron and protection with his magic club. Roberta put her foot in her mouth a few times, I lay all of my tortured ambivalence aside and busted my ass, and on Election Day I beat her by five points—115,540 to 104, 340.

It was the closest race of my career—until the last one.

So did Stratton buy me for fifty thousand bucks? Yeah, he bought me. There, I said it. And I hate the way it sounds because it shatters so many illusions. But sometime down the line, I couldn't be sure when, he was going to come to me and ask for my vote on something he *urgently* needed. And when that moment came, I wasn't going to keep an open mind, or examine the pros and cons, or gauge the effect of my action on the constituents of the 15th District. I was going to vote the way Stratton needed me to vote because I owed it to him.

If that isn't bought, what is?

Kris Lamborn Stratton

That November, he came to Columbus for the Michigan game, and on Sunday morning, he dropped by our apartment for a couple of hours. He told Rhody he was going to take him to the Rose Bowl to see Ohio State play USC. Rhody was eight, in fourth grade. He was a pensive guy who felt sad and mad and bad about what had happened between his mom and dad, and he didn't smile much. But after Terry's visit, he bopped around beaming for days. He was out of his mind with excitement.

In December, at the start of Christmas vacation, Terry called and said he had work obligations in Los Angeles and couldn't take Rhody to the game after all.

I was livid. I picked up the phone and screamed at him. "What the hell do you think you're doing?"

"I'm sorry."

"You ruined his vacation," I said. "He's up in his room right now, bawling his eyes out."

"I'll make it up to him."

"Why did you string him along?"

"I *didn't*. I had a change of plans."

"Are you taking a woman with you?"

"Please, Kris."

"Or hooking up with one after you get there?"

"For the love of God, let it go."

It was so unlike the Terry I *thought* I knew, to do something that hurtful to his kid. His wife was fair game. His son wasn't. But I didn't want to poison the well, so I ramped down my rage and backed off. We were two and a half years split at that point, and the fiercest hell of it was finally behind me. I had steady income, good health, and new friends. My kids weren't happy, but they were safe. There was no doubt in my mind that I'd made the right decision.

I feel like I bailed out just in time. Terry was changing—and not for the better. He was surrendering to his temptations.

Jaye Janis

Thirty months after I peeped on him at the *Diff'rent Strokes* taping, I ran into him again—on New Year's Eve at Frankie Hodnett's grotesquely huge mansion in Holmby Hills.

I was there by luck of the draw. An awkward, bookish gay guy who'd been a housemate of mine at Vassar knew Frankie's wife Lizzy, he was invited, and he wanted to take a woman along so he wouldn't feel too uncomfortable.

"It will be grist for your mill," he said.

What a collection of guests. Call it the Hollywood F List. Standing in the upstairs living room, on a balcony overlooking the great vaulted space where a motley pack of coked-up crazies were boogying themselves senseless, I thought, gee, they don't look much different from the folks boarding the midnight shuttle to Las Vegas at LAX, or ringing in 1985 at Grandma's Bar & Grill in Normal, Illinois.

This was inside the most extravagant house I'd ever seen. I grew up rich in Highland Park on the North Shore of Chicago, and I've been in plenty of big houses. This puppy was obscene. Twenty-two thousand square feet of Gothic-Tudor glory on four acres along Charing Cross Road. Fifteen bedrooms and nine bathrooms on three levels. As rich as Frankie Hodnett was, buying it must have been a stretch. The market value today is probably fifty million.

Our host appeared to be totally out of his element—with the guests, the mansion, the Industry, L.A. itself. He was a pale, tubby guy with a giant bald spot and crooked teeth, wrapped up in a ratty old blazer that fit him like a bathrobe. He was also a full-blown Tory, a pro-Reagan, pro-Thatcher conservative who had expressed some barbaric political opinions. "I have no problem whatsoever with decent, hard-working black people," he'd just pronounced in a *Hustler* interview. "Who I have a problem with are niggers." And a few years before, peevish and drunk in some strip club in Van Nuys, he'd inadvertently muttered something into a live tape recorder: "Hitler was on the right track with the Jews. He just went too far."

He inspected my tits and crotch and ass, apparently like what he saw, handed me a glass of champagne and guided me into the main kitchen. There, pinned to the refrigerator door with Green Bay Packer magnets, were a dozen pictures of Lizzy and his family and friends back in Stepney.

"Your wife is exquisitely beautiful," I said.

"Thank you." He sighed forlornly. "She attracts men—and women—by the busload."

"I imagine she does."

"She has to fend them off with a mallet," he said. "Truth be told, I'm not sure how long it will be before she moves on. What do you do?"

"I'm a production assistant for *Diff'rent Strokes*."

"Then you know Dana Plato."

"Of course."

"She's in the game room right now. Let's go say hello."

The room was actually a house, behind the swimming pool and barbecue area. There, on a fluffy couch surrounded by pinball machines and video games, sat Dana, hugely pregnant. Snuggled up next to her, gently massaging her neck and shoulders, was Terry Stratton.

I was stunned. I never expected to see *him* again, let alone the two of them together. Dana had left the show in August. The rumor was that the departure was triggered by her drug use, but that was not true. We simply couldn't keep pregnant, seventeen-year-old Kimberly Drummond in the story line. She was married to the rock guitarist Lanny Lambert, the father of her baby. She said he was there that night, but I never saw him. He may have been down in the music studio in the basement, jamming with Echo and the Bunnymen and the other punk musicians Lizzy had flown in from London. My own "date" had drifted off himself, no doubt to the opium den in the pool wing, to snort and smoke and shoot whatever he could lay his hands on.

Terry, Frankie, Dana and I played Trivial Pursuit. Frankie kept tapping me on the shoulder. "I'm a tad color blind," he said. "Is that a brown wedge or an orange wedge?"

"Orange."

"Is that blue or green?"

"Green."

"Thank you, love."

I edged out Terry for the win. Frankie was impressed. As midnight approached, Terry and Dana headed to the opium den, and as Frankie and I walked back to the main house, he touched me lightly on the shoulder.

"Lizzy and I have got a production company bubbling up," he said. "We're looking to do *sophisticated* adult films and we need a bright, sexy girl like you to read all these scripts we're getting and ferret out of the best ones."

"Is Terry involved in your venture?"

"He's a close friend and trusted adviser," Frankie said. "Have lunch with all of us on Sunday and let us tell you about it."

We met at Mel's Drive In, on Sunset. They were as gracious as could be. Lizzy did most of the explaining, Terry, looking resplendent, wanted to know all about the North Shore and Vassar, and Frankie kept his napkin in his lap and did his best to chew with his mouth closed. The next morning, he called and offered me ninety thousand dollars a year to become chief of development at Royal Duchess Media. That was three times more than what I was making with *Diff'rent Strokes*.

I graciously declined. My goal was to write scripts for crime dramas and night time soaps, and I was eager to find a new job that brought me closer to that. But I couldn't stomach a pornographer who had a problem with niggers, who thought Hitler had been on the right track with the Jews. Have lunch with him, yes. Touch and smell and hear and see him, in order to get a cleaner read on the kind of character he was, absolutely.

But work for him? Never. The idea of it repelled me.

As grist for my creative mill, Terry was even more intriguing —and in no way repellant. I asked him that Sunday at Mel's, "How does a guy get from Marietta, Ohio to the White House to Frankie Hodnett's castle?"

"One step at a time," he said. "With his fingers crossed."

"Tell me more."

"I wish I could," he said. "Look behind the picture and read between the lines."

That's what I tried to do.

Michael Deaver

During the first months of the second term, Stratton kept contacting me at the White House, leaving voice mails, personal notes, news clips, books, autographed pictures of Tom Selleck, Charlton Heston, Kenny Rogers. When it all got to be too much of a pain in the ass, I handed him off to Vonda. It wasn't long before she'd had enough of him, too.

I couldn't help him. Deep down, he knew that. I was the Vicar of Visuals. Tax reform was as far from my bailiwick as it was possible for a subject to be. I didn't even have anyone useful to put him in touch with, because a huge number of people weren't talking to me anymore. I'd gotten so wrapped up in myself that I'd become oblivious to the many I'd offended, alienated, enraged.

Two months later, the sad moment arrived. I was gone from the White House myself. And my sendoff wasn't much nicer than Stratton's. Yes, Mrs. R. cried at my farewell party, and the president was eloquent and gracious, as always. But that was for show. Inside, I think they were weary of me, and happy to see me go.

Twenty-four years with the two of them and I still didn't know where I stood. I had to work ceaselessly to remain in their good graces. That was all I had. My future depended on it.

Judy Zakowski

I saw a lot of Terry that summer. After the reform bill got rolling, he came to Milo's office in Cannon to talk shop. I'd told him about my standing offer with L Street by then, and that I was on the fence, but we didn't discuss it. And he never asked to see Milo. Which was good because Milo did not want to see him.

So when Terry dropped in, we ignored him and picked each other's brains in my space.

"The Buckeye Generals are coming to town on Tuesday," he said. "We'll be hitting the Hill full force, getting our message out, going to every fundraiser we can."

"When you don't pay any taxes, you can afford to go to all the fundraisers."

"I've got a one-page memo you can read in sixty seconds that will tell you how much my guys pay in taxes."

"What's Frankie Hodnett's beef with the bill?"

"He incorporated part of Royal Duchess in Puerto Rico to get a break on his income tax," he said. "Now you're trying to yank it away from him. Grandfather in the big shots who got there first but ditch the little guys who came in later."

"Frankie Hodnett is a little guy?"

"You've had dinner with him," he said. "Pretty ordinary human being, don't you agree?"

"Why the break in the first place?"

"To promote stability in the Caribbean," he said. "Sharing the pie with our neighbors brings peace. And it keeps Castro in the isolation booth with Russia."

"So if Frankie stashes his porno-dollars in San Juan, the Berlin Wall is going to come down quicker?"

"Yes, my dear. Think big picture."

Milo tapped on the door and popped his head in. "I need to see you," he said to me. "*Alone.*"

He and Terry exchanged some truly fierce eye contact. Then Terry grabbed his briefcase, squeezed past Milo's bulk and headed up the hall without looking back.

"Keep that smarmy son of a bitch out of my sight," Milo said.

"You *could* learn something," I said.

"Out of earshot, too."

"Exactly what is your hang-up with him?"

"I'm trying to get some work done," he said. "Why don't you stop yakking about Terry Stratton and do the same?"

Phil Sparrow

I was at his place in the summer of '85, in July. We were sunbathing on his back deck. It was the Saturday of Live Aid, and people across the alley on Mintwood had set up a super-sized TV screen on their own deck to take in the concert. Coked out of our gills, he and I took it in with them.

When Madonna came on stage she screamed 'I'm not gonna take shit off tonight!' She was referring to her nude photos in *Playboy* and *Penthouse* that had just hit the newsstands.

I hopped up on the back ledge of the deck and faced the crowd on the other side of the alley. "Girl!" I screamed at them, "you may not be taking shit off tonight, but I am!" And I peeled off nude as an oyster and displayed every nook and cranny of my semi-glorious anatomy to the assembled masses.

That was the craziest thing I *ever* did on Biltmore Street. The only even remotely crazy thing.

Later on inside, after we were spent, he brought up this VIP he knew, a bottom bear in his fifties who worked in the House. This bear wanted to set up a low-key, steady thing with a younger guy, who knew his way around the Hill. A well-muscled guy who looked and acted straight and liked to kick back with a brew and watch football. Who wasn't into all the out and proud bullshit and felt no urge to preen around DuPont Circle in a purple thong and a pair of motorcycle boots.

"Sounds like you," I said.

"If we can expunge your stunt out on the deck just now, it really sounds more like *you*."

"What kind of action is he looking for?"

"You'll have to hear that from him," he said.

"There's a lot I'm not into."

"There's one other thing," he said. "This guy is a Member. You'd have to be *completely* discreet."

I thought it over. I decided the next time I saw him I'd ask for the bear's number. A couple of days later Rock Hudson collapsed in Paris and announced to the world that he had AIDS. That changed my mind. I don't know why exactly. Fear, I guess. Of dying a painful, horrible, death and missing out on everything coming next, of leaving my X all alone and my kids without a dad. I'd tricked for a string of married guys in my lost years after I flunked out of Marshall. But I had no reason to get back into it—and plenty to stay away.

A couple of weeks later, I changed my mind again. I couldn't resist the idea of maybe getting a chance to top a Member. That was a prospect too exciting to pass up. I got the number from Terry and gave him a call.

Dan O'Hanlon

My first term in the House, I rented a studio apartment in a building called the Capitol Arms, three blocks east of the Supreme Court Building, on A Street. Six hundred dollars a month is all it cost—and that included a toaster oven, a mini-fridge *with* an ice tray, and a toilet that flushed a good solid majority of the time. The landlord even supplied a shower curtain.

I brought in a dresser, a metal frame cot, a couple of card tables and chairs, and I was good to go—ready to indulge in the opulent lifestyle of a rich, famous congressman.

A half-dozen other Members had places in the building, but we didn't mingle. There was a tacit rule that once you were inside the Capitol Arms, you left each other alone. It was our safe haven, the one place no lobbyist, constituent, staffer, reporter, or little old lady in tennis shoes who wanted to free the dolphins could find us. We'd nod to each other in the lobby and exchange brief banter in the elevator. That's all.

So I was jolted very late on Halloween night when my intercom buzzed. It was eleven-forty-five. I sprang off my cot.

"Who's there?"

"It's Terry, Dan. Please let me in."

"Terry Stratton?"

"*Let me in now!*"

I buzzed him through. A minute later he knocked on my door.

"Sorry to intrude," he said. "A couple of nasty-looking spades were casing me on the street, and I'm *sure* they wanted to mug me. I was right in front of your building, so I came inside."

I pulled on some clothes, popped a couple of Millers and sat down with him. He didn't look shook up, the way you'd expect a guy who had just dodged a mugging to look. In fact, he seemed precisely the opposite—calm, serene, reflective. Still, sitting five feet away from him in that dark, dumpy little room, I was inclined to believe his story. I just wasn't sure I was getting the *whole* story.

He thumbed through a thick pile of reading material on my card table. "Doing your homework, are you?"

"I'm trying to figure out what all these bills I'm voting for actually *do*," I said.

He peered at me. "Hombre, can I be frank with you for a moment?"

"Of course."

"I envy the living daylights out of you," he said. "You are the most grounded human being I've ever known in my life."

"Stop."

"The finest pedigree a person could possibly have. Beautiful wife, great kids. Integrity, compassion, an absolute dream job."

"Ten months ago I took my oath of office in a cloud of wonder," I said. "I can assure you that cloud is *quickly* evaporating."

"I saw that portrait of your uncle in the library in Longworth this morning and damn near choked up."

"Why so soulful tonight?"

"Getting the hell scared out of me on the street just now," he said. "Makes you realize the whole damn ball of wax could go poof anytime. Plus I'm just an old softie I guess. Seventeen years we've known each other, and we've had our ups and downs. But I cherish every minute of it."

"You're too good to me."

"Being good to you is a no-brainer," he said. "Like buying IBM at three bucks a share. I keep telling you that but you don't seem to believe it."

"Can the flattery. You're going to give me a big head."

He looked at his watch and bolted upright. "I'll be on my way then," he said.

"Are you driving?"

"Not tonight," he said. "A car can be a nuisance in this town."

"Need a cab?"

He drained his Miller and dropped the can in the trash. "No thanks. I'll make sure the coast is clear and slip away."

"If you can stand sleeping on the floor, you can crash here."

"No, you need to get your homework done." At the door he turned around and gave me a little jab on the shoulder with his knuckles. "Thanks for pulling me out of the deep current tonight," he said. "It's *damn* good to have a friend in the neighborhood."

As quickly as he arrived, he was gone. It was midnight on the dot.

Judy Zakowski

Terry worked like a dog to get his loopholes restored in the reform bill. But he was wasting his energy with my boss. Milo was against the Buckeye Generals, and he was against Royal Duchess Media. Chairman Rostenkowski was eliminating loopholes for corporations and special interests, and he was standing with the chairman. That's all there was to it.

The situation exposed the cold reality of the process. Terry had courted me for hours on end in an effort to gain access to Milo. And none of it had amounted to diddly-squat. Milo wanted nothing to do with him.

But he could still talk to me. And I could tiptoe into Milo's study and relay his messages.

"Terry Stratton came by with another memo for you."

"I don't give a toasted turd about Terry Stratton's memos," he said. "Haven't I made that clear?"

"You told me you wanted to *read* everything."

"You're hallucinating. I've never said that in my life."

"Could you at least look at it?"

"I *could* but I won't," he said. "I *choose* not to look at it."

"Do you know *everything?*"

"What in the hell does that mean?"

"I don't like the way you're talking to me," I said.

"I don't like the size of your rear end," he said. "Every time you shove it in my face, it looks bigger."

"Go to hell."

"Make it a *dry* salad today." He chortled. "No creamy ranch and croutons. That's a direct order from the guy who can fire your disgusting ass anytime I want to."

I left the office immediately, went home, lay down on my bed, and cried for an hour. Around midnight, I woke up from an ugly nightmare and broke down again. The next morning at work he apologized profusely, and I cried a third time, in front of him.

I tried so hard to forgive him. My career was the only good thing I had going in my life, and I needed to preserve the relationship. But I just couldn't do it. What he had said to me was too despicable. At that moment, I knew that my days with Milo were numbered, and that our time together was not going to have a happy ending.

Tax reform didn't have a happy ending, either. The bill the House passed in December and shipped to the Senate was a mess, a mish-mash, a hybrid, a stew with so many thousands of ingredients that nobody had a grasp of what was really in it. One thing I knew for sure: Terry's two amendments weren't included. They never received any serious consideration.

But he got what he was looking for over in the Senate. The Finance Committee added his amendments into the bill, and they survived the rest of the process and became law.

He wasn't a cocky guy. At least not with me he wasn't. But he must have done a bit of crowing to someone about that.

Belinda Carlisle

I met him just once, at Frankie Hodnett's Tudor castle in Holmby Hills, on New Year's Eve in '86.

The event didn't interest me. The Go-Go's were over. So were my partying days. I'd married Morgan in April, in Lake Tahoe. It was the best move of my life. My weight was down, I was working out religiously and *hard,* and I was clean and sober for the first time in years. I didn't want to tempt the beast by spending the evening with a pack of drinking, drugging wastrels.

I went because my husband asked me to. He didn't want to tempt the beast, either, but he'd been with Terry in the White House, he was a deal maker and a player, and he was always working. There were people there he wanted to see, Terry and others.

While Morgan circulated, I hung out in the green and gold living room on the second level, nursing a can of Diet Mountain Dew, nibbling salt-free bagel chips, and regaling Frankie and Robin Leach with tales of life on the road with the girls. They listened—shall we say—*intently.* And this was PG-rated stuff. I'd heard about Frankie being a boor, but he was a prince that night. Dressed like a cab driver, yes. In dire need of a tongue scraping and an aggressive flossing, yes. But as attentive and gallant as could be.

Robin headed downstairs to record the occasion for posterity with this cute, little magnetic video camera he was carting around on his belt. Frankie fetched me a fresh, cold can of Dew, walked me out to the railing that overlooked the vaulted great room, and pointed out Terry on the dance floor.

"That man is a genius," he said. "The most brilliant human being at our celebration tonight. Except your husband, of course."

"Morgan says he's very good at what he does."

"He just stopped Congress from picking three million dollars out of my pocket," Frankie said. "I'm struggling to make a clean, honest living in a brutal business, and these window lickers in Washington insist on trying to rob me blind."

"Is that Dana Plato with him?"

"Isn't she stunning?"

"Motherhood becomes her."

"Indeed it does." He slurped his mug of nut brown ale, and a dreamy look came into his eyes. "She started out as a figure skater and her body is still as hard as granite," he said. "I've asked her to take her clothes off for me and share every *inch* of her beauty with her millions of fans. But she won't do it."

Later that evening, Frankie introduced me to Terry. I told you my partying days were over. But a girl can still get weak. A heart can still get tangled up. The planet was still overflowing with sexy, enticing men, and he was one of them. I was relieved—and a little sad—when Morgan swooped in and spirited me away.

In the morning, I told him about my conversation with Frankie, and what he had said about Terry being a genius. He snorted with derision.

"You told me he was good at what he does," I said.

"He is."

"I don't understand."

"Good influence peddlers hardly need to be *geniuses*," he said. "They don't even need to have influence."

"No?"

"They just need to give the *appearance* of having influence."

"What do you mean?"

"Take Royal Duchess Media and the Buckeye Generals," he said. "The Senate was *always* going to give them what they wanted, with or without Terry Stratton. But they're too ignorant of the process to know that. Terry convinces them the sky is falling, tells them he's the only one who can stop it, and now he's getting kudos for something that was going to happen all along anyway."

"Is that how it works?"

"That's how it works," he said. "Frankie Hodnett is being fleeced. Congress may not be picking his pocket anymore. But Terry Stratton is."

Michael Deaver

That January, after the mid-term elections, Stratton called and asked to see me. He was just back from Los Angeles and he had a surprise for me.

I'd sworn off him, but I had a soft spot for the guy and thought what the hell, one last time won't hurt. He came by my office late one afternoon. I was heading to an appointment at the State Department. He climbed into my Jaguar limousine and rode with me in the back seat toward Foggy Bottom.

Planted there across from me in his Burberry overcoat and yellow power tie, he looked a bit full of himself. He'd just been featured in a segment on CNN, showing life behind-the scenes with a Washington power lobbyist. Maybe I was just jealous. Stratton made his mark reading Mrs. R.'s Ouija board and doing goofy faces with Gary Coleman on *Diff'rent Strokes*. If he was a power lobbyist, what was I?

He laid a shiny black and red gift box on the pull-down table between us. "Go ahead, Mike. Open it."

Inside, wrapped in white tissue, was a black eye patch attached to a leather strap. There was also a one-page document, a certificate of authenticity from a place called the Palace of Fame, on Sunset Boulevard in Beverly Hills.

"John Wayne wore this in *True Grit*," he said. "They used twelve during the shoot. This is one of them. I know you're a fan and I thought you'd enjoy it."

I tried not to be was touched, but I was. Not only did I adore the Duke, I especially loved *True Grit*. I held the thing in my hands and wondered how much it had cost Stratton. A thousand dollars—three, five, ten? Or maybe he'd bartered it with something out of his own collection.

We were silent for a while and then he said softly: "The L Street Team and Mike Deaver can do business together." He reached across the seat and touched my forearm ever so lightly. "Have lunch with Raj and Georgy and me. You'll be pleasantly surprised by how much we can do for each other."

I wasn't interested. I'd been gone from the White House eighteen months, and I was lobbying for Singapore, Mexico, TWA, GE, Philip Morris, God knows who else. I had so many clients I couldn't keep track of them, couldn't utter a syllable without creating some kind of conflict of interest among two or three or twelve of them.

Then there were his partners. I had no intention of exploring a relationship with either of them. Why not? Because Raj Rao was full-blooded Bushie. He was raising early money for Herbert Walker's '88 White House run, and he was close to Barbara and the children as well, some kind of cuddly brown brother they'd all adopted as kind of a family mascot. And Georgy Greco was tethered to the waist of her old boss Howard Fryer, one of the most strident liberals in Congress. He'd been chiding the president and Mrs. R. forever about everything—the White House china, her wardrobe, their over-the-top friends, all the time they spent riding horses and chopping wood at Camp David and the ranch in Santa Barbara.

The Reagans did not care one whit for Bushies. They cared even less for mouthy left-wingers who razzed their lifestyle. I still had unfettered access to the White House. I played tennis there every week and saw the president's confidential daily schedule in advance, and I wanted to keep it that way. There was no percentage for me in getting involved with either Rao or Greco.

As for Stratton himself, I'd heard bad things from Morgan Mason and some others. They were virtually certain he was dealing cocaine on the Hill. Mostly to staffers, but also to lobbyists, reporters, possibly even Members.

My sources were credible. I believed what they were telling me. I'm a recovering alcoholic, and I had a serious drinking problem during my career. I had no right to get holier-than-thou, call him a piece of druggy slime behind his back, or squeal on him to the authorities.

But I was not going to do business with a guy who was selling cocaine.

"I'm keen to meet your partners," I said. "Let's do lunch soon."

That was a nasty lie, particularly to tell someone who had just put a genuine lump in my throat with a nice gesture. But after he jumped out of the limo on 17th Street in front of the Corcoran Galley, I cut him off and never communicated with him again.

I held on to his gift, though, and I'm glad I did. After the angry Ds in the House unleashed the General Accounting Office on my firm and my life careened headlong into the toilet, the Duke's eye patch became a source of strength.

I didn't wear it over my own eye because the Duke's head was a lot bigger than mine, the strap was too long, and I didn't want to fiddle with it. Instead, I wore it around my neck, like an amulet. Just inside the house, of course, and out on the patio a couple of times. Never in public.

I think it had something to do with keeping me out of jail.

Phil Sparrow

My world fell apart on June 19th, 1987, when I got busted for selling cocaine in the Doorkeeper's Office. It was my own fault. I sold to a narc not once, not twice, but three times—a black woman who worked in the House Library, someone I thought I knew *more* than well enough.

A week after her third buy, two cops with the Capitol Police came to my desk, cuffed me in front of everybody like the assholes they are, and led me out the Documents Door into a paddy wagon.

And all of the shit on God's green earth came raining down on my head.

I was suspended from my job, without pay, until the case was resolved. The union got me a lawyer. We met for coffee at Roy Rogers on New Jersey Avenue to assess the situation.

I asked her: "Can I save my job if I rat somebody out?"

"Your supplier?"

"If I do that, I'll be dead in twenty-four hours. I'm thinking customers."

"I'd talk to the prosecutor but it would be a waste of time."

"Why?"

"This is about you, not them," she said. "The cops and lawyers have their orders from the powers that be. Clean up drugs on our turf."

"Clean up drugs by busting *me?*"

"Nail a retail dealer, take his job, scare the hell out of everyone. They're setting an example. Unfortunately, you're it."

"There is so much coke and speed and weed on the Hill it might as well be Hollywood."

"That may be true," she said. "It has zero effect on your current predicament."

"The black bitch who popped me. I bet she used to deal. Turned snitch to save her own ass."

"So what if she did?"

"If the powers that be want to scare everyone, why don't they want the names of my customers?"

"Billy Bob, my advice to you is this. Don't jump in front of a train. You are dealing with the feds, not some Andy of Mayberry out in the sticks. Take their offer. Plead guilty to two misdemeanors and resign."

"Then what?"

"Get off the Hill and start a new life. You *will* survive being busted."

"What happens if I fight?"

"They'll convict you, fine you ten grand for their trouble, and throw you in jail for five years."

"Do I get to share a cell with Deaver?"

"Deaver ain't going to jail, honey. All he did was get too rich too fast and make people jealous. He didn't sell blow twenty yards off the House floor."

"I'm sorry."

"During the fucking invocation. You offended powerful people."

"I know."

"You're dead meat. *Give it up.*"

I tried to find Terry then. I was desperate to hash things out with somebody who might be able to help. Of course he was avoiding me. Wouldn't come near me or return my phone calls. Granted, I had no product for him. But our thing had never been solely about product. He was acting like we'd never been friends.

I cornered him early one morning in the alley behind his place on Biltmore Street, dumping a load of trash and getting into his Volvo.

"I'm late," he said.

"Can we talk?"

He let me in the passenger side door and we sat there with the engine running.

"The way you're treating me," I said. "It hurts."

"I can't see you anymore."

"Why not? No one knows we're connected."

"Am I in danger?" he asked. "Do they want names?"

"Yes."

"Keep mine out of it," he said. "The press is linking me to Deaver and my Ohio clients are about to dump me. I can't handle anymore of this crap."

"How can you blow me off like this?"

"What do you expect me to do?"

"Loan me money. Help me find a new job."

"Talk to Milo."

"Three years together and it's over just like that?"

He flipped on the air-conditioning and released the parking brake. "Get out now."

"Do I mean *anything* to you as a human being?"

"Get your sorry faggot ass out of my car."

As rude as that scene was, the one with Milo was worse. I went to his office in Cannon, which I *definitely* should not have done. We'd never met anywhere except his apartment in the Capitol Arms. His receptionist stared at me like a vulture for fifteen minutes until he came out and took me back to his study.

"I told you never to come here," he said.

"I'm losing my job. I'll be broke in a month."

"You know the rules," he said. "If you get into trouble, we're finished."

"I need money."

"No."

"I'll tell them about us—and Terry. And the others. *All of it*."

He crouched down, reached into a drawer underneath his bookshelves, and pulled out a huge black handgun with a silencer attached. He pointed it at my chest from six feet.

"You don't have the guts to out me," he said.

"Are you sure about that?"

He lowered his aim to my crotch and gripped the trigger with both hands. "This will blow your balls clean off," he said. "Then I'll scrap them off the floor with a spatula and shove them down your throat."

For one long horrible moment, I really thought the motherfucker was going to drill me. Finally, he laid the piece on the desk. I left his office immediately. The next day, I went back to my lawyer and told her I wanted to take the deal and resign.

"You're making the right move," she said.

"But I want to make a statement. I'm going to name names."

"That might get you hurt—or worse."

"I lose my job, health insurance for me and my X and my kids, get branded as a coke dealer for life. And all of them are getting plastered at lunch, and sucked off in some hotel room, snorting blow they're buying from somebody else now instead of me. High as kites, free as birds. It's not right."

"No, it isn't. But there's nothing you or I can do about it."

"I'm going to tell the cops and lawyers what I know. Maybe it will trickle up to the powers that be."

She wanted nothing to do with my statement. I couldn't blame her. It was my rage, not hers. So I stayed quiet while she processed me through my resignation and plea deal. Then a month later, after I'd moved back to Warrenton, I spent two hours on my own with two detectives from the Capitol Police.

They listened with interest and took the names of my customers. Terry was on the list. I fingered him because he was such a prick to me. But I don't think anything ever came of it. The detectives did pass my information about Milo along to the House Committee on Standards of Official Conduct. That's the formal name of the Ethics Committee. Six weeks later I got a call from the committee's chief counsel. He and his staff wanted to hear more.

I met with them and got the rest of the story off my chest. There's a hell of a lot more to it than drugs, as the world found out. Then I came back to Warrenton and got on with my new life.

My lawyer was right. I did survive being busted. I even got back with my X and my kids. All of us under one roof, eating dinner together every night, going to church on Sunday. It didn't last, though. Nothing good ever does.

100th Congress, 1st Session
U.S. House of Representatives
Committee on Standards of Official Conduct
October 13th, 1987

Affidavit of Phillip Parker Sparrow Relating to Allegations of Improper Conduct by Representative Milo Forbes (D-Wisconsin) with House Employees and Pages.

Summary Version. This is a controlled document. Not to be duplicated.

1. I am Phillip Parker Sparrow. My current address is 501 Waterloo Street, Warrenton, VA 20816. My current occupation is shuttle bus driver for the Airlie Conference Center.

2. I attest that I am over eighteen years of age and that I am providing this affidavit in the absence of undue influence, fraud, or duress.

3. From July 1st, 1982 until my resignation on August 8th, 1987, I was employed by the House in the Doorkeeper's Office as Second Assistant to the Facilities Manager.

4. In September, 1985 I met Representative Milo Forbes in the Majority Cloakroom. One week later, at his invitation, I went to his apartment in the Capitol Arms, Unit 6G, 333 A Street, N.E. That was the first of approximately eighteen encounters over a twenty-month period ending in May, 1987.

5. At each of those encounters, I provided sexual services to Representative Forbes and was paid in cash. At each encounter, I provided cocaine and marijuana to Representative Forbes, which he used in my presence. At four, I provided LSD, and at three others I provided psilocybin mushrooms, both of which he used in my presence.

6. From midnight to 5 a.m. on the morning of November 1st, 1985, I participated in group sexual activity with Representative Forbes in Unit 6G at the Capitol Arms. Also present were [*****redacted**********], a 17-year old male House page,[*****redacted*********], a second 17-year-old male House page, and [******redacted**********], an adult male who was neither a House employee nor a page. During that activity, all five participants, including the pages and Representative Forbes, used alcohol, cocaine, and marijuana in my presence.

7. On July 22nd, 1987, I met privately with Representative Forbes in his office in Room 456, Cannon Building. During that meeting, he pointed a firearm at me and threatened me with death if I revealed to anyone the information contained in this affidavit.

8. I provided this affidavit in the presence of the Chief Committee Counsel, Deputy Chief Committee Counsel, Majority Counsel, and Minority Counsel.

Judy Zakowski

I left Milo's office for The L Street Team in December of '87, as the House went into Christmas recess. He wasn't sorry to see me go. Things had been tense between us since his comments about the size of my ass. We'd never returned to the level of rapport we once enjoyed.

On my last day, after the staff party was over and everyone was gone, I went into his study for a one-on-one farewell toast. He pulled two cans of Point beer out of his mini-fridge, took his mandolin off the wall and plucked the Badger Fight Song for me. I got a lump in my throat as big as a boulder, but I swore I wasn't going to cry this time, and I didn't.

"I'm worried about you," I said. "Before I go I wanted to say that."

"Why are you worried about me?"

"You're isolating yourself," I said. "I don't know you anymore."

"You know me as well as any human being alive." He lay the mandolin down, dropped his head, and massaged his temples with his thumbs. Then he said: "There's a man I'm close to. I've treated him like dirt and now he's taking his revenge."

"You treat Pete like a prince," I said. "He called me this morning to wish me good luck."

"He's always loved you."

"He's excited as a little kid about you coming home for Christmas."

"But I'm not talking about Pete."

I was stunned. "Are you seeing someone else?"

"I have been," he said. "For almost two years."

"In Washington?"

"Yes."

"Does anyone know?"

"They will soon."

"Are there going to be problems?"

"Yes."

"Do you want to talk about it?" He swiveled around in his chair away from me. "Milo?"

He didn't turn around and face me, and he didn't reply.

"Do you want to talk about it?"

He picked up his mandolin and began to pluck the *Hee Haw* theme. That's how I left him after eight years together.

Dan O'Hanlon

The Milo Forbes scandal broke in the *Post* in January, as the House reconvened for the second year of the 100th Congress. Someone connected to the Ethics Committee leaked the Sparrow affidavit. Or Sparrow talked to the *Post*. Maybe both things happened. Then all sorts of folks in Wisconsin came out of the woodwork with vivid tales about Milo's volcanic temper, his forays in disguise to leather bars in Milwaukee, and his nocturnal dumpster diving in Madison, designed to pick up dirt on his enemies. The story combusted, and virtually overnight, Milo Forbes became the poster child for decadence with a capital D in the Democratic House.

The all-male group sex tryst. LSD and mushrooms. Milo's enormous black gun, which the Capitol Police confiscated the day after the story ran. This was not just another horndog chairman carrying on with a hot young babe. The fact that the pages, speaking anonymously, called their involvement "one thousand percent consensual," turned the heat higher. The hottest topic of all: the name of the unidentified adult male at the man-boy love fest. The cheap wordplay wouldn't stop. Who was the point guard? The top spice on the five-way chili? The fifth easy piece?

Terry Stratton. He's denied it to my face and he's never been conclusively outed, but my inner clurichaun tells me every day *it was him, it was him, it was him*. Because that Halloween night back in my first term—when he burst into my room at eleven-forty-five claiming he'd almost been mugged—was the same night Milo Forbes hosted his midnight party three floors above me in the Capitol Arms.

Why did he drop by my room that night at all? That's something I've never figured out. Mugging or no mugging, why didn't he push Milo's buzzer instead of mine and arrive at the orgy a few minutes early? In his mind, I was a paragon, a peerless example of all that was good and right and virtuous in the world. Maybe he figured seeing me might keep him from succumbing to the temptation upstairs. Or maybe he was *trying* to reveal himself, creating a link in my mind to an incident that might someday go public, leaving a mark, a hint, a clue to his illicit life.

I didn't have it in me to hate him. It was way too late to change him. All I could do was try to figure out why he behaved the way he did.

Judy Zakowski

Four days after the story on Milo ran in the *Post,* the Redskins played the Broncos in the Super Bowl. Raj and Georgy hosted a party at their townhouse on Scott Place in Georgetown.

Fifty or sixty people came: staffers from L Street, clients, congressmen, colleagues in the lobbying trade, print reporters, anchormen, professors, bureaucrats, friends from Dallas, Houston, Palo Alto, Pittsburgh, Manhattan, New Haven, Cambridge, London, Mumbai. And two-thirds of us looked to be under forty. There was so much raw, youthful ambition packed into the place I thought the ceiling might explode.

Attached to the side of the garage was a spare two-room unit with a separate entrance. They used it on and off as a guest quarters. That night an auxiliary TV was set up in the front room to accommodate overflow viewers. As the Redskins scored five touchdowns in the second quarter to blow the game open, I went out there to escape the thunderous din in the house.

Three zoned out dudes from the catering crew slouched on a couch, staring at the screen. They appeared to be the only people in the unit but then, in the semi-dark back room, sitting on the edge of a bed in front of a nearly bare coffee table, I saw Georgy. Staring out at me with a robotic smile on her face, she put her finger to her lips, and waved me in to join her.

"Shut that door," she whispered. "I'm sneaking away from the rabble for my annual Super Bowl cigarette. Want to join me?"

I hadn't smoked as a habit for years, and I didn't miss it much—only twenty or thirty times a day. We fired up Lark Lights and blew our smoke out a crack in the window into the crisp evening air.

"Terry is taking on new duties next week," she said. "I want to give you a head's up before the memo comes out."

"What kind of duties?"

"Raj and I are sending him out West to drum up new business," she said.

"What brought this on?"

"We need to lower his profile ASAP," she said. "The fifth man at Milo's orgy—we're hearing it was him."

"Our Terry? The guy in your living room right now, grooving to Chubby Checker and the Rockettes?

"The one and only."

"With women literally lining up for a chance to say hello to him?"

"It doesn't make much sense, does it?"

There was a mobile bar set up on a cart in the front room. I stepped out, nodded to the catering dudes, and mixed a double martini for myself. Then I went back to Georgy and bummed another Lark Light.

"Milo detests Terry," I said. "He avoided him like the plague."

"That looks like some kind of cover to trample all the suspicions," she said. "It seems they're very good friends after hours."

"Have you confronted Terry about it?"

"He denies it," she said. "Calls it the most vicious lie he's ever heard in his life."

"Do you believe him?"

"No."

"What does Raj think?"

"That we should give him the benefit of the doubt."

"And you can't quite do it, can you?"

"Raj adores Terry," she said. "He convinced me to bring him in as a partner."

"You had reservations?"

"Being a bit of a rogue isn't a serious problem in our business," she said. "But Terry is more than that."

"What do you mean?"

Avoiding my gaze and my question, she jerked the window open and blew out two big plumes of smoke. "You must be furious at Milo," she said.

"I feel completely and utterly betrayed," I said. "And angry at myself for being so ignorant of what was going on."

"How *could* you have known?"

"I cannot envision Milo and Terry together at some orgy," I said. "Do you *really* believe that?"

She shut up the window, turned around, and snuffed out her butt in a ceramic bowl on the coffee table. "I've said all I'm going to say about Terry. Time to get back to the rabble."

The memo came out on Wednesday morning. Effective immediately, Terry would no longer be a partner *in* the firm based in Washington, but a consultant *to* the firm based in Los Angeles and Las Vegas, where he would focus on the acquisition of new clients.

There was a second item in the memo that Georgy hadn't mentioned during our smoking break. The L Street Team was under investigation by a federal grand jury, convened in D.C. at the request of the Public Corruption Section in the Office of the U.S. District Attorney. We were instructed to cooperate fully with every aspect of their probe.

Mary Quesada

I am an American, born in El Paso in 1954 and raised in Albuquerque by Mexican parents. They left Ciudad Juarez after World War II in search of a better life for themselves, and then for me, their beloved daughter and only child.

I succeeded beyond their most fervent dreams.

From St. Pius X High School and the University of New Mexico, I went to Pepperdine Law School in Malibu. After four years with a blue-chip corporate firm in San Francisco doing white collar defense work, I accepted an offer from my old law professor to work under him in the Public Corruption Section of the U.S. Attorney's Office in D.C.

Early in 1988, Public Corruption launched Operation Hired Gun. Our goal was to investigate, indict and convict lobbyists working on Capitol Hill. My office did not think Congress was doing enough to police its own domain. The stench of lucre was pervasive, and laws were being flaunted with impunity every day. I headed the probe of The L Street Team. It was my first major case. I was a single Hispanic woman, viewed by nearly all of my colleagues as a lightweight, the director's pet student from his Pepperdine days. Many of them were eager to see me fail. So while most prosecutors rely heavily on agents and investigators, I took a more hand-on approach. I read every document we obtained from L Street, and I interviewed every employee.

What did I discover? Virtually all the government needed to indict and convict Rao, Greco and Stratton on an array of counts: wire fraud, embezzlement, filing false disclosure forms, making gifts above the legal monetary limit. I also found flagrant and repeated violations of the Ethics in Government Act, which bars federal employees from lobbying their former colleagues for one year after they leave government service.

I worked sixty hours a week for three months before taking the case to my superiors. I expected to be told to go to the grand jury and seek indictments. For days, then weeks, I heard nothing. It was utterly frustrating. I complained to my old professor.

"Why aren't we moving on L Street?" I said. "We're moving on seven other firms."

"So?"

"The goal of our operation is to gather evidence."

"Correct."

"Then proceed through process, without regard to the violator's prominence, political connections or party affiliation."

"Yes."

"Is this about George Bush?"

"Whatever do you mean?"

"Bush is close to Rao, and there's plenty here that might embarrass him."

"Such as?"

"Rao's scholarship fund at the Foundation for Capitalism. His vacations with Jeb and George Walker and the Royal Prince of Brunei. His luxury box at Texas Rangers Stadium."

"What of it?"

"And then we have Stratton's pornographer friend in Los Angeles, his links to Deaver, the rumors of his decadent lifestyle."

"Ms. Quesada, you are out of line. We do not deal with *rumors.*"

"Are you putting a hold on L Street because you don't want to hurt Bush's chances in the election?"

His face turned ash gray. "You don't have the slightest idea what's *really* going on."

"Tell me then. I'd like to know."

"This isn't law school. We're not in Malibu anymore."

"I'm fully aware of that."

"I brought you to this office. I can send you packing whenever I want to."

"Yes, sir."

"And you know something else?"

"What, sir?"

"Nobody would miss you much."

"Did I do all this work for nothing?"

"So what if you did? What's so God almighty sacred about *your* work?"

The next day, I received a new assignment. Packed up and sealed in fifteen bankers' boxes, the L Street files languished in our basement storage room. That is where I thought they'd stay forever.

Frankie Hodnett

The Squire came out from Washington and spent most of that year at the mansion. I was keen for his company. I was in a deep funk and lonely for London. I missed Stepney, football, the *Eye*, my old crew. I even missed the Fleet Street bastards.

Worst of all, Lizzy had taken up with a Raiders cheerleader, a luscious, almond-skinned honey from Barbados, by way of Orange County. Across the hill along the backside of my property was a snug Spanish bungalow I'd bought for mum and dad on the off-chance I could ever lure them away from White Church Lane to come live with me. That's where the lovebirds spent their days and nights, half-nude on the screened-in back porch, toking on Lizzy's stinky, purple Hawaiian herb, talking out scripts, auditioning studs and studettes for Royal Duchess projects.

My wife was a head over heels goner for a skirt. God, it hurt. I'd been fearing the moment when that ax would swing, and when it did, it sliced out a gigantic piece of my heart. Having the Squire on the premises made it easier to salve the wound.

I gave him the run of the grounds and his own living room, bed and bath in the pool wing. He was game to earn his keep. So I figured I could show him off to my best friends, six guys I'd gotten close to in the business, entrepreneurs like me, going it alone. The Out and Outs is what we called ourselves. Not only were we out with the old line establishment, we were even out with the *other* Hollywood, the mega-producers in Porn Valley with the Mob behind them. I invited them over to my place one Friday to join us for nosh and get the lowdown on what the wankers in Washington had up their sleeves.

"Remember, these lads do *not* have a high opinion of politicians," I said. "And they don't know a thing about this investigation you've been through."

"Let's keep it that way," he said. "It's nothing but a witch hunt and I'm not sure it's over. But don't worry, L Street is as clean as a whistle."

"As a whistle?"

"If not cleaner. Nobody is going to lay a hand on us. Or *you*."

Amazingly, all the Out and Outs showed. They didn't waste any time ripping into him. They were like a Greek chorus, shaking their fists at the gods.

"Mr. Strattman, would you like to hear my plan for constructive change in Washington?"

"It's Strat-*ton*."

"Drop an atomic bomb on it, Mr. Strattman."

The Squire didn't flinch. "Cut the melodrama," he said. "I'll tell you something we can actually *accomplish.*"

"And then for good measure, drop another one."

"Cutting all the red tape in the Child Protection Act."

"I built my studio up from zilch and I now employ forty-eight American citizens. Health insurance, retirement, sick leave, paid vacations."

"Everyone in this room is a legitimate businessman."

"*Ten thousand percent* legal, by the way. We don't pimp out our girls, and we don't sell smack to sixth graders."

"I'm *gold level* with the Sherman Oaks Civic Association."

"I'm the *commissioner* of the pee wee football league in Northridge."

"So get Reagan and Meese and the rest of the motherfuckers off our backs!"

There were no takers that day. A couple of weeks later, we assembled again and the Squire pitched Bush.

"Why support Bush? He's the second coming of Reagan and Reagan is buggering us with everything he has."

"Bush is no Reagan. Not even close."

"The feds are knocking on my door every day, asking for every goddam piece of paper in my office. FBI, IRS, IN-fucking-S."

"Bush will slack off," the Squire said.

"Why?"

"He isn't taking two million bucks from the moguls at the mainstream studios. They're the people pulling Reagan's chain on all this crap you're fighting."

"So we throw a truck full of money at Bush, and he loses. Dukakis will have our balls on a platter, right?"

"When is Washington going to crack down *on their own* instead of everybody else? This pervert in Congress—the guy who threw the orgy with the pages where everybody dropped acid and cornholed each other or whatever the fuck. Why doesn't Washington crack down on *him?*"

"Dukakis is nothing but a tax-and-spend liberal," the Squire said. "He'll take more money out of *your* pocket and give it to the people who don't *do* anything. Bush won't."

It went on in that vein for a good while. In the end, he won them over, and after all that harping and bitching every one of the Out and Outs dropped a hefty wedge in the kitty for Bush. And within a month, all six of them had signed on with L Street, too.

All that new juice earned him a fat bonus, and one evening we celebrated guy-to-guy up in my quarters with a gram of blow and a bottle of Chivas Regal. I'd converted one bedroom into an exact replica of my old digs on White Church Lane, and that's where I laid out my latest acquisitions for him. Marilyn Monroe's brown and beige Pucci belt, size ten, Ray Nitschke's helmet from the Ice Bowl game against the Cowboys, a signed, original Fawcett Books edition of *Hondo*, Louis L'Amour's first novel.

He darted down to his room, brought back a small white box, and handed it to me. Inside was a black eye patch attached to a leather strap.

"John Wayne wore this in *True Grit*," he said. "There are only twelve of them in the world."

"My God."

"They look opaque on the screen, but they're really fine mesh," he said. "So the Duke could see what was going on during the shoot."

"Ah, mate. You shouldn't have."

"Something for the crew as well." He handed me forty tickets to the Raiders-Redskins game at the Coliseum in the fall. "It's the least I can do," he said. "I wish I could do more."

"There is one thing."

"I'll do what I can for my best hombre."

"Could you and Dana take off your clothes for me? The two of you look so *splendid* together. One night we can all hang out, get loose, and you can have a good long go at it while I work the camcorder."

Dana was over the moon for him, or I never would have asked. Her own marriage was ropey by then, her boy was with his dad and her mom was sick, and she joined him out in the pool wing for the overnight frequently. The Squire was her father figure, her knight in shining armor who was going to make everything good again in her life.

"I'll plant the seed with her," he said. "We'll see if it grows."

What he ended up doing to that girl was shameful. Worse than anything he pulled on me.

Dan O'Hanlon

The House came back from recess at the end of July. The Milo Forbes matter was on our agenda, and the air in Washington was fetid with the aroma of scandal.

Forbes had admitted to the drug and sex allegations, pleaded guilty to the firearms violation, and waived his right to a public hearing on the misconduct charges that the Ethics Committee had filed against him. He said he did not want to violate the privacy of the pages.

But he refused to resign. Speaker Wright's plan was to censure him with a quick vote and a minimum of floor debate, be done with the mess, and hand his fate to the voters of the 12th District of Wisconsin. That's what most people wanted, including Forbes himself.

But Newt Gingrich and his mad cows picked a fight. A mere censure would allow Milo to keep his seat, Ways & Means assignment, and seniority. They forced a floor vote on a motion to drop the censure and instead re-open and expand the probe to see if Milo had committed more misdeeds. And if he had, whether expulsion from the House was warranted.

In the midst of all the intrigue, I figured Stratton would be getting in touch. I sensed his predicament, and I wasn't eager to deal with it.

"There's an ugly rumor swirling around about you," he said.

"Let me guess. I don't have enough fun, right?"

"How *anybody* could think that is one of the great mysteries of our time," he said. "Because a semi-riotous event is in the stars for you this evening."

"I am not up for a semi-riotous event."

"I need your input on this Forbes thing," he said. "Enlighten me tonight over libations. What do you say?"

At eight o'clock, he swung by Longworth in his brand new BMW and drove us to the Gangplank Marina. It was kind of a floating trailer park along the Washington Channel, a mile due south of the Air and Space Museum on the Mall. Howard Fryer was one of a dozen senators and reps who had slips there. He liked to host summertime parties on the *Yellow Jacket*, the fifty-foot yacht he'd bought from a drug company lobbyist.

It seemed like everyone in Washington was at the Gangplank that night. The *Yellow Jacket* was not the only hot spot. Gatherings erupted spontaneously. As we wandered the docks I spotted Tim Russert, Andrea Mitchell, John McCain, Dan Quayle, Nancy Pelosi, Larry King, and George Bush the Younger with his frat boy friends. W. was forty-two then, the same age as me. The energy business had gone bust and he'd moved Laura and the twins up from Texas for the duration of his dad's campaign.

I'm pleased to report that the urban legend is true—he *is* a great guy to have a beer with.

By the end of the night, Stratton and I had found our way to the communal party barge at the end of the main dock. We tipped mugs and gazed across the Potomac toward the lights on the 14th Street Bridge.

"This Forbes thing has got me all in a pickle," he said. "Newty is *insane* to force this vote."

"It's going to come back on him."

"All these Ds I keep hearing about who are jumping the fence. *Why?*"

"Wright is not Tip O'Neill," I said. "He's a dictator, and this gives you a chance to thumb your nose at him."

"What else?"

"Forbes has even fewer friends than Wright," I said. "He's the most arrogant son of a bitch in the caucus. And ninety percent of us are on the ballot in three months. You don't want to come off as a whitewasher, protecting your own."

"Be honest with me, hombre. Are *you* jumping the fence?"

"I got a call from the bishop in Cleveland this afternoon," I said. "He wants to clean up moral decay in Washington, and he's asking me to defy my leadership and vote yes."

"It's tough to compete with a bishop," he said. "But as a personal friend, I'd *very* much appreciate your no vote."

I got after him then, and laid it all out in the open. I figured this was my best shot at getting him to come clean. "Do you know Forbes?"

"Not at all. He doesn't deal with lobbyists."

"The night of his orgy three years ago—that was the same night you surprised me at the Capitol Arms."

"Yes, it was."

"Coincidence?"

"Of course," he said. "It's like I told you. I was a couple of blocks away, having dinner with a friend. When I left his place, two spades cased me and I went into your lobby to escape them."

"Random target, were you?"

"What are you driving at?"

"Maybe you were holding something specific that they knew about."

"Like what?"

"Like a dozen grams of packaged cocaine, or a couple of thousand bucks in cash. Or both."

"If you *really* believe all the shit people are spreading around about me, why are you here?"

"Did you leave my room that night and head upstairs to G6?"

"No."

"But if you *had,* you sure wouldn't want the events of that evening back on the front burner, would you?"

"If you guys open this can of worms any further, *good* people are going to get hurt. There's no telling *who* or how many." He drained his mug and hurled it out into the water. "Yes, I screwed around on Kris, and I pay the price for that every day. I drink *way* too much, and I smoke pot and snort coke here and there, although I've never done either in your presence and I never will, because I don't want you getting a bad reputation. But I don't *sell* drugs and I *sure* as hell don't blow pages. It's like I'm the biggest sleazeball who ever lived. You know what I am? The whipping boy for everybody else's sins."

That was about the longest I'd ever heard Stratton talk at one time. Heading home in the BMW, he was morose and silent. When he dropped me off at the Capitol Arms, I said good night to a man who looked fatigued and frightened.

"I need you on this one, Dan. More than I've ever needed anything in my life."

The next day the House punished Milo Forbes. The Gingrich motion to re-open the probe went down to the wire. Heading onto the floor at two o'clock, no one knew which way it was going to turn out. The Rs needed forty-eight Ds to crossover and join 170 of them. Only forty-one did, and the motion failed—211 yes, 219 no, Speaker Wright present and not voting, four absent. Then we went back and passed the original motion to censure, 430-0.

I voted no on the Gingrich motion. At the precise instant I locked in on the voting board, I believed in my mind that I was saving Stratton's ass. That was the moment in my career when I felt most acutely like a flawed, mortal being making a flawed, mortal decision.

Yes, he'd bought me with the help he'd given me in my first House race. But I didn't have to stay bought. Three days later, I dumped L Street and hired another firm to run my fall campaign. Stratton left half a dozen voice mails, pleading with me to change my mind. I never responded. It was time to lay all the sentimental nonsense on the shelf and cut the cord for good.

Judy Zakowski

After Labor Day, Raj was on unpaid leave from L Street—on loan to the George Bush for President Committee until the day after the election. Georgy was in league with her father and brothers in Pittsburgh, working for Dukakis. She and Raj each spent one or two days in D.C. each week and the rest of the time on the road.

What was Terry doing? Tracking the Indian gaming act that was moving toward enactment, bundling money for Bush, shacking up with Dana Plato at Frankie Hodnett's mansion in L.A. It was an open secret by then that the two of them were together. There'd been a picture in the *Enquirer* of him and Dana tipping fruitshakes with O.J. and Nicole Simpson at some juice bar in Beverly Hills. Whenever he was in D.C., I only saw him in group meetings. All of a sudden, it was like he didn't want me within a hundred miles of him.

Early one morning, when there was no one else in the office and he was alone in the library, I went in and sat down across the table from him.

"You never come around and let me pick your brain anymore," I said. "I miss that."

"I can't let a good friend like you near me," he said. "I'm toxic now."

"Just this once," I said. "I'm wearing protection."

He laughed and closed his books. "Pick if you must this old, gray brain."

"Why did we get through Hired Gun unscathed?"

"Because we're clean."

"You could shake down *any* firm in this town and find *something* illegal. Did Bush step in to protect Raj?"

"That's something we'll never know."

"Is Raj leaving to work at the White House if Bush wins?"

"Not only will Bush win, he'll win *big*. But Raj is going to stay right here and make *millions* of dollars."

"What about Milo?"

"Come January, he'll be teaching Econ 101 back in Madison."

"All the rumors about you being at Milo's orgy. I don't believe them. Nancy Reagan, Mike Deaver, Frankie Hodnett, Dana Plato. I don't hold any of that against you."

"Thank you. I appreciate that."

"But do you have to ignore me?"

"I ignore everyone now," he said. "It's safer for all concerned."

*"*Please don't be a stranger."

That's what happened, though. Except for his three conversations with Georgy and me—the conversations that destroyed us all—that morning in the library was the last time I ever talked to Terry.

He was right about the election. Bush surged in late October and won forty-one states, and Milo got trounced by a pro-choice mother of two and former Badger cross country star. Terry was right about Raj, too. In the weeks after the election the rumors about his future changed daily, but he announced at the end of November that he was staying. He spent December flying all over Europe and Asia, meeting with potential clients eager for access to the incoming administration.

Georgy just looked sad. *Profoundly* sad, and dog tired. She was a tenacious competitor and she'd laid her heart and soul out for Dukakis. But it was more than that. I was alone with her a few days before Christmas, reviewing tax issues for January, and she couldn't focus at all. Wearing the face of a woman who'd surrendered, she stared past me out the window at the dreary drizzle like a zombie.

"Where in the world is Raj today?" I asked.

"London," she said. "Playing tennis with the Dragon King of Bhutan. Having dinner with the Minister of Defence from Sri Lanka."

"Why doesn't he take you with him?"

"Because I'll just get *in the way*," she said. "And I certainly don't want to get in the way."

"Has the campaign come between you?"

"The campaign and a thousand other things."

"I'm sorry to hear that."

"I hate doing this," she said. "Being a married girl who complains about her husband to a girl who isn't married."

Her desk phone chimed. It was him. She swung around in her big, beige leather chair away from me, murmured softly for a minute, then swung back.

"Raj is on his way to Heathrow right now," she said. "He's flying to New York tonight to see Donald Trump, then he'll be home Christmas Eve."

At six o'clock that night, the phone rang in my kitchen at home. It was Georgy.

She said: "Turn on CNN right now."

On the screen, an anchor was at a desk, and behind her on the monitor was a low, overhead shot of a village square at night, taken from a hovering helicopter. The ground was covered with mounds of debris, and under a bank of floodlights lay a massive piece of an airplane fuselage, as big as a house. The graphic read: *Live. Lockerbie, Scotland. 260 presumed dead on Pan Am Flight 103.*

Georgy sobbed into my ear. "Raj was on board."

"No!"

"He called me on the runway five minutes before takeoff."

"That cannot be!"

"He's gone. This is the end of everything."

The Gleam
London - February 12th, 1989

Was Lockerbie Bomb a Hit on Bush Family Ally?

America's new First Family is mourning the loss of a close friend and supporter in the Lockerbie tragedy—and a source tells Gleam he may have been the real target of a bomb that killed 260 people aboard Pan Am Flight 103 and ten on the ground.

Washington power lobbyist Rajan "Raj" Rao, 39, perished in the nightmare fireball that rained death on the Scottish countryside four days before Christmas. Theories abound about the source of the explosive device planted in the luggage hold of the 747 at Frankfurt Airport. Most finger Muslim terrorists from the Middle East.

But now a close observer of politics in the USA tells Gleam there may have been another motive: good, old fashioned greed.

"After Bush won the White House, Raj was signing up every sultan, prince, and prime minister on Earth as a client. All any of the lobbyists got were his leftovers—and a lot of them were angry about it."

The Texas-born Asian Indian first met the Bushes at Baylor University, when he worked on the president's campaign for U.S. Senate. He then served Bush for two decades as a fundraiser and advisor, while holding posts in government and the private sector.

"They all adored Raj," a source told Gleam. "They called him Bearcub. The president's face went white as chalk when he heard the news. Barbara was in tears."

Daughter Dorothy "Doro" LeBlond and eldest son George W. represented the family at a public memorial service on January 28th at the St. Alban's School Chapel in Georgetown.

Our observer is convinced more evidence of his theory may emerge in the near future: "Follow the money," he says. "Who found money when Raj Rao lost it? Never underestimate the power of the dollar."

Jaye Janis

In October of '86, I sent one of my scripts to *L.A. Law.* I was gone from *Diff'rent Strokes* by then, working as a secretary at Chaz-Dezmond Productions.

A week later, the story editor called me.

"We love this," he said. "We're going to do it—later. Right now we need something else. Why don't you and I write it together?"

Our joint effort became "Fry Me to the Moon," Episode 11 of Season 1. Nine months later, they shot my original script as "The Brothers Grimm," Episode 27 in Season 2.

Those credits got me a union card and an agent. In the next year, she sold a second script to *L.A. Law,* and two each to *Dynasty* and *Knot's Landing*. I quit my job and plunged into full-time freelancing, and in March of '89, I landed my first TV movie, a send-up of *Ocean's Eleven* called *Four Aces* that I did with Ethan Gorman Films for ABC.

Before I drafted, I booked a room at Caesar's Palace for three days to immerse myself in Sin City. On my last morning there, I wandered over to the sprawling convention facilities, not really knowing what I'd find. I poked my head into one of the meeting rooms, and what I found was Terry Stratton.

He was pacing back and forth in front of a podium, pointing to a big, bright pull-down screen, explaining the provisions of the Indian Gaming Regulatory Act that Reagan had signed six months before. A crowd of a hundred or so—half of whom looked to be Native Americans—listened.

"Unlike many in this business, we don't see Indian gaming as a threat," he said. "We see it as an *opportunity*. A tribe can't set up a casino tomorrow. You'll need federal recognition, a compact with your state, a building, staff, equipment, publicity. Alliance Entertainment can help make *all* of that a reality for you."

With his suit coat off, his tie loosened, and his sleeves rolled up, he seemed quite at home in front of the audience. His delivery was so fluid it reminded me of his old boss, hosting *General Electric Theatre* or presiding over a White House press conference.

Four years had passed since our encounter at Frankie Hodnett's New Year's Eve bash. But even with my glasses on and my hair pulled back, he recognized me right away, scrunched along the back wall with my pen and notebook, sipping a cup of java. His smile jolted me like a stun gun.

At his invitation, I dropped by the Alliance hospitality suite for happy hour that afternoon. As he schmoozed the stream of dreamers, hustlers and hangers-on who filed in, I girded myself with a couple of bourbon mists and finally corralled him into the seat next to me on the couch.

"Are you still with Dana?"

"She's back in L.A."

"But you're together?"

He grimaced and shook his head. "We tried, but we couldn't make it work. It's over."

When I got home, I found out from a girlfriend with the inside dish that he was lying to me. Yes, Dana was in L.A. to audition, because her nude spread in *Playboy* had created buzz. But she was back in Las Vegas three days after I left. And not only were the two of them together, they were co-habitating in a cookie cutter ranch house on Cinderella Lane, west of the Strip across I-15. Dana's residuals from *Diff'rent Strokes* were drying up by then, and apparently they were living off his earnings from Alliance and The L Street Team.

So did I return his hospitality by inviting him to join me for dinner? Yes. Show me a woman in my position who wouldn't have done the same thing. He claimed to be unattached. I *was* unattached, and insanely attracted to the man. And we *were* in Las Vegas. When the moment arrived to either say good night and goodbye, or ask him up to my room for a nightcap, I searched my mind for a reason to back off. I didn't come up with one.

The moment he became a lover, he exploded to life as a muse, too.

So nowadays, people ask me—is Terry the model for Jimmy Blaine in *Hired Gun*? I used to hedge, like most writers. Explain that I met ten lobbyists in the flesh and researched the lives of twenty more, and Jimmy Blaine is a composite, constructed from tiny pieces of all of them.

That's true to a point. But if you're talking about the man's essential character, I don't hedge anymore. Yes, Terry was my model. Like Jimmy Blaine, Terry was a divided soul, torn and finally ripped apart by conflicting desires. He craved men and women, work and play, fame and anonymity. He built his body up with sweat and exercise every morning, and corroded it with alcohol and drugs every night. Above all, he wanted to live within the norms of society and outside of them at the same time. I took all of that from Terry.

And of course his ass. There's a backside shot we like to use of Jimmy, nude as a peeled shrimp, feeding the squirrels on his sundeck, with his taut, bare cheeks cupped up high and tight, right into the eye of the camera.

That's Terry to a T. That's exactly what his ass looked like that night in my bed at Caesar's. The most stunning ass I've ever seen on a man in my life.

Frankie Hodnett

It happened spontaneously one Saturday morning, the way I'd been hoping it would. Production at Royal Duchess was on ten-day hiatus. Most of the crew was in London for a homecoming. The mansion was quiet and the Squire and I were in the upstairs living room, celebrating the fall of the Berlin Wall with bagels, blow, and screwdrivers at dawn.

Dana padded in barefoot, with a big, baggy USC sweatshirt covering her privates. "I want to make love with Terry in front of the camera," she cooed. "I want you to tape us, and I want Lizzy in the room with us when you do."

"Now?"

"Why not now?"

Why not, indeed. I was so ecstatic over the moment, I didn't quibble about Lizzy being invited in. Dana had always fancied her. She was still camped out in the bungalow next door, but alone. Her Raider cheerleader friend had dumped her, for a man of all things, a dashing Cuban boxer who'd seen her bumping and grinding at Joe Robbie Stadium in Miami. So the wife was feeling blue.

The four of us went out to my home studio on the second floor of the game room. Lizzy and I set up microphones and light banks and tacked my best Rock Hudson and Marilyn Monroe posters up on the walls. We wrapped Marilyn's size ten Pucci belt around Dana's waist and shot the thing in eighty minutes, smooth as silk.

No need to delve into the physical fine points. Let's just say morning is the best time to make love. They were mad for it, they gave it their all, and I got everything they gave into my camcorder. Right down to the tattoo of the winged fairy above Dana's delectable mound of Venus.

We christened it *Secret Strokes*. I burned six copies of the final edit and stashed them with the master in my collections room.

Mildred Gouyen

Born and raised on the land of my ancestors, the land on which we were placed by our Creator at the beginning, I am a Blue Mountain Apache.

When Indian gambling arose, and casinos began to be built on reservations in the West, a whole tribe of pale-faced beggars rushed hither to share their visions of magnificent wealth. Terry Stratton was one of them. He came dressed in finest clothes to our tribal council meeting in Snowflake, to make a presentation. At the end of it, he asked for questions from the audience.

I raised my hand and stood up.

"The white man wiped us out," I said. "Stole our land, destroyed our homes, raped our women, brought deadly diseases to all of us. In spite of all those crimes he committed against us, *he* is still called civilized, and *we* are still called brutes, animals, savages. Why is that so?"

He was dumbfounded. He had no idea how to respond. The audience squirmed, and the council members snarled at me in anger and disgust. The chairman slammed his gavel, called for a ten-minute recess, and walked alone with me out to the playground behind the meeting hall.

"We're going to build a casino here whether you want one or not," he said.

"I urge you and council to take a cautious approach."

"Lead, follow, or get the hell out of the way."

"I'm not the only one who feels like this."

"Where are the rest?"

"You've scared them off."

"Why don't you go, too?"

"This man here with us today collected hundreds of thousands of dollars for George Herbert Walker Bush."

"How did you find that out?"

"On the computer, at the library," I said. "They call it the world wide web."

"Why put any stock in a bunch of numbers put up on a screen by some white man you don't know?"

"The information is there for the world to see," I said. "Amounts, dates, names, organizations. This man is a lackey of Bush."

"Why do you care?"

"Because Bush's own father robbed the grave of Geronimo at Fort Sill. Stole his skull and bones and silver bridle, all for the amusement of a secret society of rich white boys at Yale."

"Mildred, you are out of your mind."

"George Herbert Walker Bush himself has kissed the skull that his father stole. Can there be a greater insult to our heritage?"

"Go bury yourself in your wide world web. Leave us alone."

"Go bury your head in shame for inviting this man onto our land."

An hour later, before he left, I spied the beggar behind the school, inside his big silver car, talking on his gleaming telephone. To a fellow beggar no doubt, reporting on the progress he was making in Snowflake, even in the face of an agitator like me.

The chairman was right. I and the people who felt like me could not stop the casinos—not on Blue Mountain or any other tribal land in America. The forces aligned against us were too powerful. But I could try to stop *this* lackey of Bush from ever reaping a penny of it.

As he sat in his car on his phone, I raised my right arm into line with my eye and clenched my fist as tightly as I could. The anger of Geronimo welled up inside me—free, defiant, indomitable.

I pointed my outstretched finger at the beggar.

The anger of Geronimo traveled from my finger through the air like a ray of fire and seared his soul.

Judy Zakowski

In the months after Lockerbie, the prospects Raj had been wooing signed with other firms. Then our existing clients began to depart in a steady stream. We made a valiant effort, but the void he'd left was too huge. As the first anniversary of the crash approached, we'd lost over half our accounts, and Georgy had laid off three attorneys and ten of our twenty support staffers.

No one knew what the future held. Were we going to stay the course, merge with another firm, disintegrate?

One Friday in late December, Georgy asked me to stop by Scott Place after work. She said she had something she wanted to discuss with me outside the office. I'd gotten close to her by then, closer than I wanted to be. But she was grief-stricken, she didn't seem to have anyone else to lean on, and she pulled me in.

When I arrived, she led me to the separate unit behind the house. In the back room, where we'd smoked our Super Bowl cigarettes, a shredder lay on the coffee table, surrounded by three cardboard boxes stuffed with paper files. I sat down on the couch. She turned the shredder on and fed its whirring mouth while we talked.

"Don't look so distressed," she said. "These are just some old files."

"You brought them home from the office?"

"Yes."

"The judge told us not to do that," I said. "*Ordered* us not to."

"You and I are both attorneys," she said. "And we know there are times when a judge's order needs to be ignored."

"Did the investigators see any of these files?"

"No."

"Please, Georgy—stop. You're making me very uncomfortable."

"Don't be such a *ninny*. Nobody cares about this anymore."

"If nobody cares, then why bother to shred it at all?"

She gave me a flinty look and then, before I realized what was happening, she started to explain the situation in her measured, methodical way. I'm glad I was sitting down because otherwise I might have fainted.

She and Terry had been diverting fee payments from Frankie Hodnett and his pornographer friends into a secret account that Georgy controlled personally. From that account, she'd made regular cash payments to an event planning and catering business owned by Howard Fryer's wife.

"What are you shredding?" I asked.

"All of my correspondence with Howard's office over the years," she said. "Bank statements for my account, invoices, notes, calendars, message slips."

"How much money have you given her?"

"Two hundred and twenty thousand dollars."

"Who knows?"

"Terry, the Fryers, me—and you."

"Why me?"

"Because I'm scared to death of Terry," she said. "He's compulsive, deceitful, secretive. And *powerfully* addicted to cocaine. At some point I'm going to sit down with him and settle this. And when I do, I want you in the room with me."

"Are you still diverting funds?"

"As much as I can," she said. "Terry is having no luck at all signing up tribes. I think some crazy Indian put a curse on him."

"What about Frankie Hodnett?"

"What he doesn't know won't hurt him." She stuffed a pile of shredded paper into a thirty-gallon plastic garbage bag. "Judy, I'm one of the *good* guys."

"I know you are."

"I help the other good guys, and they help me."

"I know they do."

"It's quid pro quo," she said. "Do unto your friends and your friends will do unto you. That's the essence of human beings, business, politics, life. You know that too, don't you?"

"Yes, I guess I do."

"I have *nothing* to be ashamed of," she said. "And I'm not doing anything wrong."

"No."

"Say it, then."

I couldn't speak.

"Say it!"

"You have nothing to be ashamed of. And you're not doing anything wrong."

She went into the bathroom and shut the door behind her. A minute later, I heard crying, then vomiting. I burst through the door. She was on her knees in front of the toilet, wiping her mouth with a hand towel.

"*Dozens* of people knew there was going to be a bomb on that plane," she said.

"That's pure conjecture."

"Then why was it half empty?"

"Every other flight that night from Europe that night was half-empty, too."

"He had a thousand friends," she said. "Why didn't *somebody* warn him about the bomb?"

Later, after she cleaned up and calmed down, we pushed all the shredded paper into three bags and hauled them back to the house.

"I know this is a lot to ask," she said. "But could you stay the night? Tomorrow is the 22nd and I'm about to lose my mind."

"If it will help you."

"There's a bedroom behind the den," she said. "You can sleep there and leave first thing on the morning."

I was alarmed by what I appeared to be witnessing: my boss and friend, one of the most esteemed women in Washington, teetering on the brink of a nervous breakdown. I didn't want to stay. But the depth of her despair made me reluctant to leave her alone.

At ten o'clock, I went upstairs to check on her. The door to her bedroom was ajar. A bookcase lay tipped on its side. Books were scattered everywhere. There were two empty bottles of chardonnay on the dresser. Georgy was curled up on the floor in her nightgown, clutching a bunch of men's pants and shirts and neckties and crying uncontrollably. Her legs were twitching and shaking.

I gently pried all the clothes out of her hands, rolled her onto her back, and put two pillows under her head. A minute later, she sat up and stopped crying. "Go down to the kitchen," she said. "Get me a big glass of ice water and a fresh box of Kleenex."

When I got back she was in bed, asleep. Or maybe just pretending to be asleep. I left the water and Kleenex on her table, and then I did something I swore I wasn't going to do. I went into her bathroom, opened the medicine cabinet, and examined the labels of all the capsules inside. What I saw popped my eyes out. Prozac, Xanax, Nardil, Parnate. I knew all of them were used to treat depression and anxiety, but I had no idea what kind of precise effects they had, how they interacted with each other, or how long she'd been taking them. With that many drugs involved, all I knew for sure was that the situation couldn't be good.

I got up at six o'clock and tried to sneak out, but she was already pacing back and forth in the kitchen in her bathrobe, gulping a can of Diet Pepsi, gobbling a hunk of coffee cake with her fingers, staring at a big picture on the wall of her and Raj on a beach somewhere.

I want to say she looked better after a good rest. But she looked worse—much worse. As if she'd spent all night with her eyes wide open and hadn't slept a wink.

She stared at me blankly. I wasn't absolutely sure she even recognized me. "Raj was alive when he hit the ground," she said.

"Excuse me?"

"He survived the explosion and the descent."

"Oh my God."

"They found him strapped to his seat in the middle of a corn field. Conscious and alert."

"I am so sorry."

"He died in the ambulance on the way to the hospital."

I broke down then. I couldn't take it anymore. We had a loud, long cry together in the kitchen and then I went home.

Mary Quesada

In early 1990, Public Corruption re-opened its investigation of The L Street Team. Again, I was assigned to lead it.

I asked my professor: "Can we clarify the mission? Last time, I felt out of the loop."

"Rephrase your question."

"What is our goal?"

"To remove a liberal from power."

"Which liberal?"

"Howard Fryer."

"Why Fryer?"

"Because we *can*," he said. "The foundation has been laid. You thought all your effort before was for naught. We're building on it now."

"What is our action plan?"

"The road to Fryer runs through Stratton and Greco," he said. "Stratton is a nothingburger, a zero. We'll use him to nail Greco. Then we'll use Greco to nail Fryer."

"She's a widow now."

"What is your point?"

"Is there a way we can do this without destroying her life?"

"If destroying her life is a concern, step aside and let someone else run the case."

I had a husband by then, and a year-old daughter of my own, so I didn't tell my professor what else was on my mind: Well over a year had passed since Lockerbie, the president's favorite brown-skinned friend was gone and largely forgotten, and now we could hunt down a choice liberal with no messy complications.

With an assistant, I flew to Las Vegas and met Stratton at his lawyer's office on Bridger Avenue, across from the Foley Federal Building. The four of us sat in the cramped library, surrounded by volumes of the U.S. Code and Nevada Revised Statutes.

Stratton looked like a sick goose about to get cooked. I laid out everything we had on him: twenty counts of lobbying White House officials within a year after leaving his job there, in violation of the Ethics in Government Act, twelve counts of providing illegal gifts to members and staff of the Senate Finance Committee during the tax reform debate in '86, eighteen counts of diverting client funds into Greco's personal account.

"I'm a Republican," Stratton said.

"We understand that," I said.

"I bundled three hundred thousand dollars for Bush."

"We know."

"Why are you doing this to me? My career is taking off again and you're going to kill it."

"We're willing to plead you down."

"In exchange for what?"

"All you can get on Greco." I said. "Especially her work with you in funneling money to Fryer's wife."

"I could make that happen," he said.

"The only person we can convict through the paper trail is you," I said. "To convict her, we need a verbatim record of your communications on the subject."

"It would have to be face-to-face," he said. "In Washington. That's the only way we talk now."

"Will you wear a wire for us?"

"What happens if I do?"

"You'll plead guilty to one count of exceeding the monetary limit for gifts, pay a thousand dollar fine, and get a year's probation."

"Why are you letting me off so easy?"

"Because we want Fryer, and we need you to get him."

He didn't decide that day. I didn't expect him to. Greco was presumably, on some level, his friend, and he was facing a momentous, life-altering decision. I suppose he examined the percentages. If he was convicted on numerous counts and imprisoned, his career was over. If he ratted out Greco and earned himself a wrist slap, his career undoubtedly was damaged—but perhaps not over.

A week later, his lawyer called. Stratton was willing, able and ready. The next three times he came to Washington, he wore a wire into his meetings with Greco and secretly taped their conversations. Zakowski was in the room, too. She came in very late in the game. I felt as sorry for her as I did for Greco.

Stratton gave us what we were looking for. Our quest to remove a liberal from power moved onward and upward.

The Red Pepper
London—October 3rd, 1990

Pretty Woman on the Loose!

Looks like America's Favorite Sweetheart may be stepping out on her beau.

Julia Roberts—currently on the outs with fiancé Kiefer Sutherland—was recently spotted by a crowd of onlookers in the midst of a make-out session with a much-older mystery man.

And they were doing the deed at high noon on a bench in Farragut Square—smack in the middle of bustling downtown Washington, D.C. The Pretty Woman was in the USA capital to co-host the American Film Institute tribute to Sir Laurence Olivier at the Kennedy Center.

"These were not pecks on the cheek," one startled eyewitness told Pepper. "The mouths were open. The tongues were churning. The chap had his paw up under her blouse, caressing her stomach."

"They were on another planet," a second witness said. "I don't think they knew a dozen people were gawking at them. If they did, they sure didn't care!"

Well, a girl has a right to be happy. Hope things with Kiefer are . . . as they should be. With Miss Julia inked to play Tinkerbell in Steven Speilberg's action flick Hook, we'll stayed tuned.

As for her cheeky make-out mate, sources tell Pepper he's a high-powered lobbyist and former aide in the Reagan White House, with ties to porn king Filthy Frankie Hodnett.

Frankie Hodnett

After I shot *Secret Strokes* and stashed it away for safekeeping, all was merry between me and the Squire until one evening in Vegas. A bunch of the Out and Outs went over for the Douglas-Holyfield bout at the Mirage, and one of my cohorts came to my pre-fight buffet with some bad news.

"A few of us hired a private dick in Washington," he said. "To check out your mover and shaker friend."

"Why the fuck would you do that behind my back?"

"To learn a few things we weren't getting from you."

"Such as?"

"He's talking to the U.S. Attorney's Office. And the rumor is he's queer."

He wanted to haul him up in front of everybody and crucify his ass. I convinced him to hold off until I talked it out with him alone. The Squire kept blowing off my calls, so early the next morning I cabbed it to his house on Cinderella Lane and banged on his door. Like a prick, he took his own sweet time opening up, hanging me out to dry on the porch in front of all his bloody neighbors peeking through their curtains. Dana was sacked out in the bedroom. Through the half-open door I saw her foot, covered with a flower tattoo, hanging out the back of the bed. The Squire and I went into the kitchen, and I told him what I'd learned.

"The Out and Outs are brassed off at you big time," I said. "They don't like having shit pulled on them."

"I talked to the law during Hired Gun," he said. "That's stale news. So did everybody else in D.C. As for being queer, I've been hearing that all my life."

"I don't care one way or the other if you're queer. Whatever turns you on, that's my philosophy. You've known that from the night we met. But some of these other guys— "

"Give the other guys a screening of *Secret Strokes* and let them decide if I'm queer."

To give us all a chance to clear the air, I set up a lunch at Thai Barbecue, on Reseda in Woodland Hills, out by the studios. I thought a public setting might dampen the animosity. I was wrong. The Greek chorus cranked up one more time.

"Fifty grand a month we're paying you."

"That's what I cost."

"A shitload of money, pal. And you're pissing it up a wall."

"I'm selling access to the system," he said. "You're buying it."

"What good have you done for us? Bush is raising our taxes. The FBI and the IRS are *still* on my ass, and now you're in cahoots with some bitch from the U.S. Attorney's Office."

"That's a lie."

"Do you happen to be of the homosexual persuasion?"

"No. Ask Julia Roberts."

"Why the hell weren't you working that day?"

"I was."

"You're on our dime, and you've got time to display yourself like an asswipe in front of the entire universe?"

"We do *not* do business with men of the homosexual persuasion."

He left then, and we had it out. They agreed to let the situation slide a while longer. But I was feeling the heat. Here was a man I'd been tight with going on ten years, and suddenly he was putting me in a very ugly light.

I say we were tight. Maybe it just seemed that way to me. It was starting to look like the Squire had been playing me for a fool.

A few months after the lunch, this brainy chick with a crew cut and orange glasses came to the mansion to appraise my collection. She picked up the John Wayne eye patch the Squire had given me and giggled.

"This is worth maybe twenty bucks," she said.

"What are you talking about? He wore it in *True Grit*."

"No, he didn't."

"It's worth ten grand or more," I said. "There are only twelve of them in the world."

"I've seen close to a hundred of these things," she said. "It's one of the biggest scams around."

The very next night Dana called me on my private line—something she'd never done. It was 2:30 A.M, closing time at the Viper Room on Sunset, and she was out in the parking lot, sprawled on the hood of some car.

"Terry is ripping me off," she whispered.

"What do you mean?"

"I signed some form he shoved in my face when I was messed up a couple of years ago, before I went to rehab. A bunch of legal mumbo jumbo I didn't understand. Power of attorney or some such bullshit. Now he's draining my account to keep himself above water. I'm desperate for money."

"That's outrageous."

"I love Terry," she said. "He takes care of me. At least he used to. But he's turning into a gigantic asshole and I want you to know."

I wanted to end things with him then, but I kept faffing around. We rolled into '91, and got another report from the private dick in Washington. He had a airtight source with the law and knew on good authority that the Squire and his chick partner had been diddling with our jack, sliding backhanders to her cronies at our expense. The next month, I blew off my fee payment. The rest of the Out and Outs did the same.

A week later he called. I didn't want him at my place anymore, and we agreed to meet at Matteo's, on Westwood. When I walked in, he was at the long bar in front, looking clapped out.

"We're letting you go," I said. "It's time for a change."

"Can we talk?"

"You're stealing from us."

"My Ohio clients are long gone," he said. "The tribes won't do business with me. I need you, I don't have anybody else."

"And the John Wayne eye patch you gave me is a fake."

"It's one hundred percent authentic."

"No it's not."

"*Yes it is.*"

"Are you going to sit there like some pitiful child and lie to my face?"

It was such a pathetic way to end things. All the fantastic times we had together, the drugs we shared because we loved them, everything he taught me. And we were down to bickering about some ridiculous piece of celebrity junk.

He bolted then, stuck me with the tab. Didn't even have the basic human courtesy to shake my hand. He got into his Mercedes and drove up Westwood, toward Olympic. I followed the car until his tail lights disappeared. That was the last I ever saw of him.

I was so bummed out I spent the rest of the night on that stool, getting hugely sloshed. So sloshed I left my car in the parking lot, took a cab home, and collapsed into bed.

In the morning I found out he'd been there. He must have left Matteo's and driven directly to the mansion. He came to the door with a gym bag, told one of the crew he needed to fetch a few items he'd left up in his quarters, and the moron let him inside, even though I'd told them all not to.

Up in my collections room, the master and six copies of *Secret Strokes* were gone. The bastard had a bit of honor, I'll give him that. He could have stolen so much more.

Mary Quesada

After we got what we needed from Stratton, we turned our attention to Greco.

She started out tough as nails. When we played the tapes of her conversations with Stratton and Zakowski, she barely flinched. It was as if she'd been expecting it. Her lawyers wanted her to tell us all she knew and wear a wire against Fryer, just as Stratton had done against her.

"My career is over whether I cut a deal or not," she said. "So I'm not going to. I won't help you take out Howard Fryer."

"In that case," I said. "You're probably going to jail."

"King went to jail. Debs, Mandela, Gandhi."

"Would Howard Fryer go to jail to save you?"

"I'm not doing anything wrong."

We proceeded without her cooperation. My professor and his superiors were supportive. The election was ten months away. Bush was riding high in the saddle, celebrating victory in his splendid little war in the desert. He looked like a shoo-in for a second term. The idea was to stomp Democrat ass while the stomping was good.

Even without Greco's wire, we had more than enough to squash Fryer. The *Yellow Jacket*—his yacht at Gangplank Marina that he'd bought from a drug company lobbyist for a price that was one-quarter of its true market value—turned out to be his undoing. The grand jury indicted him on twelve counts of receiving bribes, evading taxes, and laundering campaign contributions.

He refused to resign. Like Congressman Forbes, he cast his fate to the voters. He was defeated in November and convicted at trial the following August.

The rest of it ended like this:

Stratton pleaded guilty to one count of making an illegal gift, paid a thousand dollar fine, and received one year of probation.

Zakowski pleaded guilty to one count of destroying subpoenaed documents. She paid a five hundred dollar fine and received six months of probation.

Greco pleaded not guilty to charges of perjury, tax evasion, diversion of client funds, and destroying subpoenaed documents. She vowed to go to trial. But Stratton's tape recordings provided overwhelming evidence of her consciousness of guilt. In layman's terms, that means that she *knew* what she was doing was illegal. That was something her lawyers simply could not refute.

A week before her trial date, she asked permission to change her plea to guilty on all charges. It was ten weeks before the election. My professor and his superiors wanted to refuse her request and proceed with a public humiliation. But I asked them to accept her change in plea and stand down. Someone higher up in the chain of command must have asked them to do the same, because that is what happened.

Four months later, my husband was transferred to Denver. I resigned and went with him. That was the end of my time hunting liberals.

On my last day, my professor saluted me in front of the assembled staff. "Job well done, Ms. Quesada. You are a child of immigrants who believe in democracy, integrity, and fair play. Your mother and father must be proud of you."

They were. But for the first time in my life, that wasn't enough to make me proud of myself.

Judy Zakowski

The tables turned so quickly it was terrifying. As my friends celebrated Clinton's ousting of Bush and applied for jobs in the new administration, I became Washington's number two radioactive woman, behind only Georgy.

After she and Terry and I entered our guilty pleas, I made twenty contacts seeking work in D.C. and didn't get a single expression of interest. Three days before Thanksgiving, Marquette Law School in Milwaukee offered me an adjunct position starting in January, teaching taxation and legislation. With gratitude and relief, I accepted.

As I was preparing to leave town, Georgy called and asked to see me. She was free until her sentencing in January. She knew she was going to prison, but she did not know for how long. Her lawyers were saying somewhere between three and nine months.

She and I weren't close anymore. The emotional brutality of the criminal justice process had put an end to that. But I was touched that she'd reached out to make contact one more time, and I told her I'd drop by Scott Place the next morning.

Her money was nearly gone. The L Street Team was extinct, and Raj had left her virtually nothing. To pay her legal expenses, she was selling her townhouse. The scene in the living room that had once been so festive was grim—two shattered women, neither with a husband or children to comfort her, surrounded by trash bags and cardboard boxes and furniture wrapped up in plastic sheeting.

"I'm sorry for involving you in this," she said. "I know you can't forgive me, but I just want to say it. I should have handled it alone, but I got scared."

"It was my choice to get involved."

"We didn't do anything wrong," she said. "You still believe that, don't you?"

I wasn't sure what I believed anymore. I was beginning to think the people with the badges—not us—were the good guys. But I didn't want to sit in Georgy's empty living room and go round and round over who was right and who was wrong. I didn't want that futile, exhausting dialogue to be my last memory of her.

"Have you heard from Terry?" I asked.

"No," she said. "And I don't expect I ever will."

"I still can't believe he did this to us," I said. "I never saw him as *that* big of a scumbag."

"None of this would have happened if he'd stayed away from Dana Plato and Frankie Hodnett and cocaine and all the rest of it. The high life destroyed him."

We went silent. Now that his name had been broached, neither of us wanted to go on. We left Terry Stratton hanging heavy in the air, like a swaying corpse with a snapped neck. Down in the basement, the furnace kicked on and started to rumble.

"I've got to do some packing," Georgy said. "I'm leaving tomorrow morning."

"Where are you going?"

"San Mateo," she said. "I'm driving coast-to-coast, something I always wanted to do."

"All that time alone." I said. "Won't you get down in the dumps?"

"Not at all," she said. "Believe it or not, I actually feel quite good. I'll be house sitting for a friend. Visiting my old Stanford haunts, going hiking along the ocean."

"Goodbye, Georgy. And good luck."

I gave her a quick, awkward hug and was gone.

San Mateo County Sheriff's Office
Crime Report
Case Number 93-012-09

Victim (V) Name: Greco, Georgiana Elena
Date and Time Occurred: 01-04-93.
Location: Montara Mountain, adjacent to the Old Coast Highway, 2.7 miles south of the Higgins Way Gate.
(V) Residence Address: 3206 Scott Place, NW, Washington, DC 20007.
(V) Race: W / Sex: F.
(V) DOB: 04-18-53.

(V) DL: V9157030 (DC).

Report Submitted by: Deputy S. Chen / Badge #383.

Reporting Person (RP): Michael Reynolds—Pacifica Fire Department.

Witness (W): Cookie Dilla—Pacifica Fire Department.

Controlled Document—Not To Be Duplicated.

Awareness: On 01-06-93 at approx. 1025 hours, County Radio requested that I telephone them for a call. I immediately did so and was advised that off-duty firefighters, while biking on Montara Mountain, had discovered the body of a deceased female.

I proceeded to the Higgins Way Gate and met the Deputy Coroner, who arrived by separate vehicle. W-Dilla led us up the trail to the crime scene.

Examination of Crime Scene: The body was lying in the middle of a steep, narrow dirt path leading to the summit of the mountain.

The Deputy Coroner took possession of the body and searched it, along with a blue knapsack found next to it. He estimated that V-Greco had been dead for 48 hours.

He removed the pistol from V-Greco's right hand. The index finger still rested on the trigger. The gun was loaded with five rounds of Glaser Safety Slug ammunition. The round under the hammer was expended.

The Deputy Coroner found the gun to be a Rossi .38 special 2-inch revolver, with rubber grips, serial number #AA212657. County Radio later advised that it had been purchased in Herndon, VA on 09-17-92 and was registered to V-Greco.

V-Greco was fully clothed, lying on her back, partially on a blue foam pad and partially on bare moist ground, with her face turned somewhat to the left.

The eyes were fully open and fixed. The mouth was open and the tongue was protruding from it. There appeared to be a great deal of trauma inside the mouth. It did not appear that a struggle took place. Rigor mortis was present.

The Deputy Coroner photographed the victim and scene, taking a total of twelve Polaroid photographs. They were later booked as evidence into Sheriff's Property.

The body was then carried off the mountain and transported to the county morgue.

Supplemental Information: Early on the morning of 01-06-93, approx. five hours before the discovery of V-Greco's body, San Mateo City PD began broadcasting information on a missing female with suicidal tendencies.

They did so after receiving a phone call on 01-05-93 from Mr. Terence C. Stratton of Las Vegas, NV. Stratton described himself as a former business partner of V-Greco in Washington.

He said he had received a letter from V-Greco the previous day, postmarked San Mateo, CA, with a return address of 110 West 3rd Avenue, Unit 5. In the letter, she wrote that by the time he read it she would be dead.

With the consent of the unit owner, contacted in Flagstaff, AZ, San Mateo City PD entered the 3rd Avenue address and conducted a search. The search produced a suicide note, a will, and two crayon drawings indicating V-Greco's desire to kill herself.

Stratton said V-Greco had a history of depression and had been medically treated for it. He said her husband was deceased, she had no children, and that her siblings and parents resided in the Pittsburgh, PA metro area.

On 01-8-93, V-Greco's brothers Aristotle D. and Paul A. Greco arrived at the Coroner's Office to ID V-Greco and transport her body to PA. Body left jurisdiction of San Mateo County at approx. 1234 hours on 01-8-93.

Disposition: Case Closed – Suicide.

Five / Appalachia 1993

Ruth Toops

One gray afternoon, just after New Year's, he tapped on the front door on Warren Street, like he used to do when he picked up Freddy to go running. Except this time, he gave me the shock of my life.

"Hello, Mrs. Toops. Terry Stratton."

I hadn't seen him in twenty-four years, since the day of Freddy's funeral when he mixed it up with Jack Cutler at the cemetery. And I'd lost track of him after my husband died and his mother and Ron Polk got married and moved to Florida.

The lovely brown eyes and inviting smile were the same. What was different was the demeanor. He looked disheveled and haggard, with a week's worth of beard on his cheeks and chin, and he was wearing dirty blue jeans and skuzzy sneakers and a parka that looked like it had been plucked out of a Goodwill bin. The clothes just hung on him, because he was as scrawny as a scarecrow.

A big, fancy foreign car was parked on the street in front of the house. A BMW, I think. I could see clothes on hangars and stuffed cartons piled in the back seat. Apparently, he was in transition, living through hard times.

I invited him inside for a cup of coffee, and we caught up. Life had taken him out West after Washington, he said, and now he was migrating back East.

He had a large manila envelope with him. He opened it up and showed me what was inside: the photograph of him and Rock Hudson together on a bench behind the Hotel Lafayette, before the *Battle Hymn* debut in 1957.

"Please take this," he said.

"You don't want it?"

"I'd prefer it to be in safe hands."

"Yours aren't?"

He looked down at the floor. "Mrs. Toops, at this point, I'm not sure where I might end up."

"Have you been through some trouble?"

"More trouble than you'll ever know."

"What are you going to do now?" I said. "That's all that matters."

"I'm going to do what Rock does in *Battle Hymn*," he said. "Atone for the innocent people I've hurt. Try to correct the horrible mistakes I've made."

For a moment I thought he was going to go on, but when I didn't give him an encouraging look, he stifled himself. It sounds hurtful to say this, but I didn't want to hear his tale of woe. He'd dropped on my doorstep from a place too far away, too long ago.

He stood up and walked to the front window. "Mrs. Toops," he said. "Do you have any cash here in the house right now that you can spare?"

I really didn't. But he had such a sad, desperate look on his face, and I doubt he was eating enough to keep a rat alive. I went into my bedroom, took five twenties out of my lock box, and handed them to him. As he stuffed them into the pocket of his jeans, he wouldn't look me in the eye.

I walked him out to the porch. "Where are you heading?" I asked.

"Over to Clarksburg in West Virginia," he said. "To pay respects to the family of a late friend. Then to Morgantown, to meet my birth mother. Ramsay was always bugging me to do it, and I'm finally taking her up on her advice."

"I certainly hope that works out for you."

"At least I'll be able to buy some decent clothes, thanks to you." In the yard, he paused and gazed down the way to his old house. "Who lives in 333 now?"

"Mark and John," I said. "Warren Street's first gay couple."

"Give them my best regards," he said. At the curb, he turned around. "When I get back on my feet, I swear on Freddy's grave I'll pay this money back to you."

He never did.

Cecile Harris

Father would not receive the man. I told him it was the sin we hated, not the sinner, and that he was being un-Christian.

"On the contrary," he said. "Avoiding him is the most Christian thing I can do."

"How so?"

"If I meet him, I'll snap his neck with my bare hands."

Father had faced down gun-wielding racist thugs in Birmingham, been clubbed in the mouth in Selma on Bloody Sunday, led five congregations, and raised six children with me. But he could not summon the fortitude to face this man as a human being, shake his hand, say grace, break bread. Cletus's death was too fresh, the scar on Father's soul too raw.

An hour before my guest was to arrive, my eldest daughter pulled into the driveway, unannounced. That was Father's doing. He would not be present himself, but he was sending a surrogate to express his outrage. She was always so eager to do his bidding, and he knew I would not refuse her entrance to the house. It was the two of us who received Mr. Stratton.

His clothes were plain, and he was reserved and respectful. I was surprised. I expected someone more garish, more flamboyant. He did not look like a man who lived a perverted lifestyle.

"I'm sorry about your son," he said. "I lost touch with him many years ago, after I left Columbus, and just recently learned of his death."

"Cletus spoke of you often during his final illness," I said. "He loved to go up to the attic and listen to the rain on the roof. It was his refuge, where he poured out his heart into his tape recorder, for us to listen to after he was gone. He was quite candid."

"He was an open soul."

"Those tapes deeply upset his father," I said. "That's why he's not here today. But all of us know about the illegal drugs the two of you ingested together."

"Yes."

"And your physical intimacy."

"Yes."

"You violated him. Abused him."

"Yes, I did."

"Used him to pull yourself up the ladder of success, then threw him away like a piece of garbage."

"I regret it profoundly."

"Cletus did not die peacefully," I said. "There was physical agony. And rage."

My daughter coughed, unfolded her arms, and lay her hands on the table.

"Homosexuality is a revolt against the Creator," she said. "A man who lies with another man is an abomination in the eyes of the Lord."

"I have two children," he said. "Both conceived with sanction of clergy. Loving relationships with human beings of both sexes."

"Why do you shade words like a legalist? Do you lay with men or do you not?"

"Daughter," I said.

"And what of your wife and children? Did you lay with my brother when you were married? The down low is the deepest pit of hell because you defile not only the Creator, but your family as well."

"Daughter, leave this room now."

"You can criticize what we had," he said. "But in the short time we were together, your brother and I made each other better people. We shared passion."

"You are *not* in this world to share *passion*," my daughter said. "To satisfy every vile urge you have and spread this horrible scourge."

"I want to *stop* the scourge."

"Confess your sins," my daughter said. "Accept Jesus Christ as the Lord and Savior of your life."

She left the room, averting her eyes from us in anger and shame. She went upstairs to Father's study, slammed the door shut, and paced the floor in her heavy heels.

"It would be best if I go," he said.

"Please forgive me. I did not want this to happen."

He went out to his car, came back with a cardboard carton, and laid the contents out on the kitchen table: autographs and pictures of O.J. Simpson and many other football, baseball and basketball players I didn't recognize.

"Your son and I loved sports," he said. "It was one of the passions we shared. I want you to have these."

I didn't care a thing about sports or O.J. Simpson. I barely knew who he was. But he insisted. After he left, I took the box down to the basement and put it with the other box of Cletus's mementos that I was hiding from Father.

That night, when Father got home, he went to the basement, rummaged around, and brought both boxes up. That was my daughter again. From his study, she had spied on me going down there, and then told him what she'd seen.

He took the boxes out to the fire pit in the backyard. He dumped everything in them into the pit, doused it all with gasoline, and dropped a match on top.

Doctor King said life was hard, as hard as crucible steel. That day was one of the hardest.

Carol Archer

It was him and me at Oliverio's, on Clay Street in Morgantown, along the wharf. All dinner long I felt like I was seeing him through a pane of glass, like I saw him that night so long ago at the hospital, before the adoption agency took him away. Our connection, as strong as it was, did not seem real.

I was seventeen when he was born in Huntington in 1948. His twenty-five-year old father was out of the picture, off to Hollywood to become the next Clark Gable. I remember his calm breathing and his bright, alert eyes. I wasn't going to keep him, but my heart wasn't broken. By giving him up I was giving him a better life. At least that's what the adults kept telling me.

Two months before we met, he'd given his name and contact information to the adoption registry in Charleston. They sent me a letter telling me that he was looking for his birth mother. The next move was up to me. I could make myself available to him, or not.

I resisted at first. I thought it might become a complication, and I didn't need any more of those. But of course I relented.

I was sixty-two and my life had been hard: two abusive husbands, two ugly breakups, a son and daughter in each marriage, all four of them hooked now on drugs or booze. And here I was a newlywed with husband number three. Why *again*? You'd think a woman in my position would say *no mas*.

I'm a sucker for tall, strong, good looking men. I always have been. And the only chance at all you have of keeping one is to marry one.

He didn't want to meet my son. He wanted to squat on his scrumptious, rock-hard ass, gobble peanuts, and watch Mountaineer basketball. He did not even want him at the house.

"Case him at a neutral site," he said.

"*Case?*"

"A safe, public place."

"Is he some kind of criminal?"

"I have no idea what he is. Neither do you."

"If you're so concerned about my safety, why don't you come with me?"

"You promised not to drag me into all your family crap," he said. "I'm holding you to that."

So I went to Oliverio's alone. I figured my son had to be a looker, because I was a firecracker as a young girl, and Wyatt, my God, Wyatt was off the charts. When I walked into the bar and spotted a lean, gorgeous, fortyish man with swimming pool eyes that made you want to dive right in and a nice head of auburn hair exactly the same texture and shade mine used to be, I knew it was him. He looked so much like me I gasped.

I wanted to hear all about him right away and he obliged, although I think it made him uneasy to talk about himself that much. I was in awe of what he'd accomplished. It was difficult to imagine my own flesh and blood rising that high in the world.

After our orders arrived, he changed the subject. "Who was my father?" he said. "I've lived my whole life not knowing the answer to that question."

"A wild boy from the wrong side of the tracks," I said. "I met him on Christmas Eve, after the service at Victory Baptist Church."

"What was he like?"

"He was the most beautiful boy I'd ever seen," I said. "But he was a scoundrel. When he found out I was pregnant, he ditched me and moved to Los Angeles to try to get into the movies."

I pulled a headshot photo of Wyatt out of my purse and gave it to him. His eyes got enormous, and he just *stared* at it. It was as if he'd seen it before.

"His name was Wyatt St. George," I said. "Do you recognize him?"

He stammered and stuttered. "Actually, I do, yes."

"How?"

"Not by name," he said. "But I had a friend in Washington with a collection of Hollywood photographs from the 40's and 50's. She's got a picture very much like this one, and I saw it a couple of times."

I didn't know what to say to that. The idea that my son had actually seen, and remembered, a picture of his own father, before he knew that the man *was* his father—well, it was insane. Like something out of the *Twilight Zone.* Just about the craziest damn thing I'd ever heard in my life.

"On the very day you were born, he died in a car crash in Death Valley," I said. "He had a couple of bit parts, but never got a real chance to make it in show business. And he never laid eyes on you."

The color had drained out of his face. He stared past me out the window at the lights shimmering along the canal. Then he excused himself and headed to the restroom. I got the distinct feeling he was hiding something from me, that he knew more about Wyatt St. George than he was letting on. But when he got back to the table he'd calmed down, and he wanted to hear about his half brothers and sisters. So I didn't press the point.

After an hour passed, I gave him the headshot of Wyatt and a half dozen of me and my family. We told each other we'd stay in touch and get together again. He did call a few times over the next three or four years, and I invited him to the house to meet my kids and grandkids. But he never came.

You hear about mothers and sons who find each other late in life and create something durable, loving, real. That didn't happen with us.

My son was a beautiful stranger, sharing a moment of his existence with me on his way to somewhere, something, someone else. That's all it amounted to. And I never did find out what he knew about Wyatt.

Coach Tim Frame

The Lord delivered Brother Terence to me in a most wondrous place: on the heights above the Potomac River, where it receives the Shenandoah at Harper's Ferry, where three states meet in the heart of the Great Appalachian Valley.

Out ahead of me in the sunlight is where he appeared that March morning, at a scenic overlook on the Maryland side. He was standing at the railing in a sweatshirt, jeans and sneakers, smoking a cigarette and sipping something out of a metal flask. He looked miserable, forlorn, defeated—and oblivious to the chill. He was alone.

I was alone, too, finishing up a six-miler on the old military road and wooded paths that lead through the forests. I drove down from Hagerstown and did that run as often as I could. Thrashing the lungs and guts and thighs on those hills was where I felt closest to God—and death.

I hailed him from the edge of the overlook. He turned my way, hoisted his flask into the air, and bellowed something incomprehensible across the valley into Virginia. He was drunker than a skunk, and just about as stinky when I got close.

"You look like you're working hard," he said.

"So do you."

"I used to run," he said.

"You were fast, I bet."

"Long, too."

"You worked your butt off."

"I did."

"And now you want to run again."

"How do you know that?"

"Something about your soul," I said. "It's a diamond shining at me through this haze of poison swirling around you."

He tamped his cigarette out with his heel and took a swig from his flask. "My soul is no diamond," he said. "If it were, I wouldn't be here."

"Where's here?"

"Broke, angry, disgusted, completely ashamed of myself. Everything I worked for in my life gone."

"Forgive yourself."

"You don't know what I've done."

"Can it be *that* bad?"

We headed back to the parking lot. He said he'd been on the road nine weeks, and now he was living in a Motel 6 in Charles Town, waiting on a last bit of money coming through from some accounts he was closing out in Las Vegas. Coach Tim Frame and Mountain of Hope Church didn't mean anything to him. Or if they did, he never let on.

"Where are you headed?" I asked.

"I'm going to drive my car down the hill and into the river."

"Are you going to hop out before you hit the water?"

"Might. Might not."

"What are you nipping on there?"

"My hillbilly screwdriver," he said. "Vodka and Mountain Dew."

"I think I better drive you back to Motel 6 myself."

He recoiled like a snake. Wouldn't let me near him, said he didn't need help, insisted he was fine to drive. So many brothers are like that. In your first encounters they resist. They don't yield easily. I'd learned not to push too hard. The thing to do was prepare the soil, plant the seed, give it a chance to grow.

"Are you serious about wanting to run again?"

"I am," he said.

"Meet me right here at dawn next Friday," I said. "We'll escape the shackles of our existence for a few hours and see what kind of shape we're in."

"I don't think I've got the strength anymore."

"The Lord will give you all the strength you need."

I've counseled hundreds of wayward men, offered a hot meal and a place to crash to just about every badass, outlaw drunk and junkie who's ever passed my way. But I still can't tell the difference between one who is ready to receive the gift of the Holy Spirit and one who isn't. So I was gratified when he showed up. On the trails, I slowed down for him and figured he might hold pace for fifteen or twenty minutes. But he stayed with me for a full hour. It took every ounce of courage and stamina he had. At the end, he was on the verge of collapse.

I took him to breakfast at the IHOP on Route 340 and he told me about his life. He was modest about it all, he didn't brag, and I didn't get the feeling he was embellishing much. The more he shared with me, the more excited I got. What he wanted to do now, he said, was wipe the slate clean.

When we parted ways, I pulled a Bible out of my van and gave it to him. "There's a way to break the grip of yesterday," I said. "Live for God tomorrow."

"Is that really possible?"

"Come to Mountain of Hope and meet our family, see the work we do. We don't smoke, we don't drink and we don't do drugs."

"That's exactly the kind of place I'm looking for."

"Bring your running gear too because we've got a bunch of warriors we call the Brigade who love to go fast—and long."

The next week, he showed up at our Sunday morning service. I introduced him to the congregation and offered him a room in the men's dormitory at the college.

"For the night?" he asked.

"For as long as you need it."

He unloaded his car and moved in. He didn't have much. A rail-thin wardrobe, a couple of desk lamps, and four or five cartons of stuff. At six o'clock the next morning he came to the gym to work out with the Brigade.

I told them all: "Give a hallelujah for Brother Terence Stratton. He's our new assistant coach. He'll be leading your morning workouts from now on."

Well, Brother Terence about dropped his shorts. We exchanged some righteous eye contact. No doubt he didn't like being blindsided in front of thirty high school and college kids he didn't know from Adam. He took to the job anyhow, and to the rest of his daily schedule: taking inventory in the food pantry in the morning, host and KP duty at lunch, a second workout with the Brigade at three before dinner, and an evening of Bible study and support meetings with those of us who, like him, were fighting the demons of substance abuse.

I was grateful for his presence. I thanked the Lord every day for bringing this man to Mountain of Hope. Because I was fifty-five, and I was at a crossroads. My genetic code was not programmed for longevity, and if the Lord were generous with me, I figured I had maybe fifteen years left before He called me home. I wanted to dedicate myself to a new mission: spreading the word to the faithful about what a mess our country was in. The time for consensus and cooperation was past. With this whore-hopping draft dodger and his dyke wife in the White House, there was no telling how low America might sink.

The war ahead was going to be long and brutal. I had a vision of myself heading out I-70 into the Ohio Valley and down I-81 into Virginia and Tennessee, to issue a call to arms in any Christian church willing to give me a podium.

And because he was a man of the world with so much wisdom to share, I was counting on Brother Terence to guide me on that journey. I was humble enough to know I was going to need him at my side.

Later that spring, the day arrived when he was ready to be baptized. He was saved, he said, and he wanted to witness to that fact. Early on a Sunday morning, before services, he rendezvoused with me and four of the Brigade at River Bottom Park in Williamsport. The ground was thawed, the spring wildflowers were in bloom, and we had a beautiful service along the Potomac.

"Repent," I said. "Be baptized. Receive the gift of the Holy Spirit."

We dunked him into the muddy water. When we pulled him up, he said it felt like a thousand pound weight had been lifted off his chest.

He dried off and changed his clothes, then got into the back seat of his Mercedes and pulled out a sturdy slab of lightweight wood the size of a card table. He opened his trunk and hauled out two plastic crates. Stacked inside them were autographs, photos, and mementoes from his days in Las Vegas and Hollywood and Washington. He tossed in a cell phone, a couple of empty vodka bottles, so many vials of pills I couldn't count them, and seven black videocassette cases, each of them labeled *Secret Strokes*. I never found out what those were. He carried the slab of wood and the crates down to the water.

My driver whispered to me: "Coach, please. Stop him."

"No. He needs to do this."

He loaded the crates onto the slab and gave his makeshift barge a gentle nudge out into the heart of the river. It caught the current and floated south for a hundred yards or so before disappearing around a bend.

We got into our van and trailed his car back to Hagerstown. In Halfway, he suddenly swerved into the parking lot of a strip mall.

"Follow him," I said to my driver.

There was an elderly black couple folding up clothes in a coin laundry. He went inside, talked to them a few minutes, and handed the man his car keys.

"Coach," said my driver. "Don't let him give away that great big beautiful car. *Please*."

"Two months ago, he wanted to drive it—and himself—into the river. This is progress."

Brother Terence shook hands with the man and embraced the woman. They were weeping with joy and disbelief. He dropped a last bag of trash from the Mercedes into a dumpster, climbed into the rear seat of the van, and rode home with us.

Six / On the Road 1993-2001

Joellen Lee

My mom refuses to give you the time of day, so I'm going to step up and attempt to set a few things straight.

I love my mom. I loved her at the time of which I'm speaking, I love her today, and I'll love her until the day I die and maybe beyond, who knows? Don't let that get lost in the sordid tale I'm about to relate.

She joined Mountain of Hope Church for me. If it takes a village to raise a child, what does it take to raise a mouthy, hostile, know-it-all who gets off on vamping in your face at every opportunity? More than Pamela Keeler Lee could provide. When we started attending services in the fall of '93 I was thirteen, an eighth-grader at Mountain of Hope Middle School. By starting us in on church together, she was trying to give me structure, guidance, community.

Let me translate that: she was trying to keep me off alcohol and other drugs as long as possible. You might be thinking, thirteen? That's about *a century* too late. In most cases, you'd be right. But for me, it worked. I went to chapel every day, ran track and cross country with the girls teams in the Brigade, fed the hungry, clothed the naked, graduated college with a decent job lined up—and stayed sober through it all in the face of incredibly tough odds.

I was an outgoing, curious kid. I had many friends among the seculars. When we joined, I heard dire warnings from just about all of them. Coach Tim Frame is a con man. He's corrupting your mom and you. It's a dangerous place, full of hateful people.

They got it about halfway wrong. When it comes to churches and religion, seculars usually do.

What was Frame conning Pam out of? She'd been a ski bum leeching off sugar daddies in Aspen, a bar manager and part-time escort in Blacksburg, and a captive housewife to a coked-out, well-hung, velvet-tongued Chevy dealer in Roanoke named Rory Lee. AKA my dad. He and Pam imploded in '85, when she caught him red-handed on the couch in his man cave, receiving oral favors from the nineteen-year-old daughter of one of his golf partners. So she was forty and alone in life, except for great big wonderful me. Taking one pill to get up and another to get to sleep, riding a dead horse in a high stress, low-pay paralegal job with a ten-lawyer general practice firm. Life hadn't gone the way she'd hoped. She had nothing to lose by joining a Pentecostal church and trying her hand at Jesus again.

Trying her hand. God, that's cynical.

We'd gone to one place in Roanoke for a few years, after she and dad split. The Blood of Jesus Holy Assembly. Skin and bones preachers dressed all in black, messing around with snakes? Yep. Women with shag carpet hair down to their butts, lugging sacks of babies? Too many to count. Hillbillies in leisure suits writhing on the floor, jabbering in tongues? A regular Saturday night event.

What she learned at Blood of Jesus was that you didn't have to buy in hook, line and sinker. A Pentecostal church is like any other. The members of the congregation are at different levels of faith. There are good Christians and bad, and fifty shades in between. Pam was a tweener, veering toward bad. I followed in her footsteps. It all boiled down to how you felt about sin—*sexual* sin, in particular. She taught me to believe in Jesus, but to make my own choices when it came to sex. That's how I've lived my life.

I certainly wasn't being "corrupted." If anyone got corrupted, it was *her*. She claimed to love Terry Stratton. She said she married him because he gave her the courage to cast away the wreckage of her past and go on. So as he rose into Frame's inner circle, she played along with the rhetoric about queer lovers in the White House, the hordes from hell, the need to man our battle stations in the war to reclaim America's godly heritage.

She didn't believe a word of that crap. Not then, not now, not ever. Neither did the man who became my step-dad. Terry Stratton was beyond all doubt the biggest phony who *ever* lived.

My secular friends did get one thing right: Mountain of Hope Church *was* a dangerous place. So many people really *were* there for the hate. And the biggest hater of all was Frame.

Coach Tim Frame

Three months after I baptized him in the Potomac, I created a job for him with my executive team—Director of Outreach. He moved out of the dormitory and into an apartment a mile down Longmeadow Road from our campus and sanctuary.

By that time he was eating right again, and he'd gained back twenty or so pounds, most of it muscle in his chest and quads and hams and calves. He'd worked himself into fearsome shape. I appointed him head coach of the Brigade because I was getting too old and flabby and occupied with other matters to keep pace with our young warriors. Two or three times a week, I joined them for a quick lift in the weight room and a couple of easy miles through town, that's all. Then after showers and a bite to eat, before we headed home to our families, he and I would get together in my office and dissect the state of the union.

In October, he brought me a videotape that Jerry Falwell had put together called *The Clinton Chronicles*. We watched it together and I felt my stomach churn.

"This guy may be the biggest creep who ever lived," I said. "He's an insult to the human race."

Brother Terence chuckled quietly to himself. "The thought of Slick Willie waddling around as America's First Runner makes my skin crawl."

"What can we do to bring him down?"

"Help Gingrich and the Republicans take back the House next year," he said. "And after they do, impeach the slimeball."

We went over to his room in the Resource Center. Covering one entire wall was a huge map of America, divided by House districts. He'd planted big red pushpins in a dozen districts in Maryland, West Virginia, Ohio, Indiana, Kentucky, and Tennessee.

"These are places where Mountain of Hope has a presence," he said. "Friends, contributors, history, passion. Where our involvement could help swing a tight race to the God-fearing candidate."

"Brilliant work, brother."

"This winter, I want to visit them all on my own," he said. "Get the lay of the land, meet the key people, and set up an appearance for you in the spring to issue our call to arms."

In January he hit the road, with fifty copies of *The Clinton Chronicles* to share among the faithful. In May, he and I and three warriors of the Brigade piled into my mini-van and revisited as a group, and I gave witness at a dozen sister churches. We struck a deep, raw nerve. People were *angry* that this man had become our president, and they wanted to do something about it. It was astonishing what happened then. As the '94 elections approached, attendance at our Sunday service tripled. We had to set up speakers in the parking lot to accommodate the swelling crowds. Soon, secular media was calling us a force to be reckoned with, and Ivy League professors were labeling us Christian fascists, committed to turning America into a theocracy.

It was all so exhilarating that I was almost able to suppress the fact that I hungered for Brother Terence. Had hungered for him from the moment I saw him strung out on the overlook at Harper's Ferry. I wanted him on all fours, naked and blindfolded on my mattress in the basement of the gym, arching his tight hot pink man pussy up to me like the obedient soldier he was.

Understand two things.

First, he rejected my advances. Brushed me aside whenever I laid a searching hand on his ass or thigh or balls.

Second, I was not a *totally* depraved human being. Depressed and conflicted, yes. Struggling every minute of every day to control my sexual addiction, yes. But I possessed a conscience. I didn't want my sickness to destroy everything so many good people were working so hard to achieve.

Dan O'Hanlon

Stratton played a key role in getting me elected to the House in '84. He was just as critical in bouncing me out ten years later.

And here's the bitterest pill of all—he teamed up with none other than Roberta Tate to defeat me. She was far removed from the loose-lipped wacko who ran against me for the open seat when Uncle Bob retired. She'd tacked expertly to the center and allied herself with the corporate chieftains of Cleveland, and in '90, she won her first term as Cuyahoga County Commissioner. She was foregoing a re-election bid to take a second shot at me—this time with a facelift, a tummy tuck, and the Jesus highlights considerably toned down.

Not that she'd abandoned her roots entirely. One of her top-level financial contributors was Terence Stratton, Director of Outreach, Mountain of Hope Church, Hagerstown, Maryland. Also on that list were Head Pastor Tim Frame and five board members and executive employees of the church.

The week after Labor Day, an aide brought me a printout of a profile he'd pulled off Mountain of Hope's primitive website: "Dan O'Hanlon is a career politician and machine man, an entrenched member of the Democrat party-hearty crowd in Washington . . . bosom buddies with dozens of special interest lobbyists . . . a supporter of same-sex marriage and other special rights for homosexuals . . . a dream Congressman for abortionists and bra burners."

I couldn't let it pass. Undoubtedly I *should* have. A long silence had descended on our contorted friendship. But nostalgia and curiosity and semi-righteous indignation overwhelmed me, and I called his office and left a voice mail. I had no idea if he'd get back to me. When he did, a couple of weeks later, he was standing right in front of my face in the lobby of the Ritz Carlton in Tower City. I'd just finished a forum with Roberta in the ballroom, before an audience of three hundred.

"Greetings, hombre," he said. "Great to see a familiar face in these parts."

"Hello, Terry."

"I'm in town for Roberta's rally tonight at Briarwood Church in Parma. I wanted to pop my head in down here and say hey to an old friend."

He looked damn good. The wasted, chubby puffiness that had blossomed during his years with L Street was gone, replaced by a muscular frame and ruddy, glowing skin. We eyed each other like a pair of veteran boxers, feeling each other out after a long absence from the ring. It'd been six years since our soiree at Gangplank Marina, the night before I bailed his ass out on the House vote to re-open the Milo Forbes probe. That was the last time we'd communicated.

"I'm saved, Dan. Born again. Let me say that right up front."

"You were an atheist in the old days," I said. "You said Jesus was a crutch for weak people who were afraid to die."

"I'm getting married next month to a fantastic woman," he said. "I've got a beautiful step-daughter, and something to live for. It's called love."

"If you're living for love, why are you whaling the crap out of me?"

"Don't take it personally."

"You don't really *believe* all that garbage, do you?"

"Just trying to take care of my new family," he said. "I'm not in D.C. anymore."

"The party-hearty crowd?"

"I actually have to *work* for a living now."

"*Bra-burners?*"

"If it makes you feel better, our efforts aren't helping Roberta much."

"Bullshit."

"Her numbers are not exactly boffo."

"I'm seeing the same numbers you are," I said. "This race is a dead heat."

"The built-in O'Hanlon edge," he said. "We know what she's up against."

Our interface seemed poised to evolve from civil to testy to downright combative. I came to my senses and left the premises. The last thing on Earth I needed was an eruption of my inner clurichaun in the lobby of the Ritz-Carlton.

On Election Day, Roberta beat me, 113,600—110,198. It was the closest House race in the country. At least I didn't go down alone. Speaker Foley and thirty-two other incumbent Ds lost, too, and the Republicans took control of the chamber after forty years of Democratic rule. I managed to rise from the ashes. On Thanksgiving, Al Gore, whom I'd known for many years, offered me the position of senior policy advisor in the Office of the Vice-President, and in January I started work in the Executive Office Building, across from the West Wing.

I figured Stratton might weasel a spot for himself somewhere on the Hill under the Gingrich regime. That didn't happen. He stayed on with the God Squad, bopping around all over the country, bellowing about Monica Lewinsky's stained blue dress, waving six-shooters in the air, making a complete idiot ass out of himself.

Andrea Bonn

Stratton was hanging out one night in Rudy Rojack's houseboat, on the bank of the Arkansas River in downtown Little Rock. Looking plastic and uptight in a suit and tie and shiny black shoes, sipping a can of Diet Mountain Dew beneath the John Wayne posters, the oil portraits of Reagan and Patton and Dole and Goldwater, the Don't Tread on Me flag, the hand grenades and machetes and all the other macho crap Rudy had hanging on his walls.

Rudy was the number one Clinton hater in the solar system, and he made sure you knew it from the moment you met him. Bulky, buff guy with a Marine brush cut. If you were drunk enough or stoned enough, and didn't look real hard, the man could pass for a well-weathered fifty. In fact, he was seventy-two, seventy-three, something like that.

He'd invited me over to meet his guest and recite my gallant tale about the Leader of the Free World. I'd been there before several times on the same mission. But the Whitewater trial was underway at the courthouse, the Clintons were under the microscope again, and a fresh batch of assorted sleaze was passing through town. Hillary got ridiculed when she said there was a vast right wing conspiracy working to destroy her husband. But I know exactly who she's talking about. At one time or another, I'd met most of them on Rudy's houseboat. And they all seemed to be acquainted with each other.

What was Stratton doing there? Christ, I don't know. What were *any* of them doing there? Maybe paying homage to the king of the Clinton-haters was some kind of rite of passage for all these dickheads. Stratton specifically might have been playing monkey move-up on the other bottom boys in the Mountain of Hope posse. Clawing up the food chain by delivering his commandant some *choice* intelligence picked up during his trip down South. At that point, Frame was preaching on the Lighthouse Network on cable TV. The ridiculous stunt with the cross was a couple of years down the road, but Mountain of Hope was starting to catch fire. All the big wigs—Falwell, Schlafly, Robertson, Ralph Reed—were streaming to Hagerstown to pray with this ornery old bat of a running coach who was going the distance every day for righteousness. So there were a lot of people around Frame elbowing each other in the ribs—deputies, counselors, advisers, aides. All angling for a slice of a pie that showed every sign of getting sweeter.

Anyway, here's my story. I saw Bill Clinton go down on a man. In May of '73, in a farmhouse on Summer Rain Road out by Lake Sequoyah, in the middle of a hellacious thunderstorm.

This was after Georgetown and Yale and the Rhodes scholarship at Oxford, when he was a wonder boy professor, teaching at U of A Law School and getting ready to run for Congress against Hammerschmidt. Hillary was up North, I'm not sure where, and he was trying to convince her to come down to Arkansas and marry him. In the meantime, he was getting his rocks off with the likes of me.

It was him and me and another guy in a threesome. On an old four poster bed that squeaked like a rusty seesaw and barely survived the workout we gave it. They traded off, went two rounds apiece as the water pounded the roof. Pumped shaft and seed into every orifice I had, boned me to exhaustion, and then some.

About three o'clock in the morning, the rain and thunder stopped. I woke up in bed alone. The door out to the living room was half-open. Through it, in the semi-darkness, I could make out Bubba, on his knees in front of the fireplace as the other guy stood over him, hands on hips. After the boning they'd laid on me, I was surprised either of them had any juice left.

Myself, I can take or leave giving blowjobs. Mostly leave. But Bubba looked and sounded fully engaged. He was inhaling—*for sure.*

When I stopped talking, Rudy spoke up in a hushed voice. "Mr. Stratton, I have always felt deep down in my heart and soul that Bill Clinton is a cock sucker." He raised his beer mug in my direction. "This young lady is confirming it for us."

Another example of Rudy's bullshit. I wasn't *confirming* anything. There was no proof—no video, photographs, audio, fingerprints, stained blue dress. And no one to corroborate my story except Bubba himself, because the guy he went down on died two years later.

No, he wasn't rubbed out by some Clintonista. He just got monumentally ripped one night and spun out his Harley into a pine tree on Dixieland Road in Apple Spur.

But my story is true. It happened. And I imagine as you're hearing this right now—up to *this* point in the story—you *probably* believe me. Most people seem to. But whenever I go on and drop my bombshell—

that the other guy in the threesome was every inch of six-foot-six and absolutely pitch black—a lot of people scoff. It sounds *too* incredible. They think I've *got* to be making it up.

Stratton was one of the ones who believed me. That was my gut instinct at that moment, and I haven't changed my mind. All I knew about him then was what I'd seen and heard on the houseboat that night. But knowing what I know about him today, after all the revelations, how in the name of God could he claim with a straight face to hate Clinton?

Take a hard look at the totality of the situation. If anybody has a right to hate Clinton, it's me, right? But I voted for the man every time he ran for governor and president, and I'd spread my legs for him again in a heartbeat to thank him for everything he's done to help keep abortion legal in America.

So maybe Stratton was faking it. Going through the motions for his own, gnarled, personal, fucked-up reasons. But what about Rudy and Coach Tim Frame and the rest of their ilk? Where does *their* hatred for the man really come from? Could somebody, somewhere, somehow kindly explain that to me?

Joellen Lee

Is Frame is talking to you? If he is, he's no doubt pontificating. I am not a homosexual. I am a heterosexual man having sex with another heterosexual man. I'm acting out father hunger. I suffer from lack of touch. I am wounded and want to embrace the healing power of holding and being held.

Self-serving gibberish. Mindless psycho-babble.

Gay or straight, straight or gay, what difference does it make? This isn't just about males. Frame was a full-service sexual predator. Men, boys, women, girls. For all we know, he may have been banging heifers and chimpanzees and black Labs, too. It was about him fulfilling his need for domination. He did not care about his partners. All he cared about was the sex act itself and sating his own lust, no matter who he hurt.

One August night, a couple of years after Pam and Terry got married, I was out in the garage, sorting through a bunch of junk to ship over to the high school for the big garage sale they had every year. Terry was on the road. Mom was out shopping for a new dining room set. I heard a car engine idling out front, and I looked up and saw Frame at the foot of the driveway, behind the wheel of his monstrously huge SUV. He was gaping at me like an imbecile. I turned my back on him and went into the garage. He lingered forever. I started down the driveway, shooting him the nastiest look I could muster. He smiled, gave me a thumbs up, and roared off.

When Mom got home, I told her about it. "What is he *doing?*"

"Making his rounds," she said. "Checking on his flock."

"It's *weird.*"

"He's been by to check on me many times."

"Does Terry know?"

"He tells me it's harmless," she said. "Next time, just give a thumbs up back. Nothing to get hot and bothered about."

"The hell it isn't."

"You could be thankful for a simple act of compassion."

"Simple act of compassion my ass."

"Tone down your language."

"A complete and total control freak is what he is."

That fall, at the start of senior year, I was alone in the kitchen of the chapelteria, the giant eating space adjacent to the main sanctuary. All of the other girls on crew had left, and I was mopping the floor and closing up after the Brigade team banquet. He dropped in to thank me for my efforts and proceeded to pin me up against a wall.

OK. Didn't exactly *pin* me. But he maneuvered his bulk so I couldn't take a step in any direction without shoving him in the stomach.

"Your dad tells me your workouts this fall have been *fabulous.*"

"He isn't my dad."

"I don't use the word step." He looked down into my face. "I'd like to run with you alone some time," he said.

"That isn't going to happen."

"Take you down to the overlook where I met your dad and destroy ourselves in a good kind of way on some hills together."

"Why did you drive by my house this summer?"

"I'm concerned about your well-being."

"I'm seventeen years old."

"Does it upset you?"

He pressed in on me and for an instant I felt his thick, bulging cock through his pants. I pushed away from him, left the mop and bucket in the middle of the floor, and ran home in a volcano of rage. Terry was still at work. Pam was in the living room, watching a taped replay of Frame on Lighthouse TV, preaching at some halfway house for heroin addicts in Baltimore.

"That bastard just pressed his cock into my crotch," I said.

She ignored me, keeping her eyes on the screen.

"Do you hear what I said?"

She still wouldn't look at me. "You say a lot of silly things," she said. "But that takes the cake."

I got angry then. The cavalier way she just blew me off, like I was making it up. This is my own *mother* talking.

"I don't like this place anymore," I said. "I've had it with you and Terry and Frame and everybody else. I'm going to Frostburg State next year and I'm getting the hell out of here."

"Mountain of Hope is offering you a full scholarship to run track and cross country."

"Has it ever occurred to you that I might be sick to death of running?"

"You'll have to pay your own way then."

"Terry makes a hundred and twenty grand a year," I said. "Enough for *you* to quit your job and sit in the bubble bath and eat bon-bons all day."

"Shut up, Joellen."

"But not enough to send me to college. Is that it?"

"You just said you didn't want anything to do with him."

I ran upstairs and slammed my bedroom door. A minute later, I slammed it again to make sure she'd heard. Then I opened it, stood on the landing, and called down to her through the stairwell.

"I found the Dexedrine and Valium in his gym bag," I said. "I thought the two of you were off that shit."

"You had absolutely *no* right to look in his gym bag."

"The body is a holy temple, right?"

"That was a despicable thing to do."

"Aren't you tired of living a lie? It takes so much *energy*."

"Lying has its place," she said. "If it keeps a family together and spares people lives of misery."

"Thank you thank you thank you for sparing me a life of misery!"

The tension eased up after that, because Terry was out of the house a lot. My senior year he was hardly ever home. He passed his coaching duties with the Brigade on to one of the college guys, and he and Frame started going everywhere together—Nashville to hobnob with country music stars, New Orleans to raise AIDS awareness, northern Virginia to scout sites for the eight-thousand seat mega-sanctuary Frame was itching to build with his humongous pile of money. Hagerstown wasn't big enough for him anymore. He wanted to move closer to Washington and thrust himself into the heart of the action.

In fact, the two of them were in D.C. the day Clinton wagged his finger at all the reporters: *I did not have sexual relations with that woman, Miss Lewinsky.*

Terry came home that night with startling news. "Coach Tim and I are going on a mission," he said. "We're going to carry a cross across America."

I looked at him like he was out of his gourd. "News flash: Jesus already carried the cross."

"Jesus carried the cross to Calvary," he said. "We're carrying it from Calvary to the world. Would you like to come with us?"

Mac McKenzie

The missus and I had driven up north from Sanibel in our scarlet and gray Cadillac for the funeral of my high school football coach. I ran into Bob Lamborn in the clubhouse bar at Scioto. He was hosting a party the next day for Kris and Terry's son Rhody, who'd just graduated from Kenyon, and Terry was in town for the occasion. Did we want to stop by the house on Club Road and say hello?

I felt no huge urge to reconnect. But the missus was game and she won me over. She'd always been intrigued by Terry.

Greeting us on the Lamborn patio the next afternoon, he was gracious enough, squeezing me on the shoulder, kissing the missus on the cheek, introducing us as dear, old friends to his young, supple blonde wife. But I didn't get the impression he was overjoyed to see me. I suppose I was a ghost from his long ago past that unsettled him, and I imagine he viewed a lot of the other guests that way, too. It was like he was on auto pilot that day, or some sort of tranquilizer, sliding robotically through the house and yard with his wife on his arm, playing a minor role in an event that belonged to his son and ex-wife and former in-laws.

I knew something about Cross America. I'd seen Frame hyping it on TV. In September, he and Terry and a gang of kids from Mountain of Hope were going to mount a sixty-pound wooden cross on a pair of rubber wheels and run it the length of the continent, arriving just before Election Day in front of the White House. They were taking to the highways to spread their message, what Frame called the holy trinity: Ban same-sex marriage nationwide. End all abortions forever. Impeach Bill Clinton.

Terry looked rapturous as he sipped a glass of lemonade on the patio and filled us in on the details. The cross had been built for them at some Pentecostal church in Glendale, outside of Los Angeles, and it was waiting there, with a flat-bed truck, a ten-passenger mini-bus, and an SUV. The plan was to surge out of L.A. to Barstow and follow a rough path along I-40 all the way to Nashville, veer north through Kentucky and Ohio, then east across the old National Road to Washington, where they'd end up with a rally on Clinton's front stoop on Pennsylvania Avenue.

I hadn't seen Terry in sixteen years, since the morning he flew into Columbus on Air Force One with Reagan and chatted with me in the statehouse rotunda. I can't claim to know a thing about his inner life. But the notion that his religious conversion was genuine struck me as preposterous. Frame was a vehicle for his own advancement. As he'd done with Jim Rhodes and Ronald Reagan and Raj Rao and Frankie Hodnett, he was attaching himself to a powerful man, exhibiting steadfast loyalty, and positioning himself for a comeback of one kind or another in Washington.

It wasn't a bad strategy. Spend the Clinton years in the field building new alliances, let your foul odor of notoriety inside the Beltway fade, work like a mule to get Bush the Younger into the White House in 2000, then head into town and claim your share of the spoils.

As we left, I caught one more glimpse of him in the front yard, posing for pictures with Kris and Rhody under a giant oak tree. It was a benign image of the man to take away. I figured that would almost certainly be the last time I ever saw him.

I had no idea we'd up end being beach bums together down in Sanibel—if only a few months.

Joellen Lee

People always call it a run. They didn't literally run twenty-seven hundred miles hauling a cross. That's an urban legend that's taken hold. Tons of people probably still believe that.

Cross America was really nothing but a mobile sermon, with a big, fancy novelty prop. They'd reach the outskirts of the town where they were going to stop, pull the cross off the flatbed, and parade it up the main street on foot behind the SUV while the guys in the bus and equipment van moved on to the rally point to set up and work the crowd for contributions. When the cross arrived, Frame delivered his spiel, mingled with the faithful, schmoozed whatever media was hard up enough for a story to show up. Then Frame and Terry and the others would jog the cross three or four miles to the other side of town, rendezvous with the truck and bus, repack the cross, and motor on.

My original plan was to be with them. Quit my locker room job at the gym, make Cross America my grand finale with running, and start at Frostburg State in January. Pam and Terry were so excited that I'd signed on, but I was faking my enthusiasm for their benefit. I didn't want to go. As the day of the launch came closer, I began to hate myself for being such a coward.

A week before we were all going to fly to Los Angeles, I said to Pam. "I'm not going."

"Of course you're going," she said. "You made a commitment to Terry and Coach and the rest of the team."

"I'm breaking it."

"Why?"

"A bunch of men with out-of-control egos is what they are. Displaying themselves to the world like a bunch of strippers. And all the time telling women how to live their lives. It sucks. I'm sorry."

"I didn't know you felt that way."

"I don't *say* it. That doesn't mean I don't feel it."

"Let's talk this out a little more," she said. "Pray on it, and not tell Terry just yet."

She did tell him, though. That very night. I wanted to slap her face. He took it badly. "You *have* to come with us," he said.

"You'll survive just fine without me."

"You're the heart and soul of the team."

"What I am is your token female."

"Run with us for three weeks," he said. "Then fly home. Or meet us in Nashville and do the second half."

"No thanks."

"Why are you changing your mind?" he said.

"There are two girls in the Brigade who happen to love each other very much," I said. "Did you know that?"

"No," he said. "I did not know that."

"Why shouldn't they be allowed to get married?"

"Because it's a sin," Pam said.

"When did you start believing that?"

"It isn't natural," Pam said.

"You taught me to make my own choices about sex."

Terry snorted at me. "This is the chance of a lifetime for you and you don't even realize it."

"A chance to do *what*?"

"Be part of one of the greatest events to ever happen in this country."

"All this hate you pretend to have on Clinton," I said. "It does nothing but make you look stupid." I started up the stairs to my room and stopped halfway up the stairwell. "As for saving the fetuses, it's my body—not yours. I'll save what I want to save. And no hick with a dick is going to have a damn thing to say about it."

Oh, my God. Talk about in your face. I don't know what made me blurt that out. Years of frustration welling up, I guess. Frame sent a message through Terry that he needed to pray with me, counsel me, enlighten me, *correct* me. I sent him a message back through the same channel that if he knew what was good for him, he'd better back off and accept the fact that he'd lost this one.

Message received. Feast never made any kind of move on me. Three days later, when the twelve-man contingent of the Brigade flew out of National Airport for the launch, I was on my way to Frostburg to enroll for fall quarter.

Mountain of Hope was crumbling. A lot of women were fed up with what was going on. They were comparing notes, hiring lawyers, complaining to the board. We weren't sure if anyone was going to care. We had no idea it would turn out the way it did. I mean, a bunch of females at some Holy Roller church, mouthing off about how they'd been hit on and hassled and abused by a creep and a bully masquerading as a man of God. How many times has the world heard that story?

But at the very least we could nick up Frame's flesh, make him bleed. He was so wrapped up in his war against queers and liberals he never saw it coming.

Coach Tim Frame

I want to tell you how magnificent the launch was, that when our motorcade left Desert Reign Assembly of God in Glendale that September morning, we were lifting Cross America together toward the light of a just, righteous God.

But the news from home wasn't good. In the midst of what should have been the most uplifting experience of my life, my wife was calling me every morning with news of yet another dried-up, titless hag betraying me.

My only solace turned out to be the delicious body of Brother Terence. Alone in a hot tub with me at a Holiday Inn in Texas after an exhausting day, he finally, at long last, surrendered. And once he did, he was eager for my firm touch. I forced nothing on him. He craved a strong master. By the time we'd navigated through the blistering heat and arrived in Arkansas, he was coming to my room every evening to offer himself up. As we got into the final leg of our journey, he'd bring along one of the energetic, young warriors for me to savor as well.

It was insane and horrible. The most self-destructive act I could have committed, short of putting a shotgun in my mouth and pulling the trigger.

I wasn't playing with fire. I was sprinting headlong into an inferno.

Jaye Janis

I was in Memphis for a getaway, feasting on filet mignon and bourbon with Cybill Shepherd, talking about hot men, dreaming up movie and series ideas. And I got the idea into my head that I should go see Terry.

The Cross America crew was setting out from a church in Memphis on the next segment of their trip east. I hadn't planned to be in the same city with him at the same time. It just worked out that way. But the fact that he was only seven miles away from Cybill's place seemed like a message from the gods of creativity to seek him out.

Crazy, I know. Even crazier when you think I was a wife by then, with a husband and four-year old son eager for me to get home to Santa Monica. But I was thirty-nine, and all of a sudden I was too old for Hollywood. The writing assignments were drying up, and my thirteen-year track record seemed to mean nothing. It was a perfect time to swing for the fences.

Cybill was all for it. "The point of your visit is to get outside the box," she said.

"I want to write something just for myself and *nobody* else," I said. "Totally different from anything I've ever done. I think this guy is it."

"What are you going to make him?"

"The man at the center of the action on Capitol Hill," I said. "The one everyone talks to, the one with head count, the one who remembers everything. He knows who's drunk or high, in or out of love, broke or rich, on the take or clean as a whistle. He knows other people's secrets. And he has many himself."

"Drop in on him cold tomorrow," she said.

"That's my plan."

"Catch him raw in his element," she said. "Don't give him a chance to tidy up. Or blow you off completely."

The next morning, I kissed Cybill goodbye, strapped on my emotional armor and headed out in my rental Corolla to Blood of Christ Church on Lagrange Road, by JFK Park. It was a neat, tidy red brick structure at the top of a long hill that sloped up from the street. In the parking lot, a couple of hundred people were assembled in front of a low, small stage, around a wooden cross maybe twelve feet high, mounted on rubber wheels. A bunch of young dudes in matching red, white, and blue sweat suits moved though the crowd, collecting donations in plastic buckets.

Inside, in the noisy fellowship hall, I spotted Terry standing behind an aluminum table brimming with Cross America merchandise: bumper stickers, CDs, cassettes, books, key chains, pens, T shirts. He was in the company outfit, too, looking frail and fatigued, as if the trip across the country was taking quite a physical toll on him.

That was the moment of truth. Approach or not approach? I hadn't driven out there to observe the man from a discreet distance. I went to his table, took a breath, and stuck my hand out.

"Terry Stratton?"

I've gotten a healthy number of dumb stares in my life. This one had to the dumbest of the dumb.

"Jaye Janis," I said. "Caesar's Palace. Summer of '89."

He shot me a nasty scowl, looked down, and rearranged some of the trinkets on the table. "What are you talking about?"

"Frankie Hodnett's New Year's Eve party," I said. "You and me and Dana Plato playing Trivial Pursuit."

He looked up at me again with vacant, bloodshot eyes and hugely dilated pupils. "Why don't you get out of here?"

"*Diff'rent Strokes*," I said. "The Just Say No Episode with Nancy Reagan. I was the chick on crew who kept mussing up your hair to make you look like a nerd."

It all came back to him then. Or for some reason he decided to pretend that it had. He bounced out from behind the table and awkwardly shook my hand. Underneath his shirt, I could see his ribs and the thinness of his torso.

"Where are you headed today?" I asked.

"Let me check that for you." He cupped his hands to his mouth and yelled into the crowd to one of the sweat suit guys. "Where are we headed today?"

"I just told you," the guy yelled back.

"Tell me again."

"Why don't you listen the first time?"

"Don't be a jerk."

"Up Route 70 through Brownsville and Milan."

"Thank you!"

"We'll be in Nashville tomorrow night."

"So sorry to bother you!"

He turned around and gave me a totally creepy smile. "That's where we're headed. Want to ride along?"

For one long bittersweet moment, I was tempted. I was still clinging to the idea that I could flip on my tape recorder and get him to spill out the latest sordid chapters of his life to me. There seemed to be plenty to spill: his ethics conviction and the sorry demise of The L Street

Team, the thousands of dollars he'd supposedly embezzled from Dana, Georgy Greco's gruesome suicide, Tim Frame's incendiary sermons on Lighthouse TV.

But that was a writer's delusion. Because the Terry Stratton I'd known was gone now, dissolved in a haze of drug addiction. I'd worked in the Industry for fifteen years, I was well-acquainted with drug culture, and there was no doubt in my mind that I was staring at a speed freak, a man exhibiting virtually all of the visible symptoms of Dexedrine dependence: exhaustion, memory loss, agitation, aggression, frailness, disorientation.

Our tryst at Caesar's Palace had been a once-in-a-lifetime experience. There would be no sequel.

"No, I don't," I said. "I'm flying home this afternoon."

The people in the hall started streaming outside. Terry stayed behind to close up the table, and I followed them. In the parking lot, Frame was up on the stage, waving out at the crowd pressing in on him. A couple of minutes later, Terry and the sweat suit guys lined up behind him, and the pastor of the church introduced Frame.

"I made a deal with Bill Clinton," Frame said. "I'm going to meet him in front of the White House next month, and one of us is going to get out of town."

From a waist holster beneath his sweat pants, he pulled out some kind of handgun and waved it in the air. I had idea if it was real or not. "It's high noon!" he yelled.

Behind me, a woman screamed: "Shoot him, coach!" Down front, an old man squealed: "Get over there to Washington right now and blow the piece of shit away!"

The crowd whooped and applauded, then broke into a spontaneous version of "Onward Christian Soldiers." On the stage, Frame raised his arms to the heavens, and Terry and the rest of the gang exchanged high fives. The cops rimming the crowd looked quite amused, and as the song went on, the TV cameras zeroed in on the cross.

I'd seen enough. The hatefulness of the scene was repulsive. There's a time to get outside the box, and a time to climb back in. I didn't even bid farewell to Terry. I'm not sure he would have remembered me from fifteen minutes before.

I drove to the airport and turned in my Corolla. As I waited to board my flight, I wrote a thousand-word biography of a character named

Jimmy Blaine in pencil on a legal pad. On the plane, I roughed out my first Jimmy Blaine script. I finished it the next week at home, and called it "Kingmaker."

Five years later, after being rejected by twenty producers, it became the pilot episode for *Hired Gun*.

Dan O'Hanlon

Three days before the mid-term elections, Stratton and his insane clown posse arrived in Lafayette Square across from the White House. The authorities would not give them a permit to assemble on a weekday, and they settled for Saturday, which was fitting because it was Halloween. I was in my office in the Executive Office Building, and at noon I crossed Pennsylvania Avenue, stood at the edge of the action, and took in the spectacle.

There was a handful of TV cameras rolling, giving the thing an air of importance. Five or six hundred Mountain of Hope people were there to make noise. They formed a ring of bodies around the upright cross. In the midst of it all, I caught glimpses of Stratton, decked out in a red, white and blue sweat suit, whooping, clapping his hands, pumping his fist in the air.

From a platform in front of the statue of Andrew Jackson on his horse, Feast screamed into a microphone. The mob wailed. A big, fat guy mounted a blue dress on the tip of an aluminum pole and waved it in the air.

The House was going to impeach Clinton in December. The Senate was going to come back to town after the New Year, put him on trial with all kinds of silly pomp and circumstance, and acquit him. The Republicans had nowhere near the sixty-seven votes they needed to boot the man out of office. Nothing this pitiful gang of degenerates or anyone else could do was going to change that.

Stratton was all in his glory for a couple of weeks. George W. Bush offered the opening prayer at the groundbreaking for Mountain of Hope's new sanctuary out in Springfield. Then Stratton went back to the hinterlands to raise money for W.'s 2000 presidential run. A few months later, I left my post in Gore's policy office and joined his campaign staff.

Stratton and I were on a collision course—heading for our final showdown at the Tallahassee corral.

Joellen Lee

Spring quarter of freshman year, this lawyer came to my dorm at Frostburg, left her card in my mailbox with a note, telling me to call her when I was ready to talk about Frame. I told Pam, and she warned me to keep my mouth shut.

As much as I despised the bastard, I couldn't go through with it. Pam had so much to lose. Because if I lashed out at Frame, I lashed out at Terry. And she'd given over her life to Terry.

I spent the summer in Frostburg working as a lifeguard at the city pool and didn't go back to Hagerstown until December. All was relatively cool until a couple of days before Christmas. Mom was shopping and Terry was home, off the road for a couple of weeks, going stir crazy. He was slumped in a recliner in the living room in front of the tube, staring at CNN news, shivering, grinding his teeth, coming off of his Valium. A segment came on about Frame donating two hundred thousand bucks to a shelter for abused women in Prince George's County. He could afford it. With the new sanctuary going up in Springfield, Mountain of Hope was raking in half a million bucks a month from the happy idiots in Lighthouse TV Land. I lingered behind the recliner and felt a wave of disgust as Frame embraced a sobbing black girl on the screen.

Terry jerked his head around and zinged me with this smug, arrogant grin. His eyes were all glassy and glazed over, and his speech was slurred. "Imagine that."

"Imagine what?"

"Coach Tim actually doing some good in the world," he said. "He just *might* not be the monster you think he is."

"He's a monster all right, and I'm not the only one who thinks that. Fifteen people have signed affidavits against him. There'll be more."

"Are you going to be one of them?"

"I haven't decided yet."

He turned back to the TV. "If you know what's good for you, you damn well better not be."

"I really don't like the tone of that comment."

He sprang up, pulled a ceramic bowl off the coffee table, and hurled it against the wall behind the TV. It exploded into dozens of pieces. Without taking my eyes off him, I backed slowly up the stairs. He hopped up onto the bottom landing and stared up at me with a look of hatred I'd never seen before.

"I pulled you and your mother out of the garbage can," he said.

"She was sober before she met you."

"Gave you the best life you'll ever have."

"Her own job, her own place, her own money."

"A far better life than a piece of scumbag trash like you deserves."

"You're an asshole, Terry."

"Who do you think you're talking to?"

"A creep faking his entire life, that's who."

"If you don't like it here, go leech off your dad."

"Maybe I will."

"Let him pay your fucking tuition bills."

His gym bag was on a table in the upstairs hall, where he couldn't see it. Before he could grasp what I was doing, I stepped out of his view, unzipped the side pocket where he kept his stash of Dex and Valium, and wrapped a dozen or so pills in my clenched fist.

He bounded up the stairwell. "What the hell are you doing?"

I turned around and threw the pills into his face. "Hypocrite!"

He came at me fast, and before I could get my arms up he slapped me hard across the mouth with his open palm. I balled my fist and smacked him in the eye. He exploded with rage, slammed me onto the floor and straddled me with his hard, bony thighs.

"I'm trying to help you!" he screamed into my face.

"Let me up!"

"All I've ever done from the day I met you is try to help you!"

"I can't breathe!"

He spit hard in my face. His saliva mixed with my tears and rolled down my cheeks to the floor. Then he climbed off me.

I left then, didn't even wait for Pam to get home. Packed up in less than an hour and drove the Chevette my dad had given me for high school graduation to Roanoke and spent the rest of break with him. Pam kept calling, begging me to come home and forgive and start over fresh with Terry. But I wouldn't do it.

When I got back to school in January, I called that lawyer who'd left a note in my box. I went to her office in Hagerstown, gave my statement about the night with Frame in the kitchen of the chapelteria, and signed it. Then I called Pam and told her what I'd done.

"You just made the worst mistake of your life." She slammed the phone down in my ear.

We didn't communicate for almost a year after that. Call it the year from hell and say no more. Neither of us would back down and make the first move. Finally, in November, two weeks after the election, the phone in my dorm room rang around midnight. It was her.

And as I lay on my bed in the darkness and said nothing, the whole sickening tale came pouring out of her. She and Terry were split. A month after our fight, he moved out of the house and into the guest lodge on campus. That's where he stayed when he came in off the road. In July, she filed for divorce.

"You're better off without him," I said.

"He and Frame are losing their minds," she said. "They're heading to Palm Beach County in Florida right now. Trying to stop Gore's recount of the ballots."

"Enough about those bastards," I said. "I'd like to have you back in my life. Is that possible?"

"I hope so," she said. "That's what I want, too."

I missed her so badly I ached. But it wasn't time yet. She needed to break completely free from Terry. And I needed to see the lawsuit through to the end.

Dan O'Hanlon

In Tallahassee, I was holed up in the Gore command post in the Governor's Inn on South Adams Street.

We were pressuring the Florida Supreme Court to order a recount of all disputed ballots in all counties. Squadrons of D and R lawyers were running loose in the streets, doing battle with each other like street gangs. Instead of flashing switchblades, we brandished briefcases and cell phones. Late on Friday afternoon, December 8th, the court announced a four-three party-line decision that gave us what we asked for. You could almost hear the screams of rage echoing across town from the Bush camp.

Stratton showed up on the tube early the next morning, on a hill outside the Leon County Public Library on Park Avenue, where the disputed ballots were being stored. A bunch of right-wing crazies had set up an encampment there, cordoned off by yellow crime scene tape, and I could clearly make him out in the middle of it, decked out in the same sweat suit number he'd worn on Lafayette Square. Next to him was Frame, wearing the same garb, making a live statement in front of a CNN camera.

"My brothers and I caravanned in from Palm Beach last night because this judicial aggression cannot stand," he said. "If Gore is allowed to prevail, we will no longer live in a country with a rule of law. What his storm troopers are doing here should scare the daylights out of everyone in America."

A few hours later, I slipped out of the command post and headed over there. In a parking lot half a block from the library I spotted Stratton, huddled around the open trunk of an SUV, sipping coffee with five or six other men. Frame was one of them. Someone recognized me as I approached.

"Traitor!"

"Queer loving faggot Democrat bitch!"

"Baby killer!"

Some jerk across the lot started screaming at me through a bullhorn. "O'Hanlon, we're not going to let cockroaches like *you* and the *media* steal this election. You're shit out of luck!"

I thought Stratton might show some courtesy to an old pal and ask the apes to back off. But he looked right through me, like he didn't know who I was.

"It's Dan, Terry."

"I don't know anybody named Dan."

"Dan O'Hanlon."

"I never have."

The face that had always been open and kind was contorted with rage. A vein throbbed like a worm on his temple. The vacant eyes revealed nothing.

"What do you want?" he said.

"I want you to go home," I said. "Pack up your ignorance and leave and go back to where you came from. Your day is done."

Frame reached into the trunk of the SUV. He pulled a semiautomatic rifle out of a black case and pointed it at me from ten feet. He unlocked the chamber and it made a loud pop.

"Move on," he said. "You're not welcome here."

Hands on hips, Stratton stared at me in silent contempt. I backed down the hill and walked away.

That was it. Our sad, ignoble, pathetic last encounter.

Three nights later the U.S. Supreme Court put a stop to the recount. Gore conceded, and Bush and his henchmen marched into Washington over our bruised and battered bodies. We never found out who really won that election, and we never will.

I lost so much that day. It hurt worse than getting bounced out of the House by Roberta Tate. I was in line for a major job in the White House. Some people were even pushing me for chief of staff. It would have been an eerie, ironic delight to tread the same turf Stratton had, two decades before me.

At least I was right about him. His day *was* done. He'd made a deal with Jesus, and Jesus had ripped him off blind.

Coach Tim Frame

My enemies say I went to Florida not to save America from Gore, but to run away and hide. My enemies are wrong. By that time there was no place to hide. I had trusted sources inside law enforcement who were telling me everything they knew.

Two men and two women who'd been minors at the time of their encounters with me had given affidavits to secular authorities. I was under investigation in Virginia and Maryland. Indictments were imminent. It was the prospect of facing justice on those charges of sodomy and assault and kidnapping that terrified me. Not the civil harassment suits from Brother Terence's bitch of a daughter and the rest of the whores. I wept a river of tears, begged the Lord for forgiveness, prayed for the strength to face the coming ordeal.

I was numb to it all by the time the election arrived. The struggle for righteousness in Florida would be my last hurrah. I wouldn't be ascending to the right hand of power. Neither would Brother Terence, and that was unbearably sad. Here was a man who'd faced down and conquered his demons by himself, and turned his life around. He'd vowed to give up unholy sex when he married Pamela, and he was upholding that vow until I broke down his resistance to satisfy my own sick urges.

I let him down. I let so many people down. That's what I most regret. We did so much good at Mountain of Hope, and all of it is obscured now because of my crimes.

You're not a failure if you fall. You're a failure if you don't get up. So I'm going to get up every day, walk to the wall at the end of my cell, look out my window at the yard and fence and guard tower, and thank the Lord for everything I have.

Joellen Lee

Why Frame insisted on going to trial at all is something I'll never understand. If he'd plea bargained instead of spending four days on the witness stand displaying his fucked-up self to the universe, he might be doing fifteen years now instead of the thirty the judge gave him. He might have given himself a shot at getting out of jail before he died.

And he might have saved Mountain of Hope. Instead, the church disintegrated. Members quit in droves, and after Lighthouse TV pulled the plug, contributions dried up. They'd borrowed big bucks to build the new sanctuary, and when they couldn't come up with the jack to make the loan payments, construction came to a dead halt. If you cruised down the Beltway that summer, you could see this enormous slab of concrete where they'd laid the foundation. It sat there like that for years until they turned it into a Home Depot.

What did I get? Seventy-five grand tax-free, which is almost exactly what my lawyer said I'd get. As much as anybody else who got felt up or shabbed in the crotch or shoved up against a wall. The really big money went to the victims he'd actually pushed his dick into. My lawyer took twenty-five for her fee and another six as payback for the off-campus apartment she'd provided to me rent free until the case was settled. I used the forty-four I had left to pay for my last two years at Frostburg and get into a condo in Frederick after I got my physical therapy degree and a job at Harley Hospital.

Terry slid through under the radar, because there were bigger creeps at Mountain of Hope who got flushed out. The financial officer was embezzling gobs of cash to cover massive gambling debts. The head lawyer was an Internet porn addict with five thousand images stored on his office computer. And the human resources chief turned out to be a good old-fashioned white racist who'd made a practice of derailing black, Asian and Hispanic job applicants. Terry got a little pile of money together, no doubt pilfered from some account or other, and flew the coop to Florida. As big a prick as he was, he did find the decency to lay fifty grand on Pam. No doubt to keep her quiet and make up for the hell of being married to him for six years. She moved into D.C., got a paralegal job, and a brand new life.

She got me, too. I finally found the strength to stop obsessing about my messed-up childhood. We're both sober, solvent adults now, and we're good friends.

As for those two girls in the Brigade who happened to love each other very much, one of them was me. We're in Vermont now, we're married, and I'm going to make Pam a grandmother next year. That's the greatest gift a mother—and a daughter—could ever hope for.

Seven / Sanibel Island 2001

Mac McKenzie

 He sold sunglasses at the tip of the island, on Lighthouse Point, perched on a stool under a red, white and blue umbrella.
 He'd flash his smile at everybody who came by. It was still one hell of a smile, and it was about all he had left. The eyes looked glassy and bewildered, the skin was mottled and pock-marked, and his body was wasting away to nothing. He moved around gingerly, often with a wince and always with a trace of a limp. Some of it was simply age. He was into his fifties by then. But I imagine Cross America had ravaged his knees.
 One morning on the beach there was another man with him at his cart, a squat, darkish guy in his thirties or forties. The missus whispered to me 'looks like Terry brought his boyfriend today.' I said 'go get your head examined,' and she said 'look harder, they're making eyes at each other like a couple of teenagers.'
 I looked harder. Damned if she wasn't right.
 The young, blonde wife he'd brought with him to his son's graduation party seemed to be out of the picture. His Jesus phase appeared to be over. But I didn't pry. In Florida, the rules are different. You don't inquire into people's dark chapters. You wait for them to broach the subject, and if they don't, you carry on blissfully ignorant of how they've mangled their lives. Unless, of course, you hear about it from someone else.
 I didn't hear much about Terry from *anybody*, including him. All he told me about being on Sanibel was that Jean Polk and her husband were over in Fort Myers, and he wanted to be close to her. I found out

from a mutual acquaintance that he lived alone above a little hole-in-the-wall gym on Rabbit Road, in a studio apartment that probably rented for twelve hundred a month. And he confessed to me that he made two hundred bucks a week selling sunglasses. Where the rest of his money came from, I have no idea. He may have been mooching off his mother, or burning through a pile of cash he had stashed away. What you hear today is that he was toiling in the drug trade, and selling sex to men.

I can hardly believe the last thing. Terry Stratton, a homosexual hustler? That strikes me as somebody's idea of a sick joke. He talked, looked and behaved as straight as any man I ever knew.

But who am I to say? I'm an old fart, eighty years old sitting here shooting the breeze with you today. The sexual revolution came after my time. It's something my kids and grandkids are into. I wouldn't know gay from Doris Day in a toupee.

It was odd, seeing him again after twenty years. When we crossed paths during happy hour at the Jacaranda two or three times a month, he gave the impression that he was through with big-time politics, that he was content to sell sunglasses on the beach for the rest of his days. That was hard to swallow. I don't think he was completely out of the woods with the Mountain of Hope situation. This was only four or five months after the scandal erupted, and there was still some chance he might be implicated. If he skated through that cleanly—or even if he didn't—he must have been angling to land *somewhere*.

I must say on that last night at the Jacaranda, the night before he died, he seemed to be at peace with himself. Any demons he may have been wrestling with looked to be well under the surface. But what is a *look*?

"I want to run for Sanibel city council next year," he said.

"My goodness. What a surprise."

"I need a campaign manager. Are you interested?"

"What do you stand for?"

"Truth, justice and the American way."

We had a chuckle and toasted truth, justice and the American way. I told him I'd ponder his offer and get back to him in a couple of days.

Reena Diamond

It was gusty from the get-go that morning, but the situation didn't get outrageous until seven or seven-thirty, about an hour after I started work. I'm day shift manager at the 7-Eleven on Periwinkle, across from Bailey's.

The burst exploded without warning and the freakiest thing is, it was *just* wind. I never felt a single drop of rain.

He was jogging slow up the bike path, toward the store. A gaunt, rawboned guy in a red singlet and baggy gray shorts. The wind was knocking him around real good. Bent low over the path out ahead of him was this tall sabal palm that looked like it might come down any second. It seemed like he was going to get by it safely, but then the trunk snapped ten feet from the base, and he *wasn't* by, and I'm like sweet Jesus Christ in heaven, the thing is going to land right on *top* of the man.

He hit the pavement like a sack of concrete. People ran into the store screaming 'call 9-1-1, call 9-1-1.' I went out to the parking lot. The wind threw me onto the hood of a Mustang. In the road, a bunch of kids were milling around—like fools, considering the danger they were in. Sand and trash was flying everywhere. Down the way, four more trees were lying across the bike path and Periwinkle. A couple of cars were smashed in.

He was right there in front of us, maybe the length of a bowling alley away. I wouldn't go an inch closer. I didn't have the guts. I knew he was dead. The trunk had landed square on his neck and head. He was splayed out on his back, motionless, and there was mucky pink and gray gunk—not just blood—oozing out the side of his head. This Hispanic dude ran down there and knelt over the body. He made the sign of the cross, took off his windbreaker and covered the head as best he could, kind of wrapped the whole mess up.

That was such a humane gesture, giving up his windbreaker to shield the head from all the gawkers. If I ever get my brains smashed in by a falling tree I hope someone does that for me.

What a God-awful way to die. Completely and totally unfair. They said later the tree was dry, but otherwise healthy. There was no rot, no disease. The gust was that strong—one hundred miles an hour is what we kept hearing.

Nobody died in any of the cars that got smashed, or anywhere else on the island. He was the only one. That was the first corpse I ever saw. I don't care to ever see another one.

Ramsay Stratton Karnes

His body was at a funeral home in Fort Myers. Jim and I left the airport, picked up Jean and Ron in our rental car, and drove there. This was Wednesday morning, August 1st, twenty-four hours after the accident.

I'd already decided that I was going to look at him. If I didn't, I'd be haunted for the rest of my life by what I missed. If I did, I'd be haunted by what I saw. Choice two seemed better, I'm not sure exactly why. Jean felt the same way.

A young guy with a crew cut took all of us into a back room. The body was lying under a sheet, face up on a metal table, with bare feet hanging out the bottom. The guy pulled the sheet down to the waist. His eyes were closed. The neck was crushed almost flat, and the left side of his head was caved in. There was a big, tan gauze wrapping over it, but you could see that a huge chunk of the brain was gone.

My heart stopped, my knees buckled, and if my rock of a man hadn't been there to catch me I would have hit the floor. I was very happy at that moment to be a married woman.

I rallied. I had to. Jean was grieving too hard to function, Ron was taking care of her, and Gale was lying in a hospice in Atlanta, a month away from dying of lung cancer. That afternoon Jim and I drove out to Terry's apartment on Sanibel. The manager of the gym let us inside. I was expecting it to look like his bedroom on Warren Street—clean, spare, neat as a pin. But it was a godawful mess—dirty clothes scattered all over the floor, food-stained dishes stacked in the sink, dozens of junk food cartons stashed in the plastic trash can. In the stinky, mildewed bathroom, the shower stall was jammed with trash and cartons of sunglasses. I had half a mind to fumigate the place and burn the sheets.

He'd laid a wooden door over two sawhorses to use as a desk. On it, in a plastic crate full of books and papers, we found a simple, two-page handwritten will, dated April 10th, 2001, leaving all of his meager assets to the Sanibel Public Library. There was also a virtually complete draft of an obituary laid out on a yellow legal pad. Both of those documents spooked me. They made me think that maybe he'd been seriously ill, anticipating death, or even planning to commit suicide.

What spooked me more was that he'd named his birth parents in the obituary. At some point, he'd found them, and he never told me. He didn't tell Jean, either. Yes, he was a secretive man, and we hadn't been close for decades. But I was his sister. I'm adopted, too, and I was the one who'd urged him to pursue them in the first place. And he never uttered a word to me to about it.

God, that hurt.

I took some small things I could haul home easily on the plane. His class ring from high school, a white running singlet, and a photograph of him on the White House lawn with Dan O'Hanlon, Raj Rao, and Georgy Greco. He looked fabulous—robust, happy, confident, at the pinnacle of life. They all did. Now, except for Dan, they were all dead.

Terry wrote in his will that he wanted to be cremated. I went to the funeral home the next morning to sign the consent form. After I did, I went to the back room again, by myself. The door was locked. The guy with the crew cut was out on the loading dock, smoking a cigarette. He unlocked the door for me, waved me inside, and left me alone.

The body was still there, under the sheet. I pulled it down and kissed him on the forehead.

"Goodbye, my brother. I'll see you in the next world, wherever that may be."

Fort Myers News-Press
August 2nd, 2001

Terence Charles "Terry" Stratton, age 53, unexpectedly on Sanibel Island July 31st, a victim of Mother Nature's random fury.

Preceded in death by father Wyatt St. George, who died February 12th, 1948, the day of Terry's birth. Survived by mother Carol Archer; adoptive mother Jean Polk and husband Ron; adoptive father Gale Stratton and wife Tanny; sister Ramsay Karnes, husband Jim and their daughter Erin.

Also survived by former wife Kris, their daughter Carol and son Rhodes Reagan; former wife Pamela and her daughter Joellen.

Graduate of Marietta High School, Class of 1966; and The Ohio State University, Class of 1970. Aide, Ohio House of Representatives (1969-1973); Executive Assistant to Governor James Rhodes (1975-1980); Director, Ohio for Reagan Campaign (1980); Office of Communication, The White House (1981-1983), Partner and Consultant, The L Street Team, Washington, D.C. (1984-1992); Director of Outreach, Mountain of Hope Church, Hagerstown, MD (1994-2000).

Runner of the Year, Ohio Valley Striders, 1965; Cross Country Coach, Mountain of Hope Brigade (1993-1995); Team Member, Cross America (1998), 'Running for the Glory of God.'

A Celebration of Life Service will be held at the Sanibel Lighthouse Beach, Point Ybel, August 4th, 9 A.M. Contributions to the charity of your choice. Arrangements by Horizon Funeral Home, Fort Myers.

Vonda Vance

The *Washington Post* ran an AP story on Terry's death, and picked up the obituary from the Fort Myers newspaper. When I saw Wyatt St. George named as Terry's father, with February 12th, 1948 as his death date, my heart about jumped out of my throat.

The name was so distinctive. I knew instantly it was the same Wyatt St. George. Mrs. R.'s tragic, departed lover who'd smashed into a Joshua tree in Death Valley half a century ago, the man she and Terry were communing with on the spirit board in her office, the subject of the vicious argument between her and the president that I'd overheard in the White House the morning before Terry resigned.

I called Mike in Bethesda. I would have called Mrs. R., but she'd cut me out of her life. I'd been too loose-lipped in an interview I gave to NBC News in '94, when she and the president announced to the world that he had Alzheimer's disease. She wasn't talking to Mike anymore, either. It was clear that she wouldn't be providing any more details regarding Terry to either of us.

I asked Mike, "Did Terry ever tell you he was adopted?"

"No."

"Nor me. Do you think he ever told Mrs. R.?"

"I don't have any idea."

"Could he possibly have known at the time he was with Mrs. R. in the White House that he was Wyatt St. George's son?"

"The only people who can tell us that are him—and her."

Dragging her into it seemed like a bad idea. Mike agreed. It was all too long ago, too painful, too personal. Maybe she knew Terry's full identity then, maybe not. Did she know *now*? Had Terry revealed the fact to her some time after she'd left the White House? Or had she discovered the connection by reading Terry's obituary? I couldn't be absolutely sure that she was even aware of his death.

I clipped the story and obit from the *Post*, put them in an envelope and addressed it to Mrs. R. out in Bel Air. It sat on my desk for a day, a week, a month before I finally dropped it in the mailbox.

I never heard a word back from her.

Jaye Janis

Nine months after Terry died, I did another rewrite of the "Kingmaker" script I'd first drafted on the flight home from Memphis four years earlier. I showed it to Lizzy Cherry. She was split from Frankie Hodnett by then, out of porn entirely, just starting her own production company. We'd kept in touch after the partying years were over, and she'd long been a fan of my work.

"This is the cleanest script I've read in ages," she said. "We could shoot it tomorrow, right off the page. And you nailed Frankie perfectly. Right down to the dandruff flecks on his shoulders."

I showed her the ten episodes I'd outlined, and the dossier I'd compiled on Terry, and recounted the night I'd spent with him at Caesar's Palace.

"I have a confession to make," Lizzy said. "I've spent the night with him myself."

"When?"

"Two nights before Charles and Diana got married in London," she said. "I was going steady with Frankie at the time."

"But Terry waltzed in and swept you off your feet."

"Just like the tornado in *The Wizard of Oz.*"

So we two former lovers of Terry Stratton honed our pitch and got a meeting with HBO. They didn't love the idea. *K Street* had just tanked after ten episodes, and they were wary of doing another show about Washington. But they didn't say no. *Sex and the City* and *Six Feet Under* were coming to an end, and they were searching for a new hit.

The project hibernated for a couple of years, and in the spring of '04, they asked for a pilot. We shot "Kingmaker," and two months later they ordered a full season. The first episode of *Hired Gun* aired in October, three weeks before the Bush-Kerry election.

Six years and eighty episodes later, we're still on the air. Jimmy continues to revel in the seamy side of life, but it's not a show about Washington anymore. He's a globe-hopping rogue now, a cohort of kings, criminals, and celebrities on seven continents. Yes, he's even been to Antarctica. I'm sorry Terry's not alive to see it, because I think he would be amazed by what he's turned into.

First, Terry Stratton reinvented himself.

Then I reinvented him.

the end

Benjamin A. Cohen

Will I Ever See Another Butterfly?

Chicago 2012

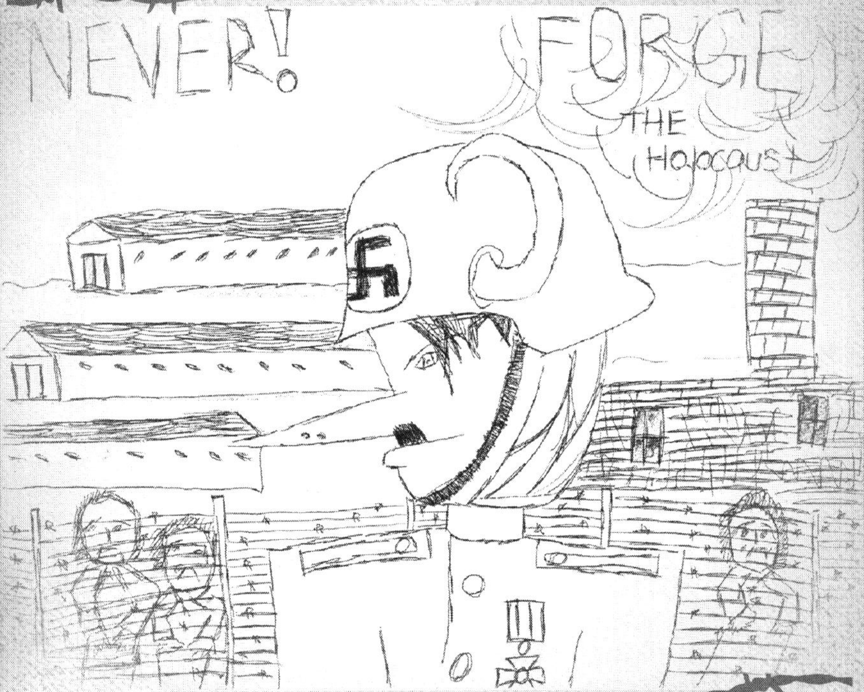
NEVER!
THE
Holocaust

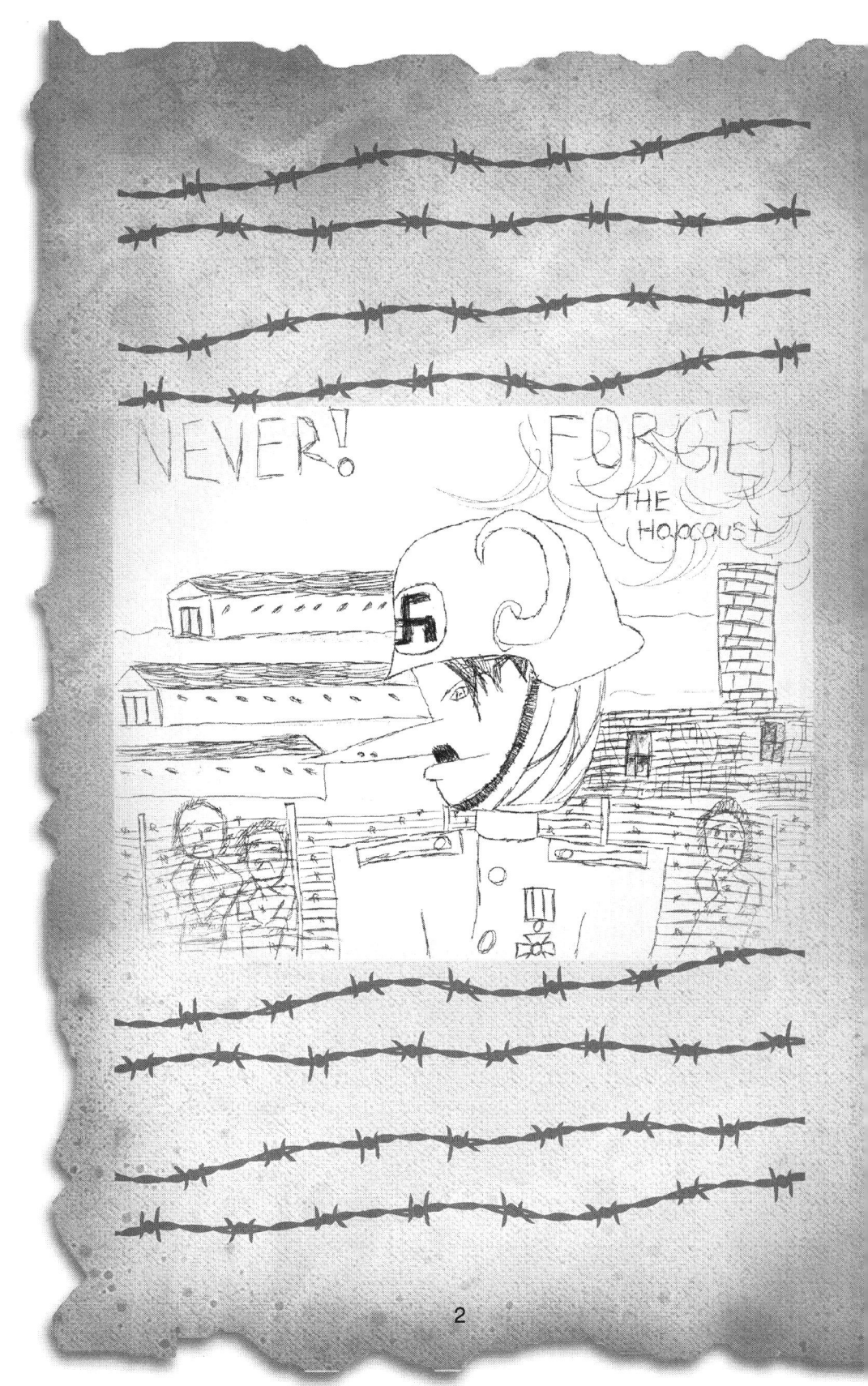

To all of the innocent victims who did not have a chance to start their lives.

INTRODUCTION

In 1939 Czechoslovakia was taken over by the Nazis. Now this beautiful country was under the command of the Nazi party. The new Governor of Czechoslovakia was a Nazi named Reinhard Heydrich. On May 23, 1939, Prague was occupied.

Nazis broke into homes and forced the men to part with their wives and children. Then they were taken to the Horak farm and shot.

Meanwhile, the women were sent to Dachau labor camp. Hundreds of girls and boys were herded into boxcars for a five-day train ride to Terezin concentration camp.

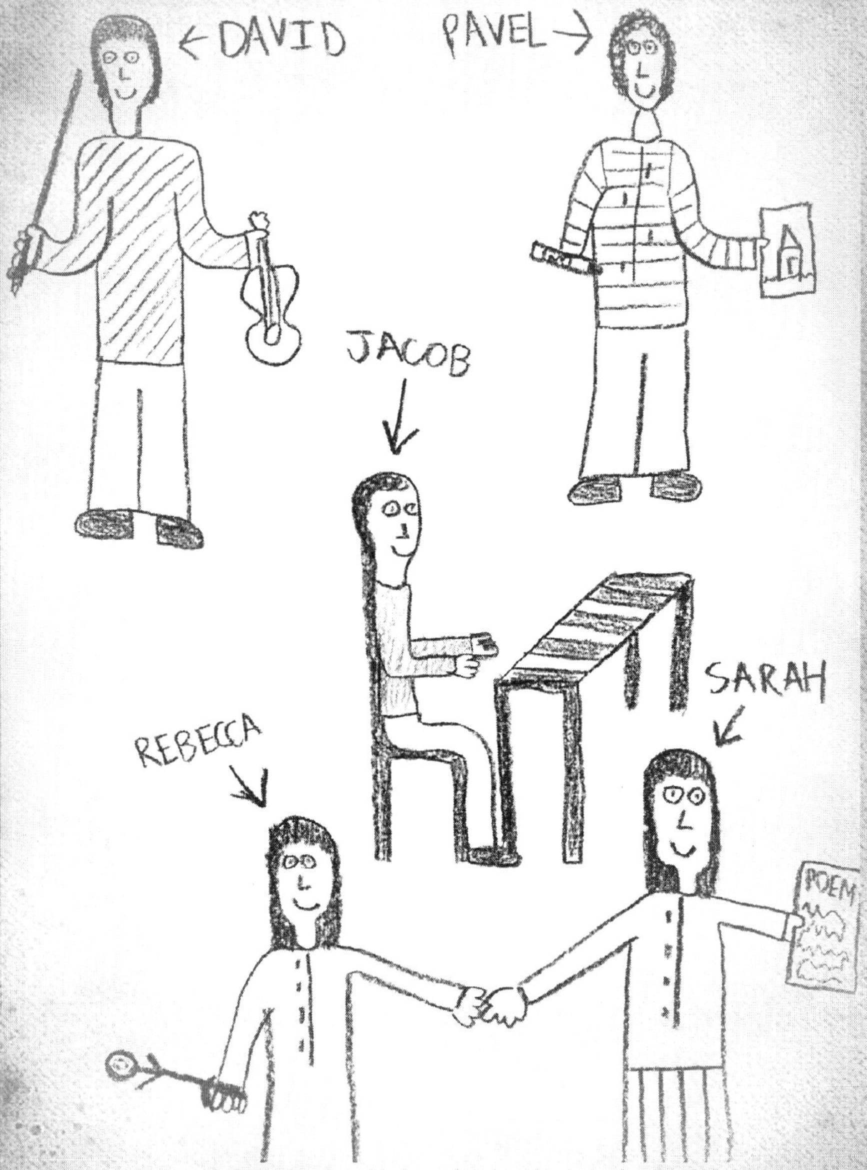
DAVID
PAVEL
JACOB
SARAH
REBECCA
POEM

CHARACTERS

David is twelve years old, born in Prague. The violin is his favorite musical instrument. He is a good listener and writer. Also, he has an eye for details.

Pavel is an eleven-year-old who grew up in a small town eight kilometers from Prague called "Roztoky". Later he moved to Prague. He is an expert at drawing and enjoys playing with other children.

Jacob is ten years old, and comes from a suburb called "Velen". It is approximately thirteen kilometers from Prague. He lived there with his mother and grandma. Jacob likes to play piano. Before he was sent to the camp, he took piano lessons. He is very shy but if you talk to him he will open up. Beethoven is his favorite composer. He especially likes "Moonlight Sonata".

Sarah and **Rebecca** are sisters. Sarah is fourteen years old and Rebecca is seven. They lived in Prague with their mom and dad before arriving at the camp. Sarah entertains herself by writing poems about things she sees around her. She plays the flute as a way to relax. Rebecca plays with paper dolls and cradles. Even though they fight over who gets to play with the dolls first, they know that without each other they wouldn't survive.

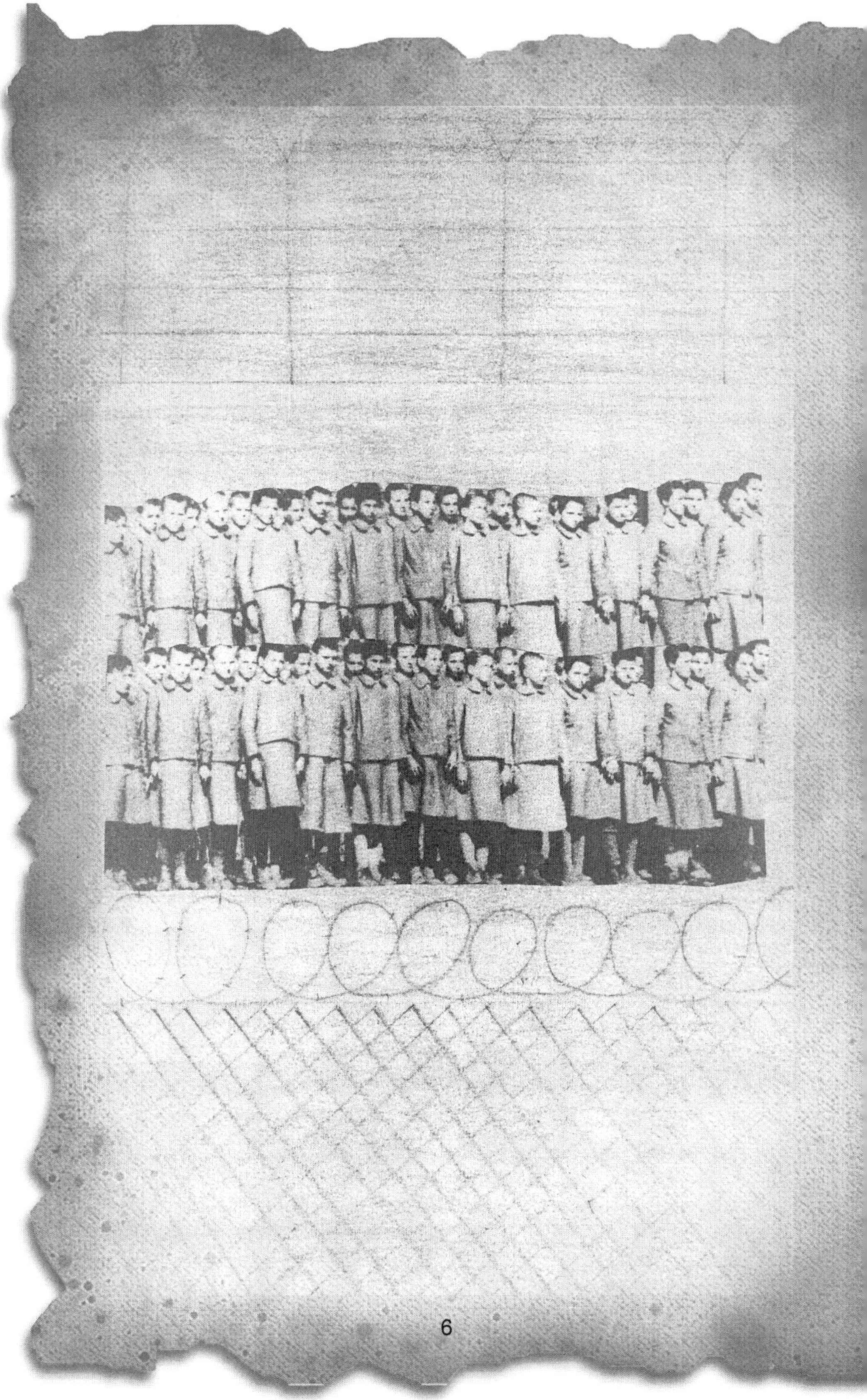

Fall 1941

We took a boxcar for five days. I fell asleep but was awakened by the sound of loads of children crying. I said to a woman on my right, "Gee, I wish it wasn't so smelly here". We had only one small bucket to use as a toilet.

I thought I saw a dead man. After looking at him for about five minutes I realized he was alive. He was only sleeping. When he woke up, I was still staring at him. "Whatcha lookin' at, huh?" he asked angrily. I was so embarrassed that I didn't look at him for the rest of the trip.

When we came to the camp, it was beautiful and ugly at the same time. The trees had different colored leaves but the camp was all barren. About a dozen soldiers in uniform shouted, "Raus, raus, get out, get out!" as they pushed us off the train. When I looked around, I thought that I was in prison. There was barbed wire all around and high walls. I started to panic. "Where am I? Where am I?" I asked myself.

I barely understood a soldier who said that we were sixty kilometers from Prage.

We were marched to our barracks. My bed was just a long board that could fit five or six people. We didn't have any bed sheets, or mattress... When I saw it, I fainted.

Fall 1941

When I woke up, I noticed that I was not alone. I saw a little group of children playing "house", with paper dolls and cradles.

When I stood up I immediately fell back down. I murmured "Please help me, please..." A girl heard me call for help and came up to me. She helped me up and we went to the spot where all of the children were playing. Soon everyone introduced themselves. I had a feeling that Rebecca, Sarah's younger sister, was on the train. "Didn't I see you on the train eight days ago?" She smiled, admitting that we had seen each other in the boxcar.

I went back to my barrack and thought really hard about everything that happened today. I couldn't understand what I did wrong and why I was in this camp...

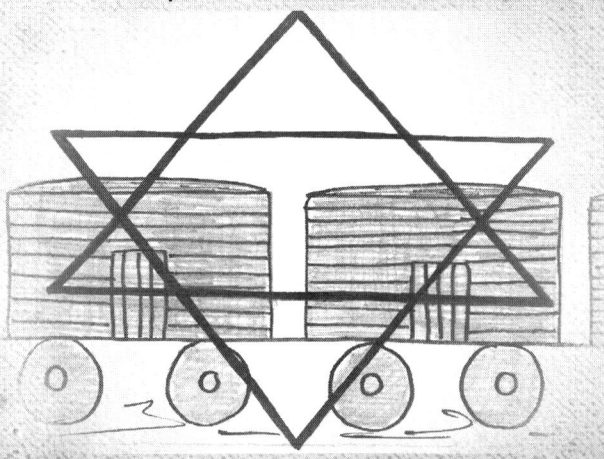

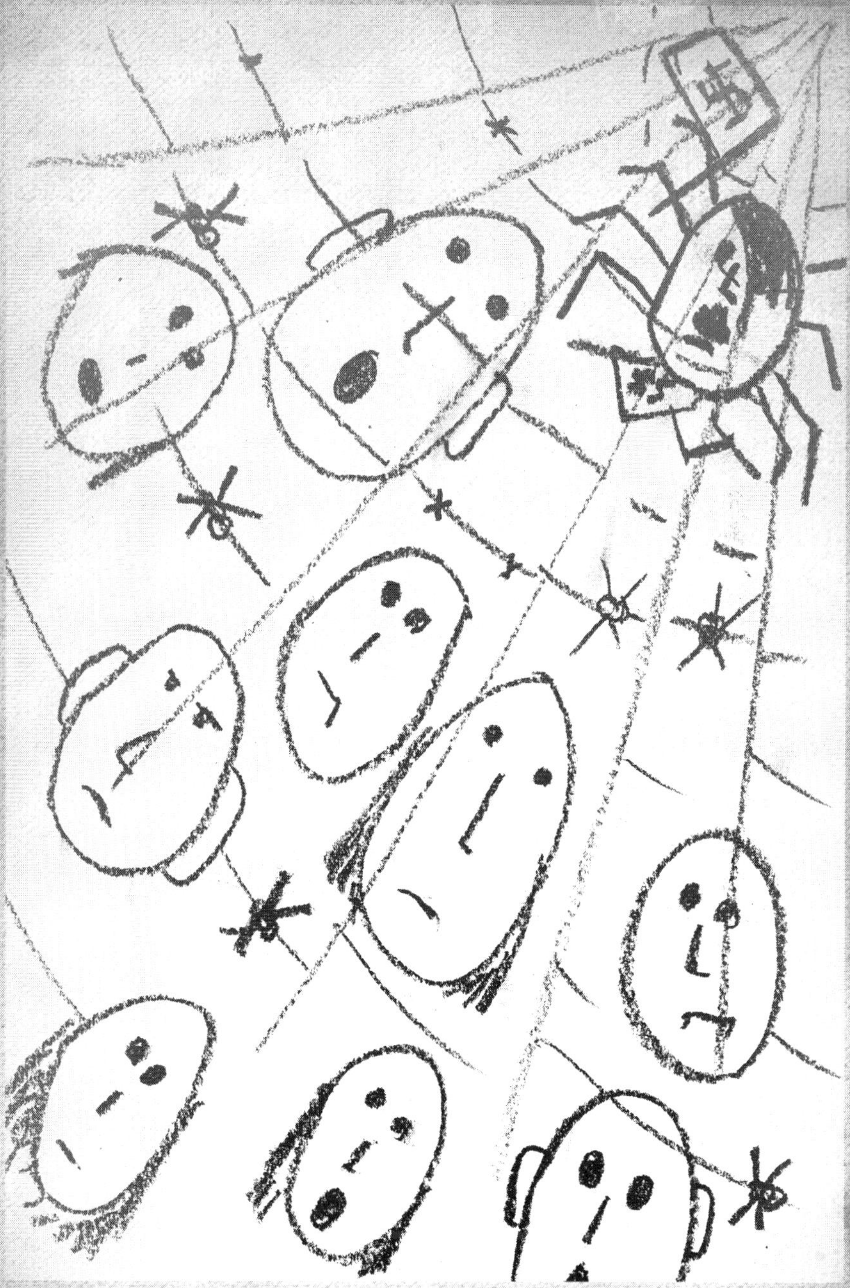

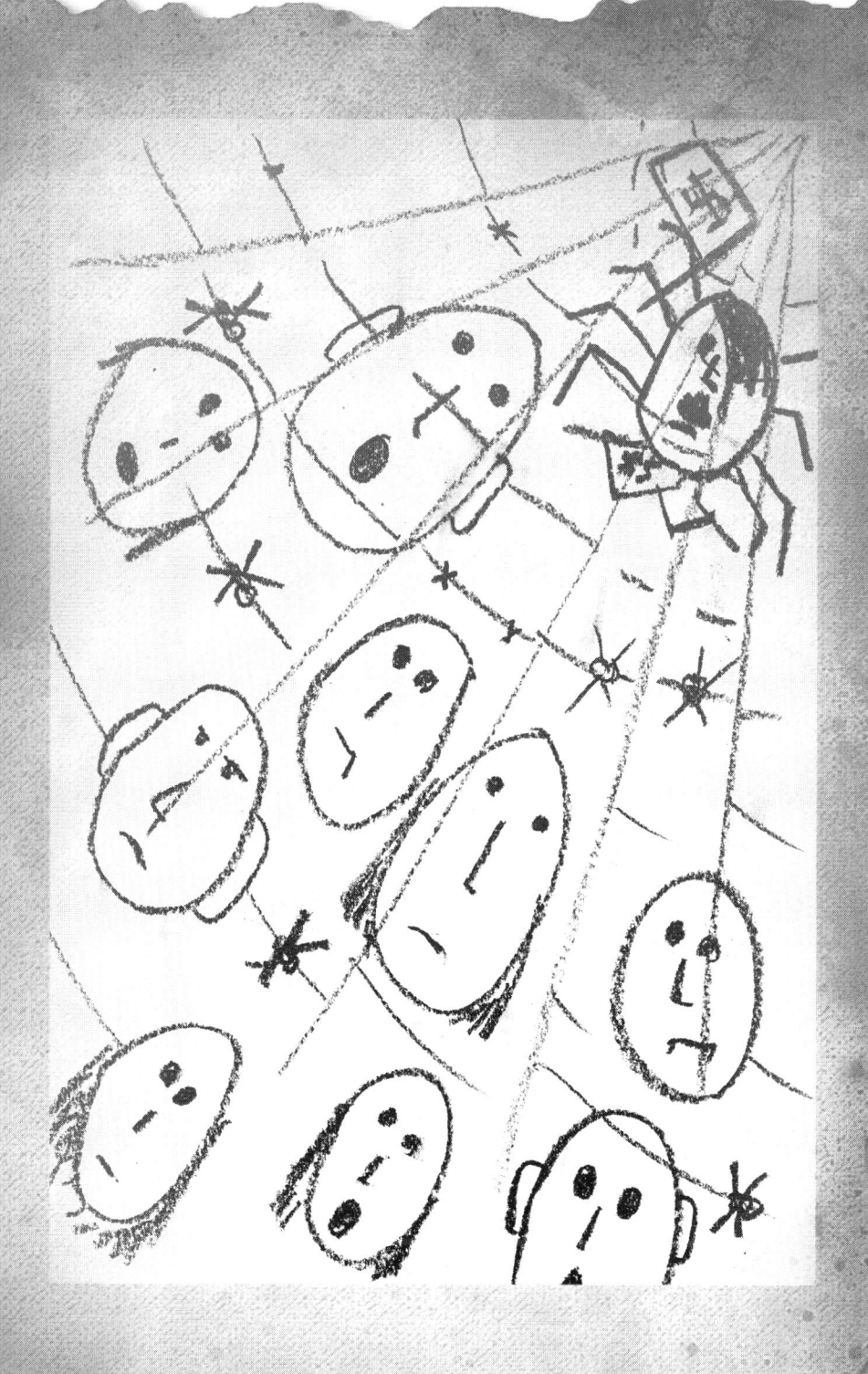

Fall 1941

We made a newspaper called "The Prague Times". It was about how the Czechs would win the war with all of the other resistance forces.

Pavel got paper from Sarah who wanted to use it to write letters to her mother who was in Dachau. On these sheets he drew propaganda pictures.

I wrote about what mistakes the Nazis had made. "Mercy, isn't this fun?" I said to our drawing star, nudging him on the shoulder.

Sarah made the front cover. She put our names on it. The interesting thing about this is that she took a quote from every article and wrote them on the back cover. I patted her on the shoulder and said "Good job!"

We were so excited with our project that we decided to make an issue every four days. This work of art that we made gave us hope that someday we would be liberated.

We must be cautious. If the Nazis find out that we are making a newspaper, we will all be executed. To avoid this danger we hid the pencils and paper under the bed and the newspaper was hidden in a suitcase under all the other belongings. If the Nazis checked our barrack they would never find the newspaper!

Fall 1941

Conditions in our barracks were very difficult. It grew cold and many people slept very close to each other: head to head, arm to arm, shoulder to shoulder.

When it rained and stormed the barracks flooded. People ran to get their suitcases and belongings. Many slipped and fell. Some screamed: "Oh, gosh!" or "What is going on?"

We were treated so poorly. I couldn't understand what the Nazis were thinking. Definitely they didn't think about us!

Soon our life in the barracks flipped over and we did not even notice.

I looked out the very small window and saw a man walk by. He was all wet and suddenly he stumbled to the ground. I just closed my eyes and never looked out the window again. As my head dropped, I noticed that leaves were falling off the trees and bushes.

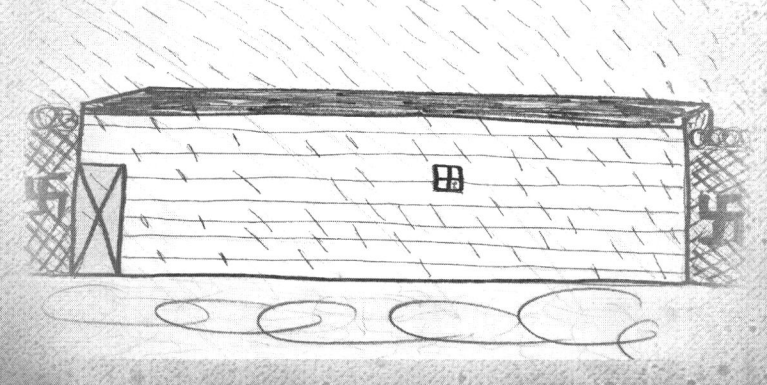

Fall 1941

In the morning I tried to look for my suitcase after yesterday's storm. After about thirty minutes, I realized that my stuff got carried away by the unstoppable flow of water. Everything I had was gone. I should've looked after it. It was my responsibility to keep my belongings. It would be stupid to check all of the barracks. There are thousands of suitcases in the whole camp. I told my friends about my loss but they couldn't help. I was completely helpless.

I cried sitting on my bed. Soon I began to write about hatred against Jews. I wrote that it was wrong, and would someday end. This gave me hope that soon we would be liberated.

I kept my hopes high while I was writing my diary. Being a prisoner in a concentration camp made me sad. What if I did do something wrong?

Fall 1941

In the evening we celebrated Hanukkah. Since we didn't want the Nazi guards to hear us, we sang in a very low tone. Luckily, an adult in our barrack had a candle which she spared to use for lighting the Hanukkah lights. Pavel took two boards and rubbed them together to make a small fire. Then he used the fire to light the candles.

We sat down and said the Kaddish and Brachot (blessings). Later on we had a small Hanukkah party. Pavel and Sarah danced a waltz while Rebecca and I were in the audience.

In the late evening we had lots of fun. We drew pictures, wrote poems, and even made another newspaper. The very last thing we did that day was to pass out presents. It was amazing that everyone had a present for someone else. Pavel gave everyone a small stone with the words joy, freedom, home, family, and happiness inscribed on it. Sarah made Rebecca a paper doll. I decided to tell everyone that I was writing a diary and I even got to read part of it to them. Then we all danced the Hora.

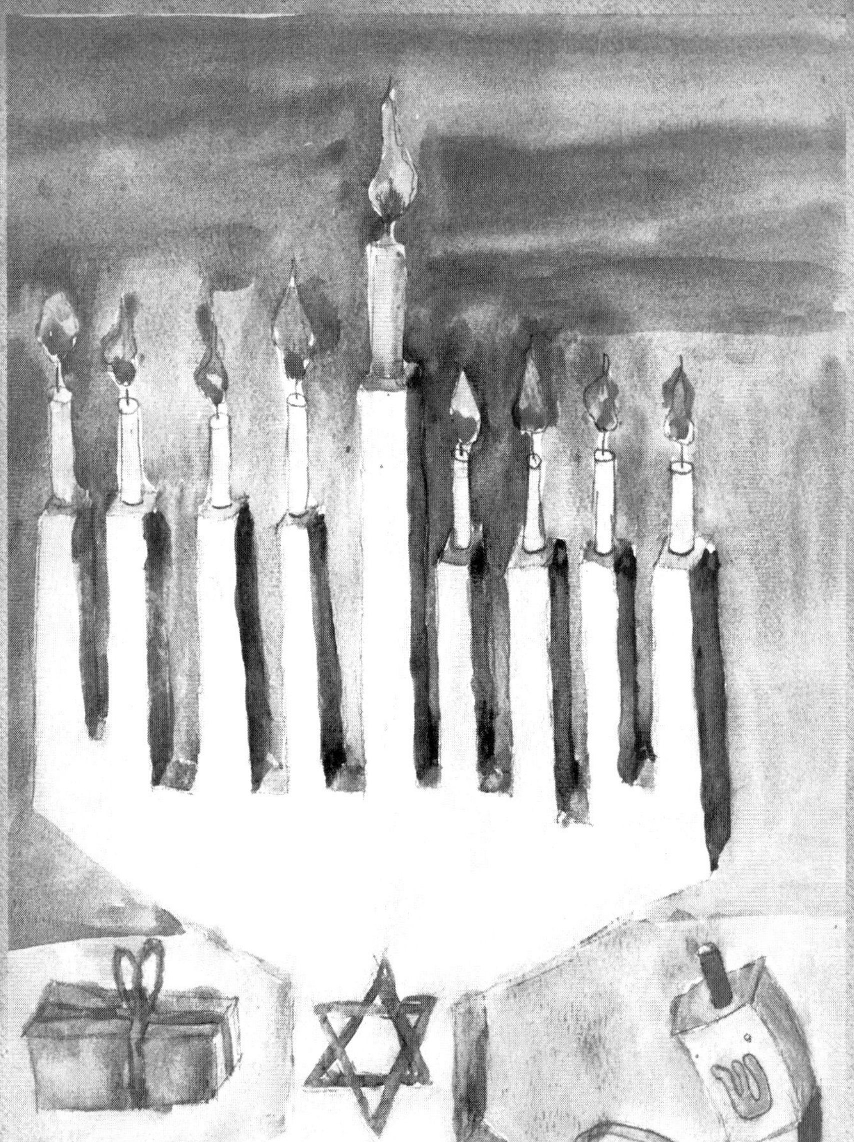

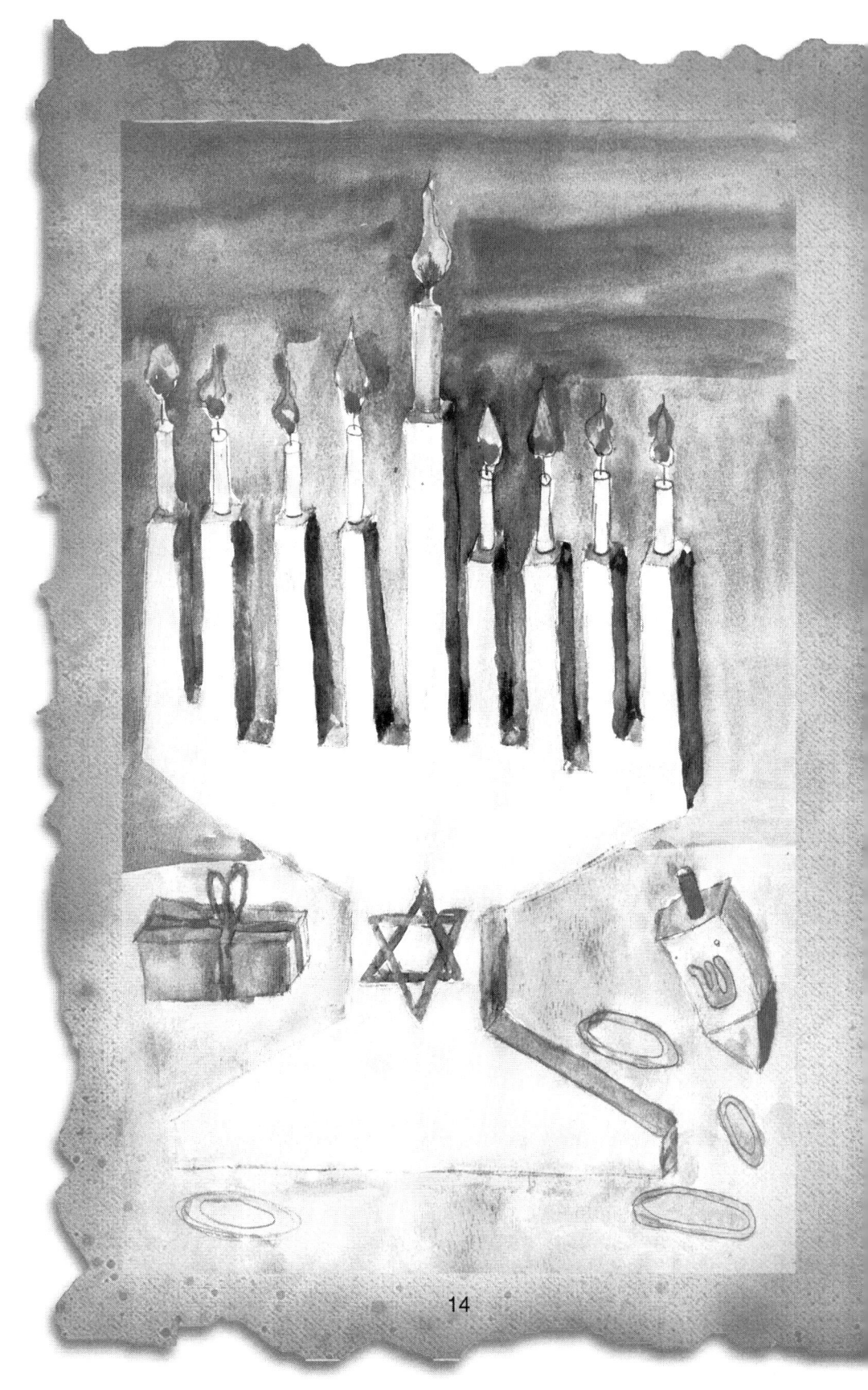

Pavel told some hilarious jokes. We laughed so hard that we couldn't stop for ten minutes! Rebecca had tears coming from her eyes that were sliding down her cheeks.

Pavel was so grateful that he didn't laugh anymore. He just had a faint smile.

We quit joking just in time to find out that a Nazi guard had come to check on us. After fifteen minutes of questioning he left. I was relieved that we could stop the jokes in time before the guard came in.

We were so excited about our Hanukkah party but now we were ready to go to bed.

Winter 1941-42

I was awakened by the sound of a train whistle. I looked out the window and saw more people climbing out of the train. I couldn't imagine that more than sixty more people would be added to our barrack. I thought I saw a boy, but I wasn't sure. When the new people came in they looked frightened and exhausted.

Suddenly I saw the same child, no older than ten, walk by. He seemed shy. I felt that someday we would become best friends.

I came up to him and asked, "What's wrong?" he said that he didn't know where he was or where his parents were. I hugged him and said goodnight. I stayed up the whole night thinking. That young boy showed bravery.

The next time I looked out the window, I noticed that the trees had snow on them. It was a beautiful sight.

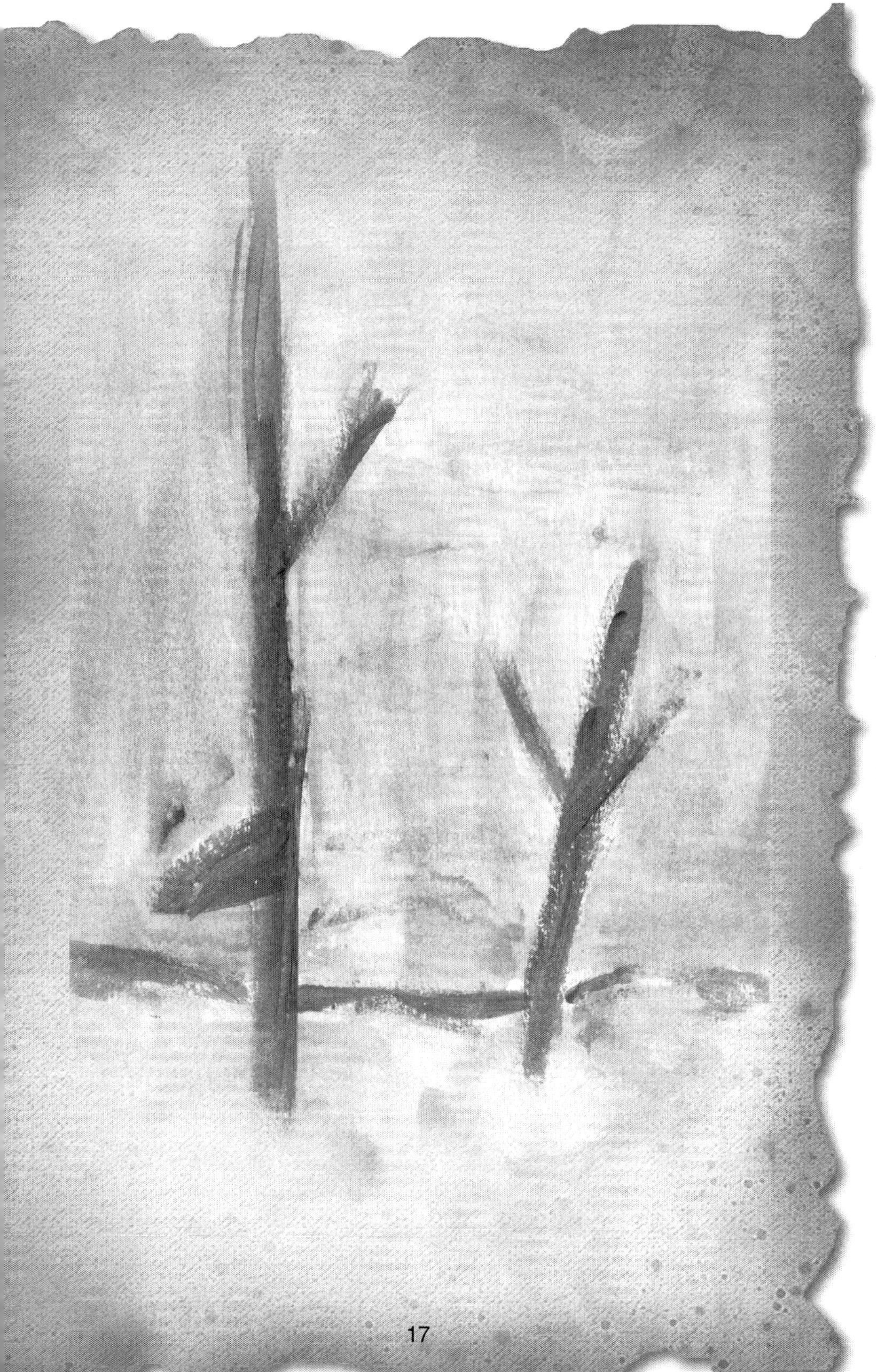

Winter 1941-42

Today was a very serious day. About midday an announcement was made that Peter, Rebecca, Wolfgang, Chase, Ella, Madison, Benjamin, and Max, had to board boxcar NO. 15.

In our barrack there was only one person crying - it sounded more like fifteen. Rebecca was leaving with other kids on a train. Sarah hugged Rebecca and kissed her one hundred times. The weeping grew louder when a guard in heavy boots pushed Rebecca away and shoved her towards the train. It was such a tragedy to separate two sisters.

Sarah wanted to run after the train but she couldn't leave the barrack.

Now, not only is she without her parents but she doesn't have her younger sister.

Another bad thing happened today. In the evening Pavel ate his bowl of soup. Later he started vomiting.

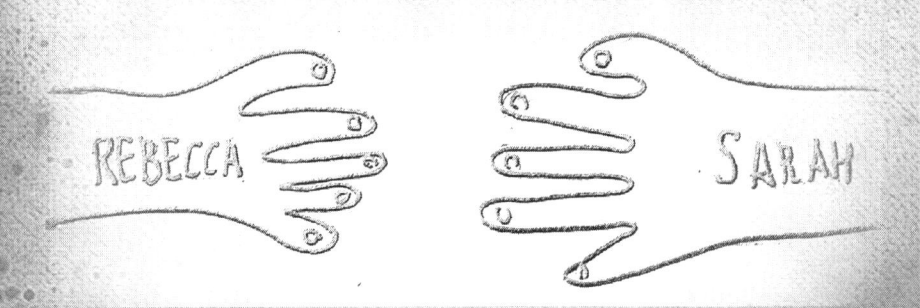

Winter 1941-42

The ten year old kid's name is Jacob. He likes to play the piano. Too bad there isn't a piano in the camp.

It grew severely cold. Our cheeks were all blue and purple. Our fingers were all numb. I tried to keep writing my diaries but the pencil kept slipping out of my grip. We sat in a circle thinking we would be warmer. "Gosh, I wish it wasn't so cold", said Pavel. Suddenly I felt a warm sensation. I scooted closer to the circle and I felt warmer. I really didn't realize that I had dozed off for a while.

Winter 1941-42

After our tiring work in the field we returned to the barrack exhausted.

Jacob taught us how to make stone drawn pictures on a piece of wood. I asked him how he learned to do this. He told us a story about how he was in the basement with nothing to do. But he did have a stone and a piece of wood. He told us the best way to make a picture easier is with a sharp stone. "I think I will do this for the rest of the day!" I said to Jacob.

I didn't do it for the rest of the day but I enjoyed learning something new.

I love Jacob. I think he is one of those kids who can fit in without disturbing. "Man, where are my parents? I thought that we would see them soon! They lied, didn't they?" said Jacob.

Winter 1941-42

At night I dreamed about how our house stood in front of our big yard. My friend and I are on the swing while my mom is hanging up our laundry. My dad... How I miss him. I would love to touch his soft mustache. I would love to see again his friendly eyes.

I woke up thinking that everybody was awake but I was wrong. I went to Jacob and woke him up. He got scared, and I calmed him down. "Heavens, you could've done that the nice way".

We sat down and talked about life in the old days. We were so busy talking that we didn't notice that the other children had woken up and were listening to our conversation. I noticed that Sarah's eyes filled with tears.

Spring 1942

Today when I opened my eyes only Pavel was awake. I went to him and asked what he was doing. He said that he was drawing a picture for his dad who was in the Czech Resistance Forces. He asked if I was good at drawing. I said "yes", so we decided to have a drawing contest.

I thought that I should draw a dog but later I realized it was boring. Instead I drew eyes filled with tears that dripped on the people at the Terezin camp. Pavel drew a beautiful house. It was his family house with many trees and a big garden in Roztoky. He lived happily in that place. He won the contest but I knew that we were both very good artists. We were so busy drawing we didn't even notice that the sisters and Jacob were up. They saw my drawing and hugged me.

We talked more about each other. It turns out that the sisters are from Prague and Jacob is from Helen. They haven't seen their parents since the war began and don't know anything about them.

We stopped talking and had a little moment of silence.

After that we went to bed. As I was lying there, I heard Sarah sniffle.

Spring 1942

The Nazis took us to a dirty field where they told us to dig "holes". I knew that we were really going to be digging graves for the dead.

It was very hard work. The hole had to be ten feet or more. Suddenly I saw a child no older than ten drop to the ground. I tried to tell him to stand up but he was too sick. A Nazi guard noticed him and started beating him with a club. At the same time he screamed "Aufstehen, Aufstehen, Get up, Get up". The boy didn't move. In anger the guard took out his pistol and fired.

It all happened in front of my eyes. I broke into a cold sweat. I was so scared I tried not to look at the scene.

I kept on digging holes. I wanted to fall to the ground like the boy but I was way too scared to get myself killed. In one day I dug about fifteen holes.

When I came back to the barrack, I started filling in pages of my diary. Suddenly I felt a cold finger running down my shoulder. I turned around, panicking. "Woo. It's Sarah". She was holding a piece of paper in her hand. She said it was a poem. She read it to me and I thought it was very impressive.

That murdered kid,
It was a crime.
We need to get rid,
Of the Nazi slime.

Spring 1942

This morning the Nazis sent us to collect potatoes in the fields. We would walk up to a dirt mark which symbolized where a potato would be growing. Then we would use a spade to dig it up. When our bag was full, we went to the closest wheelbarrow and dumped them in there. To make sure the bag was full a Nazi guard stood watch so there was no way to dump the potatoes without having a full bag. After I filled about six bags the Nazi let me go back to my barrack.

I sat down on my cot and started writing my diary. I was so tired that I slumped over on my hard bed.

Today I did very difficult work but I cannot give up hope of liberation.

Spring 1942

Outside it grew warmer, but in the barrack it became more crowded. More trains were coming into our camp. Now I had to share a bed with more people.

After the day of the huge storm, I never found my suitcase. It is such a tragedy since that was the only thing I had from my house.

At night I would always think about my parents. I miss them as much as they miss me.

I just spent time alone thinking about how unfortunate I was to be in this place. How long am I going to be in this prison? Where are my parents? Are we going to die? Are my parents alive?

Spring 1942

Today I was much more exhausted than usual. There was a new Nazi guard in the field who instead of six bags ordered us to fill up twelve bags. While I was working, I noticed that the soil was fresh and soft. That meant that summer had arrived. We returned to our barrack in mid-evening. We ate some soup and a piece of stale bread.

It has been about a year since I was sent to the camp. It meant a year of suffering and loneliness.

Spring 1942

This morning we were ordered to clean the floor and the walls. We did not know why we had to do it. Usually we would sit and wait until we got our food and then we would go to work.

A Nazi came in and told us that today we would be putting on a show for the International Red Cross.

We put cloth sheets onto suitcases with the words WET PAINT. That way the camp hid the fact it was crowded. We painted the walls so they looked much better.

When the Red Cross came, all of the survivors stood in the front of the camp. Yet, many people were hidden in prison cells to avoid showing the crowded conditions. After the introductions and the camp tour, the Red Cross came to watch our show. It was all about how "good" it was to be here.

It was embarrassing to make the show when it was all a lie.

After the show I ran back to my barrack and started crying. How could I have participated in such a hoax?

SHAME

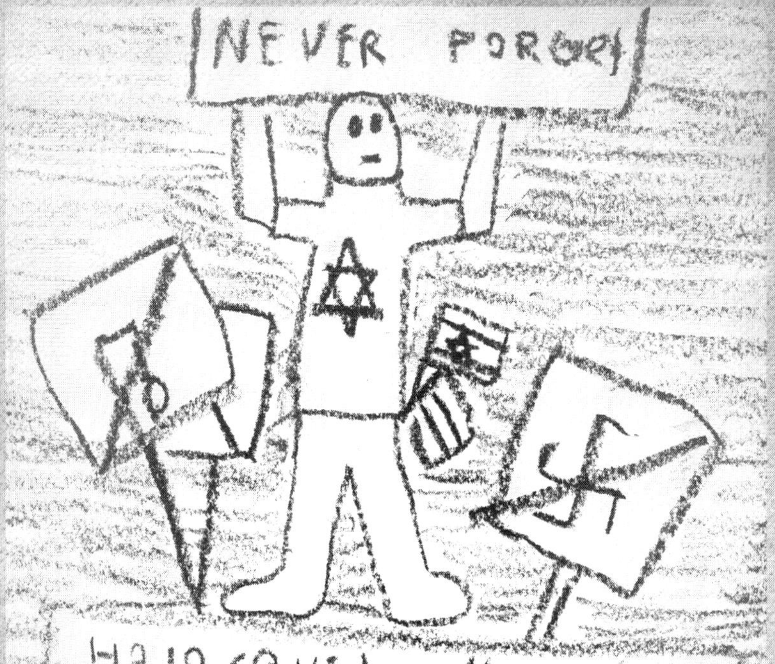
NEVER FORGET
Holocaust Memorial

EPILOGUE

Pavel died of typhus fever at Terezin camp.

David died at Auschwitz from starvation.

Rebecca was never found. Either she was gassed or shot. No one is sure.

Jacob was hanged for being caught sending letters to his brother.

The only survivor was *Sarah*. The camp was liberated by Russian soldiers in 1945. She had survived the Holocaust and she still has hope of finding her lost sister someday. Sarah promised herself she would never forget about the Holocaust.

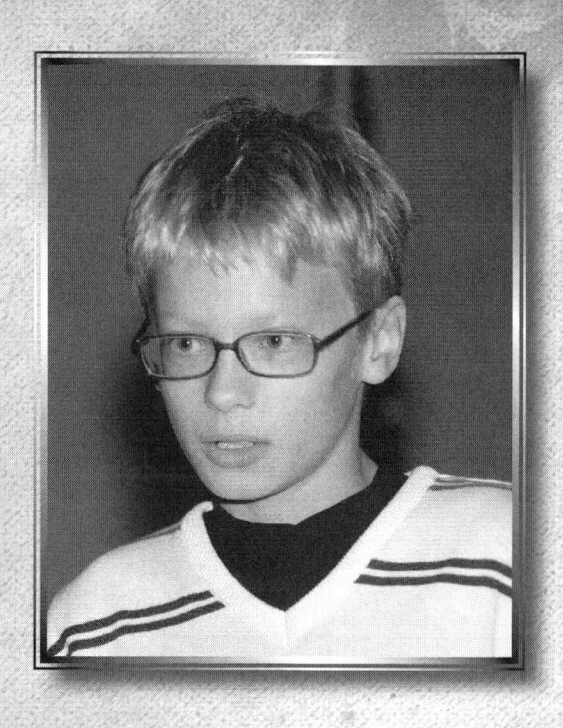

ABOUT THE AUTHOR

Benjamin Cohen is twelve years old and is in sixth grade at James G. Blaine Elementary School. This is his fourth novel. His favorite color is navy blue, and his favorite food is pel'meni (Russian tortellini with meat).

He was influenced by Markus Zusak and Susan Bachrach, as well as a theatrical play called "...And a Child Shall Lead". This gave him the idea to write about the Holocaust.

Ben's hobbies include cinema and literature. He is a big fan of Harry Potter and The Secret Series. He also enjoys art, music and foreign languages. Ben is a gifted athlete. His favorite sport is swimming. He hopes that his book will help children understand better tragedy of Holocaust.

PROJECT NEVER FORGET

Benjamin Cohen, a twelve-year old student from Chicago, received a Certificate of Recognition from Russian American Jews for Israel (RAJI) for the best literary work dedicated to the memory of the victims of the Holocaust in summer 2011. The book, «Will I Ever See Another Butterfly?» is about the children imprisoned in the concentration camp Terezin.

Benjamin is fluent in Russian and English and studies French, Spanish and Hebrew. He loves history and is an avid reader. Ben is a member of a Chicago Park District swim team and takes art classes at the Russian Sunday School at the ORT Institute (Professor Yakov Shames). Currently he is preparing for his Bar Mitzvah. He is a student at the religious school of Anshe Emet Synagogue.

Two years ago, Ben's mom took him to the Vittum Theater to see the play «And A Child Shall Lead». It was about the child prisoners of the «model» Nazi concentration camp Terezin in Czechoslovakia. This camp was created to fool the International Red Cross. It was a meticulously produced lie of the propaganda minister Josef Goebbels. In the camp the inmates – adults and children – were allowed to draw, make theater performances, receive food and get medical treatment so that later, when the charade was no longer necessary, they would be deported to the gas chambers.

Ben was so moved by this performance that as soon as he got home he began to draw and make notes so that he would not forget a single detail or a single story from the play.

«For several days Ben was under the influence of what he saw, and began asking questions about the Holocaust and the war», says his mom Svetlana. A week later, at Ben's insistence, his father Michael took him to the Museum of the Holocaust in Skokie, IL.

In Ben's school the students were assigned to write a literary work on a subject of their choice. Ben knew what he wanted to write about – the Holocaust and the children of the Terezin camp. Although this was a tough subject for elementary students, his teacher and principal approved. Thus was born the book «Will I Ever See Another Butterfly?»

The students unanimously voted the first prize to Ben's project.

Ben was invited with his parents to the presentation of the Album to the Memory of the Victims of the Holocaust organized by the Russian community of Chicago. The presentation, which was organized by the newspaper Reklama, took place at the Museum of the Holocaust. At the ceremony Ben read a chapter from his book. Even battle-scarred war veterans, survivors of the Holocaust, and victims of Stalinist repression had tears in their eyes.

Ben Cohen's book "Will I Ever See Another Butterfly?" was published by Chicago Connect - Reklama's not-profit organization on the initiative of Reklama's Women's Board.

This book was published by Newspaper Reklama
with the support of Chicago Connect, a non-profit organization.

Illustrations:
Benjamin Cohen, Joseph Puchinsky (cover page)

Acknowledgements
This project would not have been possible without the support of

- Newspaper Reklama
- Reklama's Women's Board
- Bright Future International
- Association Evidence of Holocaust
- Chicago Russian Community

All Rights Reserved @ Copyright by Benjamin Cohen, Chicago, IL, 2012
ISBN 978-1-4675-3161-0